Praise for *The Backbone of the World*

"Frontiersmen have always been out there, in remote ranches, in the hills and valleys beyond the whir of the interstate, making their living on horseback and adjusting uneasily to the latest in the incarnations of the New West. Frank Clifford found them along America's great spine, in Wyoming, Montana, Colorado, New Mexico—and he describes the nature of their lives and the rugged country they still cherish with clarity, irony, and just the right amalgam of attachment and detachment." —*Smithsonian*

"The reporting found in *The Backbone of the World* is substantial and of the most wonderful kind, with the numbers, dates, and statistics woven carefully into the stories. And the breadth of the book . . . is considerable. Clifford's book captures the tenor and angst of the time, and the voices are reported and presented fairly, even in their desperation. Our desperation." —Rick Bass, *Los Angeles Times*

"A wonderfully readable book, moving but never angry, tough as its subjects, sometimes funny. It puts us in touch with an elemental part of our natures that, in most of us, civilization long ago repressed. When the vigorous, flawed, and casually courageous people Clifford writes about disappear, his book will endure as their memorial—and, in an indefinably sad way, ours." —*The New Mexican* (Santa Fe)

"A well-told tale of a place that breaches the centuries—a place to measure what has been lost." —*Kirkus Reviews*

"Like an old-time circuit rider Frank Clifford journeys up and down the spine of the Rocky Mountains, taking down the very twenty-first-century joys and woes of its inhabitants, among them sheepherders, conservationists, ranchers, miners, and outfitters. He listens with an accurate ear. His prose is lucid and unsentimental, as surefooted and knowing as those who inhabit these fine pages." —Gretel Ehrlich

"Clifford is a compassionate ⟨...⟩nd eloquence to his self-appoin⟨...⟩m the Canadian Rockies to southw⟨...⟩d's cu-

riosity provides many eye-opening visions of this magical land, its scoundrels and its defenders." —*Seattle Times*

"A writer in the plain style, Clifford is an able judge of character, providing a refreshingly unsentimental portrait of the loners along the continent's spine." —*Outside*

"For Frank Clifford, the Continental Divide is more than a geographical reference. It is also the dividing line and mystic mid-region between a West (and a nation) forever vanishing and a West (and a nation) enmeshed in the multiple meanings, losses, and gains, human and environmental, of change, change, change." —Dr. Kevin Starr, State Librarian of California

"Clifford masterfully brings out the contradictions in the struggles of the people who live and work in the public lands along the Continental Divide while compassionately and fairly giving us their perspective on the battle . . . His prose is like a naturalist poet's." —*New York Sun*

"Clifford's storytelling is straightforward; he doesn't garnish the people or places he visits. There is a kind of raw poetry, however, in the starkness of his descriptions as they reveal life on the edge, embraced for hardness." —*Portland Oregonian*

"Honest, lovely writing that catches the scents, sounds, sights, and significance of the high West. There aren't but a handful of people who can write this well about these people and places." —Roger Kennedy, Director Emeritus, National Museum of American History, and former Director, U.S. National Park Service

"Clifford's book is a poetic portrayal of the last human links to the pastoral lifestyles that gave America its virtues, values, and identity. His subjects' heroic human struggle to maintain their place on the epic landscapes of the Great Divide is a battle over our nation's soul." —Robert F. Kennedy, Jr., President, Waterkeeper Alliance

"A readable, thought-provoking book of what's-left-of-the-Old-West essays." —*Denver Post*

The
Backbone
of the
World

A Portrait of the

Vanishing West

Along the

Continental Divide

BROADWAY BOOKS · NEW YORK

THE
BACKBONE
OF THE
WORLD

FRANK CLIFFORD

PRINTED IN THE UNITED STATES OF AMERICA

BROADWAY BOOKS and its logo, a letter B bisected on the diagonal, are
trademarks of Broadway Books, a division of Random House, Inc.

Visit our website at www.broadwaybooks.com

First Broadway Books trade paperback edition published 2003

Book design by Chris Welch
Title page photo by Kaz Mori/Getty Images
Map designed by Jeffrey L. Ward

The Library of Congress has cataloged
the hardcover edition as follows:
Clifford, Frank, 1945–
The backbone of the world : a portrait of a vanishing way of life along the
Continental Divide / by Frank Clifford.— 1st ed.
p. cm.
Includes bibliographical references.
1. West (U.S.)—Description and travel. 2. Continental Divide National
Scenic Trail—Description and travel. 3. Clifford, Frank, 1945—Journeys—
West (U.S.) 4. West (U.S.)—History, Local. 5. West (U.S.)—Biography.
6. Frontier and pioneer life—West (U.S.) 7. Natural history—West (U.S.)
I. Title.
F595.3 .C57 2002
978—dc21
2001052705

ISBN 0-7679-0702-7

1 3 5 7 9 10 8 6 4 2

For Barbara

Contents

This book is a subjective account of the author's travels and encounters along the Continental Divide. A few names and identifying details of individuals and places mentioned in the book have been changed to protect people's privacy.

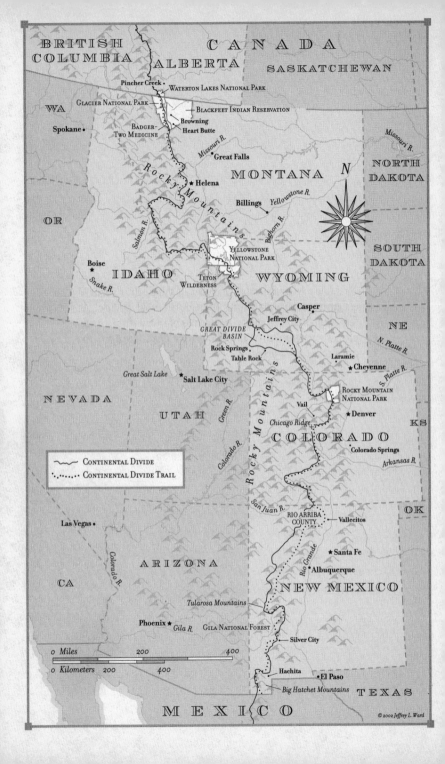

PROLOGUE

THE CALLER SAID his name was Jake. He was telephoning from
Colorado Springs, where he was living in a friend's trailer, his
packhorse tied out back. He had made his way down the Continental
Divide from Canada, intending to ride all the way to the Mexican border. He had come as far as southern Colorado when an early winter
drove him out of the mountains. He planned to resume his journey in
the spring. In the meantime, he wondered if the newspaper I worked
for, the *Los Angeles Times*, would be interested in publishing an account of his trip. He offered to show me his diary. We talked for a half
an hour. He regaled me with stories of grizzly bears and blizzards, of
getting lost in the mountains and finding shelter in places that most
travelers don't encounter—pinpricks on the map, like Heart Butte,
Montana, and Jeffrey City, Wyoming. As much as the mountain
scenery, he said, such places had captured his fancy. He had lingered
longer than he ever expected in cabins and cow camps, doing a little

work and a lot of talking with strangers. No offense, he said, but people are more interesting and life richer than the news media would lead you to believe sometimes. I encouraged him to send me his diary and promised to stay in touch. I never heard from him again. When I tried to call him back a month later, the telephone had been disconnected. I did what you do when someone ignites a small campfire in your imagination. I thought about it at night, feeding it bits of kindling, listening to L.A.'s eerie chorus of car alarms, police sirens, and coyotes. I knew a bit about the territory Jake had explored. I'd taken overnight hikes in Glacier and Yellowstone national parks, ridden a horse over the Divide in Wyoming's Wind River Range, camped in the high desert in northern New Mexico. But mostly, I had read about places along the Divide. "There is something in the country . . . in the vastness and emptiness of it, that resists knowing," Rob Schultheis wrote a quarter of a century ago in his book *The Hidden West*. Did such a country still exist? Was there still a world out there capable of living up to the expectations of the overstimulated armchair traveler? I had Jake's testimony that there was.

A few months later, a friend handed me a press release about a project to build a Continental Divide Trail, from Canada to Mexico, across 3,200 miles of mountain and desert. The trail provided the sort of organizing principle you need when you are looking for an excuse to drop everything, lock the door on your life, and light out. It also gave me a route to follow. I found a website for people hiking the trail and got in touch with three men who would be starting north from the Mexican border the following spring. They invited me to join them. I planned to walk with them for a few days and then branch off on my own. I was less interested in the Divide trail than I was in the Divide country and its inhabitants. I wanted to spend time around people who have tailored their lives to fit into exposed places where adventurous travelers spend only a night or two. I wanted to find them while they were still there.

I knew how to start the search. I had been reporting on Western politics and environmental issues for twenty-five years. I had notebooks and index files full of the names of politicians, activists, artists, country lawyers and doctors, small-town newspaper editors, game wardens, and forest rangers. They could help me find the people I was looking for—the ones who shot their own meat, who made a living on horseback, who were still trying to adjust to the twentieth century on the verge of the twenty-first. I didn't draw up an itinerary. The less structure the better. I had been tethered to an office for thirty years and I looked forward to breaking its bonds. I had an urge to drift. I would travel by horse and mule, by truck, and occasionally on foot. I would finagle rides and employ pack animals.

I started out on a nameless dirt road in southwestern New Mexico. I was headed for an expanse of desert once described by the explorer John Russell Bartlett as an "unbroken waste, barren, wild and worthless." The three other hikers and I met in Hachita, a speck of a town twenty-five miles from the Mexican border. From there, we caught a ride to the border, where the dirt road ended. The beginning of the Continental Divide Trail was marked by a windmill, the bones of a stockman's cabin, and a barbed-wire fence. From the trailhead, the three of us planned to walk north to the Big Hatchet Mountains, our first day's destination. Under hazy April skies, the low, jagged mountains shimmered like a sculpture garden of razor blades.

The Continental Divide, which runs the length of North and South America, is where nature separates the waters that flow to the Atlantic and Pacific oceans. In the United States, the Divide traces the crest of the Rocky Mountains from their spiny genesis just north of the Mexican border to their majestic exit into Canada. It reenters the United States in Alaska above the Arctic Circle and extends across the state to the Bering Sea. People have been hiking the Divide for years; the trail is an effort to establish an official route woven from the braids of old wagon tracks, logging roads, stock trails, and footpaths.

Great trails breach the centuries. Nearly 500 years ago, the desert would have looked much the same to Coronado's army as it does to us, especially at midday when the dusty glare erases detail and flattens color, let alone any glimmer of the mineral wealth the conquistador hoped to find. Propelled by visions of seven cities of gold, Coronado resolutely ignored the barrenness of his surroundings, placing his trust in tantalizing rumors. The four of us were more interested in finding water as we pondered the route to our evening destination, a nameless spot on a United States Geological Survey map that held out the only possibility of water within a day's walking distance. Quite a number of people die of thirst and exposure in this desert every year. Most of them are the descendants of Coronado. They are the torchbearers of the eternal golden dream bound for the seven cities— Los Angeles, San Diego, Tucson, Las Vegas, Phoenix, Albuquerque, Denver—and beyond. Recently, one of them showed up on a nearby ranch and dropped to his knees, believing he had reached the end of his journey after a scorching seventy-two-hour slog. The exhausted pilgrim thought he had made it after sighting the faded sign on the ranch's water storage tank that read: CHICAGO PUMP CO.

THE CONTINENTAL DIVIDE Trail does not adhere strictly to the Divide. The trail meanders down a corridor that extends out fifty miles on either side of the Divide, avoiding terrain where only mountain goats can travel and detouring around man-made obstacles. I planned to take full advantage of that latitude. My goal was not to hike the trail from start to finish. I wasn't going to follow a hiker's timetable or triptych, north to south or vice versa. On newspaper assignments in the past, I'd rarely had the chance to linger. Swooping in and out, as newspaper reporters tend to do, teasing a comparatively simple story out of life's complexities, I had been avoiding some undistilled truth, some murmuring ambivalence. In the midst of researching environmental stories about the damage done by grazing or logging or mining, I realized I frequently enjoyed the company of the people who were most responsible. I did not overlook the messes they had made. Often as not, I differed with their politics. But I could not quite accept the notion that things would be better when these people were gone, when the slate was wiped clean of their wagon ruts.

JUST OVER 100 years ago, historian Frederick Jackson Turner wrote that the strength of American democracy grew out of its experience of the Western frontier. The "Great West," said Turner, became the forge of America's vaunted resourcefulness and ingenuity. His 1893 essay, titled "The Significance of the Frontier in American History," was the opening salvo in a century-long debate among historians, environmentalists, Native Americans, and feminists on the legacy of the pioneer experience. Where Turner had seen heroic enterprise, others saw reckless expansion and exploitation. The Indians were dispossessed and exiled. The beaver and bison were exterminated. The rivers were poisoned and the forests plundered.

The scholars got a little ahead of themselves. The subject of Turner's eulogy wasn't quite dead yet. As defined by the census takers in Turner's time, the frontier was a region of fewer than two people per square mile. By that definition, close to 13 percent of the landmass of the lower forty-eight states still qualified as frontier in 1990. All of it was west of the Mississippi, much of it scattered along the Continental Divide.

My journey along the Divide did not get under way until 1999, not a moment too soon. The decade came closer than any other did in the past century to filling in the empty spaces. If I was going to find traces of that old world of remote ranches, one-room schoolhouses, volunteer fire departments, of mule packers, gyppos, trappers, prospectors, and range riders, it was time to start looking. By 1995, the Western mountain region had become the fastest growing in the country. The changes were most conspicuous in rural counties. A quaint outpost like Yuma, Arizona, once famous for its territorial prison, was suddenly classified as a metropolitan area, leaping past the city stage altogether in its overnight metastasis. The economic changes were more dramatic. By 1995, less than 5 percent of employment in the Rocky Mountain states was still in farming, ranching, and mining. Wyoming might have a cowboy on its license plate, but barely 3 percent of its population made a living raising sheep and cows.

For the anti-Turnerites, these were signs of a long overdue transition. The sooner the Old West died, the better. "We must put our agrarian sympathies aside," wrote economist Thomas Power in his 1996 book *Lost Landscapes and Failed Economies*. Agriculture does not step lightly on the land, Power said. According to Power, there is nothing uniquely wholesome about people living on the land and harvesting its riches by the sweat of their brow. Just look at what the old-timers have left us. "Landscapes stripped bare, silted streams with dead fish, fragmented ecosystems devoid of wildlife."

Like Turner before him, Power only fueled more controversy. Some of the most thoughtful criticism came from the environmental movement, from people who had condemned the destructive impulses of the Old West but could not bring themselves to embrace Power's vision of a new order where subdivisions and office parks are cheek by jowl with national parks and wilderness. Richard Knight, a Colorado State University wildlife biologist who studies the effects of development, contends that the most carefully planned subdivision can unleash more destructive energy on fragile environments than the worst-run ranch. Knight argues that we will not heal the land by treating it as a suburban playground, by letting the dogs chase down the deer or caravaning through the forest in all-terrain vehicles. We merely compound the sins of our much maligned forebears as we colonize the open space, crowd out the wildlife habitat, and draw down the water table.

A lot of the pioneers didn't know any better. They came west with an evangelical optimism stoked by land promoters who said that the arid, stony ground was the most fertile on Earth, that you could farm it without capital, and that rain would follow the plow. During the course of the last century, a lot of people gave up and left. Of the ones who stayed, some learned to work with the land and modify their expectations. They settled for unquantifiable riches. Those were the people I was going to see. I wanted to know more about the secret of their good fortune. Such intangible wealth is hard to describe and harder yet to promote at a time when it does seem possible to get rich without investing much capital, let alone sweat equity. Why grub around in the ground when all you may need is a modem and a broker's tip sheet? Aside from the mountain views and the vaulting sky, what's so special about the natural world that can't be reproduced in a laboratory or relocated safely in a park? As the late economist and environmental contrarian Julian Simon liked to say, the only thing that society hasn't figured out how to clone is water. Simon neglected to mention experience. Progress may have liberated us from the need to work the land, but it has not freed us from the impulse to do so. Disconnected from nature, we become strangers to our senses. But the senses are like smart dogs that grow restive when they are ignored for too long. They need work to be happy. Pay is not an issue. It is the experience that matters.

I come by these notions honestly. I am the son of a gold miner who knew something about the glittering promise of toil that produces little. I have a picture of the unheated cabin my father and mother lived in the first winter of their marriage in 1935. It sat on a forested mountainside about ten miles southeast of the Continental Divide. The Second World War cut the life of the mine short. By the time it

was over, the price of gold had fallen and the mineshafts had collapsed. My father went on to a career in the Navy and in business. He
and my mother retired to a comfortable house in the suburbs. But
when they reminisced, it was about that other life they had abruptly
and logically deserted. To the end of their days, that life trailed after
them like an orphaned dream. "In the woods," wrote Emerson, "a
man casts off his years, as the snake his slough, and at what period
soever of life, is always a child. In the woods is perpetual youth."

Like many of the nineteenth-century wayfarers who assembled at
the great Western trailheads in Independence, St. Joseph, and St.
Louis, the four of us gathered at the Mexican border that April afternoon were strangers to one another. We had different goals and itin-
eraries but decided to band together through the Big Hatchets, where
there was no marked trail. We would hike together for a couple of
days, sharing snacks and water, then shake hands and part company.
The group included Fred Nollan, an unemployed waiter and aspiring
novelist from Seattle who planned to walk as far north as he could
before the anxiety of joblessness interrupted his idyll. He figured to
get as far as the Colorado border, about 400 miles away. Joseph
Gendron, a surveyor from Silver City, New Mexico, was on a volunteer assignment from the Continental Divide Trail Alliance to plot
the southernmost segment of the trail. Gendron's neighbor, an ami-
able jester named Herbie Marsden, said he needed a break from his
job as a contractor and planned to walk for two or three days.
Marsden wore rubber thongs, tennis shorts, a tank top, and the sort
of cheap plastic sunglasses you can find at the five-and-dime next to
the rack of novelty postcards picturing people who are dressed like
Herbie Marsden. He carried the smallest backpack I had ever seen.

Setting off on a cross-country journey over mountain and desert
can be a forbidding prospect—a bit like setting off on an ocean voyage

in a small boat. You stand on the shore, making one last mental in-
ventory of your meager provisions and your precious supply of water.
It doesn't matter that you've performed this ritual several times already. Nor will it do any good to discover you have forgotten something essential, since the truck that dropped you off is long gone. But
taking stock one more time is a form of relaxation, a mild opiate for
the fluttering gut. Squatting in the sand, we discussed our course. We
would follow a series of intersecting arroyos about twelve miles to the
edge of the mountains, then switchback over a steep saddle through
trousers-shredding thickets of ocotillo, yucca, and crucifixion thorn,
down a long, doglegged canyon to another windmill, which, if working, would be pumping fresh water into a stock tank. Even if it
weren't working and the water in the tank turned out to be stagnant,
we could filter it. We did have a filter, right? Yes. Two hands went up.

Still, we dithered.

Next to the border fence, Herbie Marsden uncovered the stubbly
remains of a monument to past times. The barely legible inscription
read: FRANK EVANS, BORN JUNE 12, 1865, KILLED HERE MAY 1, 1907 BY A
CRAZY COOK. MURDER IN COLD BLOOD WITH AN AX.

How fitting. Where the Rocky Mountains make their southern de-
but, where the West begins . . . a killing. Marsden suggested we do
something to mark the occasion. "Let's be outlaws," he said, stepping
through the border fence and back, violating the laws of two countries. The rest of us followed him through the barbed wire, bonding
in international trespass and beginning our journey with the right
note of don't-fence-me-in Western defiance. Only a dozen scrawny
cows witnessed the crime. Then we shouldered our packs and started
north.

THE CONTINENTAL DIVIDE Trail has been on the drawing board of
federal land management agencies for more than thirty years. The

trail is a grand idea. It is a third again as long as the Appalachian Trail, longer than the highway distance from Los Angeles to Portland, Maine. It meanders through alkali badlands, climbs to the roof of the Rockies, dips and rises again as it snakes north along the zigzag course of one of nature's more sublime feats of engineering, the Continental Divide. In geographical terms, the Divide is the part in the hair of a hemispheric watershed that reaches from Alaska to the Strait of Magellan. The map of Manifest Destiny was written by the explorers, emigrants, surveyors, and engineers who forged the wagon roads, mail routes, rail corridors, and highways across the Divide.

The Continental Divide Trail intersects with history at Lemhi Pass on the Idaho–Montana border, where Lewis and Clark crossed the Divide in 1805. The most heavily traveled crossroads lie several hundred miles to the south, where the Wind River Mountains give way to a nearly treeless, sage-clad prairie at South Pass. That's where the Pony Express raced through on its way to California and where some 400,000 emigrants made their way by horseback, oxcart, and wagon to Utah, California, and Oregon between 1840 and 1870. Farther south, in Colorado, the trail scales heights first described by the explorers Zebulon Pike and John Frémont. In New Mexico, the trail meets the old Spanish Trail blazed by Francisco Atanasio Domínguez and Silvestre Vélez de Escalante, two strapping, cigar-smoking priests who set out in 1776 to establish a route from Santa Fe to Monterey. Heading out almost 100 years before John Wesley Powell made his daredevil voyage of discovery down the Colorado River and the Grand Canyon, the two priests became the first white men to see many of the geologic marvels of the Colorado Plateau, though they never made it to California.

Here and there along the trail, the New West intrudes. The trail crosses interstate highways, skirts oil fields, power plants, and sub-divisions. It winds through the outskirts of Silver City, New Mexico, and, some 300 miles to the north, enters the town of Grants. In Colorado, it takes hikers down the main street of Grand Lake. Still, it would be hard to find a route in this country that offers a more extensive immersion in time travel. The trail passes ghost towns, abandoned mines, Indian reservations, and 300-year-old Hispanic villages. It runs through three national parks, Glacier, Yellowstone, and Rocky Mountain, a dozen wilderness areas, and a score of national forests. There is one section of the trail through Colorado that does not meet a paved road for 100 miles. Hikers hoping to make the entire trip in a single season must be prepared to walk 20 miles a day, sometimes in terrain that requires 5,000 feet or more of steep, uphill walking. Move any less briskly and you risk being marooned by autumn snowfall. The modern traveler faces many of the same hazards confronted by Domínguez and Escalante, including blizzards, lightning storms, flooding streams, and hungry bears, although people are more likely to get in trouble as a result of losing their way, running out of water, or twisting an ankle.

In 1966, Benton MacKaye, the father of the Appalachian Trail, presented the National Park Service with a proposal for a *Cordilleran Trail* along the crest of the Continental Divide, according to MacKaye's biographer, Larry Anderson. MacKaye was eighty-six at the time and the hard work of promoting the trail eventually fell to Jim Wolf, a Baltimore lawyer who first saw the West as a boy attending summer camp near Yellowstone. As an adult, he found himself going back every year and eventually began writing guidebooks for people who wanted to explore the Divide country in Montana and Wyoming. In 1978 he formed the Continental Divide Trail Society to prod the government into building the trail. But Wolf was more comfortable in the mountains with a map and a compass than he was raising money or lobbying and the project languished. Moreover, his vision of the trail as a quiet footpath through the Rockies was a bit old-fashioned for the times—as legions of Lycra-clad bicyclists were discovering the West and sleek advertisements for a new generation of off-road vehicles were luring motorists to mountain trails.

By the mid-1990s, the project was starved for money and 1,000 miles short of completion. At least $10 million was needed. A new organization, the Continental Divide Trail Alliance, set out to capture the imagination of the new Westerners and accommodate their outdoor tastes. Under the direction of Bruce Ward, a former official of the American Hiking Society, and his wife, Paula, a landscape architect, the Alliance built a base of corporate support that Wolf and his group had shunned. New sponsors included ski resorts and condominium developers, eager to publicize the proximity of their property to a national scenic trail. They included outdoor clothing and equipment companies such as L. L. Bean and Recreational Equipment, Inc., better known as REI. Even Wal-Mart contributed.

Privately, the Wards endorsed pretty much the same trail as Wolf did. But they were primarily interested in getting it completed, and they did not want the fractious politics of wilderness recreation to get in the way. The Wards said they didn't like the idea that at least one third of the trail would be open to off-road vehicles, but they weren't going to pick a fight over that issue, or any other, if they could avoid it. When I visited the project office in 1997, the Wards had made considerable progress. The trail had become a perennial item in the U.S. Forest Service recreation budget. Hundreds of volunteers were turning out each summer to work on sections of the trail. Only about a dozen people were walking the entire 3,200 miles every year, but the more accessible segments of the trail were drawing thousands of hikers. While much of the trail was still poorly signed or not marked at all, about two thirds of it was in good shape.

Still, the Wards were uneasy. Too often, the trail was bumping into local resistance and requiring lengthy detours. Only about 20 percent of the trail actually coincided with the Divide. The architects labored

under an unusual handicap. They agreed to forgo any power of emi-
nent domain that might help them secure rights-of-way. But the
concession did not go far enough. Members of Congress from
Western states blocked the trail builders from purchasing rights-of-
way, even when landowners were willing to sell. Private property is
jealously guarded in the West because it is in relatively short supply.
The state and federal governments control close to 50 percent of
Western land. Any subtraction from the private stock can reduce the
tax base and erode the region's sense of autonomy and independence.

The trail encountered its first roadblock just west of the route I was
following from the Mexican border. Rancher William Hurt was one of
the first to object. Hurt manages a herd of cattle along a mostly law-
less, waterless stretch of border country that he said was no place for
city-bred sightseers. "You see a stranger walking around and you
don't know if he's drug smuggler or a cattle thief. Just about everybody down here is armed and on edge. It would just make matters
worse to have backpackers wandering through, looking for water and
scaring the livestock."

West of Hurt's operation, another New Mexico ranch manager,
Ben Brown, refused to let the trail come across his land. "The only
places a trail could go through is beside stream banks and riparian
vegetation, which we're trying to protect," Brown said. At the north
end of the state, the Divide leads to the Jicarilla Apache Reservation
and another barred entry. Next door, in New Mexico's Rio Arriba
County, the trail becomes entangled in land rights politics. Hispanic
residents don't want the trail to cross either private property or national forest land, which they believe was taken illegally from them by
the U.S. Government after the war with Mexico. In Colorado environmentalists threatened lawsuits and stopped the trail from going
through areas favored by wolverine and bighorn sheep. In south central Wyoming, more objections by ranchers, oil companies, and en-

vironmentalists forced the trail onto a road for many miles through the Great Divide Basin.

The reactions seemed out of character, a violation of the country code that welcomes visitors and extends a helping hand to travelers in need. Isn't this the place where a warm pot of coffee is always waiting and the refills are free, where the gas stations let you pump first and pay later, where people leave their keys in the car and their front doors unlocked, where the farmer's field is open to the hunter in the fall, where you bring unruly city kids to learn some manners?

It seemed to me there was a time when people were proud to show off their history. In ranching towns along the Divide, in places like Eden, Farson, Big Sandy, Boulder, and Pinedale in Wyoming, there are leatherbound books kept next to the Bibles that record the lineage of pioneer families and their descendants, that tell you who married whom, who drove the cattle to market, and what the calves sold for every year for 100 years. The story of the West is in large part a compilation of these records. The toil and sacrifice, rarely mentioned but easily inferred from these family chronicles, is what Turner was paying tribute to and what Hollywood later romanticized. Now, just as technology, the siren song of the future, is wooing us away from our romance with the past, along comes an epic trail to the old days. Yet, the very people whose culture and history would be on display don't want anything to do with it.

To be sure, not everybody is against it. Here and there, slumping old mining and railroad towns see in the trail a chance to revive their economies, if they can figure a way to lure the backpackers to cafés and shops. Yet, even in these places, there are misgivings. Amid the forces homogenizing, uprooting, or obliterating rural Western culture, a path over the mountains can seem like a small thing. But often it's the small things that get our attention. In many parts of the West, this has been a period of bitterness and blame, of selling out and forting up. The fights have been over gun control and religious freedom, over the fate of mighty rivers and national forests. But some of the angriest battles have been waged over the fate of desert tortoises, minnows, kangaroo rats, ferrets, and pygmy owls.

The trail was also was my excuse for making my own twilight ramble across God's country, for visiting some of the last lonely outposts of a time and place that were slipping away like dust spilling out of a clenched fist.

Bʏ ᴛʜᴇ ᴇɴᴅ of the first day, the four of us had walked six hours, slowly getting used to the unexpected pitch and yaw of journeying through desert terrain that does not reveal its steep contours until you are well within it. We had come barely ten miles.

Just before dark, standing on a high ridge, we spotted the windmill marking the water hole. The windmill was turning slowly. We plunged ahead, our nearly empty canteens flopping on our belts, oblivious of the one essential ingredient missing from the picture. Cows. Where there is water on the open range, there are cows nearby. There were none here. A quarter mile closer and we could see the empty spout that should have been spewing water into the tank. Closer yet, and we could make out the greenish cast of the stagnant substance in the tank. Oh well, we did have a water filter. But dipping it into the murk quickly fouled the mechanism. That was that. We would have to save what little water we had left for tomorrow's hot morning hike to the next windmill, another ten miles to the north. It would be pumping fresh water, we told ourselves, too tired to worry about it. For now, we would have to satisfy our thirst by passing around the bottle of beer Marsden had stuffed in his pack. Warm beer and cold snacks. It was too windy to light a fire.

We found ourselves in one of those places, bare ground chock-ablock with desiccated cow turds, that environmental groups point to in their campaigns against cattle ranching. They refer to places like this as sacrifice areas, where the cows have trampled or eaten the vegetation in all directions around a water hole. Over time, with enough wells, windmills, and livestock, it's a good way to turn a living desert into a dead one. Ranchers say the wells provide a critical source of water for desert wildlife, particularly bighorn sheep. Environmentalists counter that the man-made water holes have become easy ambush sites for mountain lions who prey on the bighorn, thus contributing to the sharp decline of sheep herds across much of the West. And, so it goes.

We didn't worry about mountain lions jumping us at the water hole. They rarely attack people. Still, we might have moved farther out into the desert, if only to get away from this derelict oasis. For some reason, we didn't. Instead, we booted out the cow flop and spread our sleeping bags next to the water tank.

We lay there looking up at the decrepit windmill, poking like some ironweed out of the primeval garden. Silhouetted against the Big Hatchets, its slowly turning blades caught the moonlight as they clanked and rasped and sawed the wind.

"What's that tune it's playing?" someone asked.

"Home on the Range," someone answered.

MYTHOPOLIS

Once, finding a wilderness trailhead was like looking for the entrance to a secret passageway. You got there by following a homemade map that resembled a child's crayon drawing of barns, churches, and hay fields until you got to the end of a dirt track with weeds growing down the middle. You peered into a green wall of forest, searching for the spot where the trees parted and a wisp of a trail took off. For those of us who get slightly giddy at the idea of a week-long trip into the wilderness, a proper trailhead can hold all of the pent-up excitement of New York Harbor or Grand Central Station in the grand old days of ocean crossings and transcontinental rail trips. Poised at the edge of the world, you waited for the snap of the conductor's watch and the lurch of the locomotive to bear you off to the exquisite unknown.

I'm looking for Turpin Meadows, a flat spot along the Buffalo River, in the upper left corner of Wyoming about eight miles southwest of the Continental Divide. Turpin Meadows is a popular trail-head and the gateway to the largest contiguous spread of wilderness in the lower forty-eight states. Drive into the parking lot, I was told, and search out a red Dodge pickup pulling a trailer full of mules, driven by an old coot wearing red suspenders. Those were my instructions for finding Dick Inberg, from Inberg himself.

I HAD NOT intended to start my journey on the Mexican border only to hopscotch 2,000 miles to northern Wyoming. But fate had intervened in the form of drought and forest fire, temporarily closing off a chunk of countryside in between, and so I was forced to go where nature permitted. The pattern would repeat itself. I'd go where I could: from New Mexico to Wyoming and back, then north to Colorado and Montana before doubling back again. I'd get used to it. I have always had a nomad's indifference to a well-planned future. I like waking up in unfamiliar places. I am a city dweller, a "dude" in the old-fashioned sense of the word. But as Oscar Wilde and Rudyard Kipling, among other famous dudes, discovered a long time ago when they toured the American West, city dwellers often have more in common with country folk than they realize. They are not risk averse. They thrive on the unexpected.

BRUCE WARD OF the Continental Divide Trail Alliance told me about Dick Inberg. He said he had been roaming around the mountains of northwest Wyoming for a long time, and no one knew the territory better. For the past two summers, Inberg had been volunteering for the Alliance, working to complete a section of the Continental Divide Trail through the Teton Wilderness. He invited me to join him in exploring one of the few stretches of this country he had not seen—the lower reach of Two Ocean Plateau, a long barrier ridge that rises above timberline to just over 10,000 feet. He planned to go in from the south, just below Yellowstone Park. He suspected that the only trail that went up the plateau petered out on top amid glacial rubble and shallow tarns. "I want to go and find out just how lost you can get up there," he chuckled over the phone. "Sound like a good plan to you?"

Turpin Meadows is a large campground perched at the head of a narrow valley that leads into the Teton Wilderness. The afternoon I get there it is as busy as a truck stop on an interstate highway. I drive in circles, dizzied by the crush of vehicles and horse trailers and the steady drone of diesels and the *thump-thump* of generators. There are at least 100 people milling about. Some are camped here, as close to the wilderness as they can get and still live out of a motor home. Others are clients of commercial outfitters preparing to ride into the mountains. They stand by their horses, fiddling with unfamiliar trail garb, chaps, and spurs, applying sunscreen to children's faces, waiting for a signal to mount up. Some of the larger ones require assistance. The horses bear up stoically. They are already heavily laden, camera bags tied to saddle horns, folding chairs and fishing rods strapped to their flanks, and water bottles and sack lunches bulging out of saddlebags.

Ah, wilderness.

Eventually, I spot a large man wearing red suspenders. He is standing in one of the camping alcoves, having a furious argument with another, much smaller man. The two are standing toe to toe, snarling at each other like a pair of lunging dogs. Inberg, 6' 4", with a wide slab of a torso, towers over his pudgy antagonist, but the little fellow doesn't back off. He calls Inberg a scofflaw. Inberg calls him a puffed up little Hitler. They are arguing over a $5 admission fee, which Inberg doesn't think he should have to pay. The other man is the campground "host."

All the while, Inberg's wife, Judy, is pulling gently at her husband's sleeve and attempting to point out that the golden age card he thinks entitles him to free admission is not valid here.

"Dick, Dick, your card is only good at Department of Interior campgrounds. This camp is run by the Department of Agriculture."

There is a pause as Inberg looks at his wife and fingers his golden age card.

"OK, Adolph, I guess you win. Satisfied?"

"Not until I get your money," the little man says, but he is retreating now. "And not until I get his," he says, waving disdainfully in my direction.

Inberg, who appears invigorated by the fracas, extends a big paw in my direction and grins. He has a broad, coarse-featured face with liquid eyes, arching brows, and creases that make him seem like he is smiling, even when he isn't. He introduces his wife and suggests we go over to the corral and meet his mules.

"I want you to meet Stuart. You'll be riding Stuart. The two of you will be spending some time together, and it's a good idea for you to get to know each other. A mule needs to be talked to, see. Ya, he does."

At the corral I meet Trouble, Inberg's mule; Apollo and Hay Boy, two magnificently muscled pack animals; and Stuart, who looks morose and potbellied and reminds me of Eeyore, the dyspeptic donkey in *Winnie-the-Pooh*.

"The thing about a mule," Inberg says, "you can count on him for life. If he likes you. But if he don't, God help you."

"Hello, Stuart. How you doing? Looking forward to the trip?" I give his fat, sleek rump a friendly pat. He moves away.

AT SIXTY-THREE Inberg has been riding his mules around the mountains for forty years. The son of a Finnish farmer, he grew up in a little town in northern Wisconsin where hunting and trapping were the normal pursuits of rural kids trying to earn pocket money. He came west in the 1950s, lured by a uranium boom, to prospect in the Gas Hills in central Wyoming. After a few years and not a whole lot of luck, he went into the land-surveying business. He married Judy and built a house in the irrigated farm country outside Riverton. In the early 1960s, he began exploring the Absaroka Mountains that fold around the southeast corner of Yellowstone Park. Over the years, these humpbacked massifs became Inberg's second home. At first, it was just a summer playground where he took his kids to hunt and fish. But in time the Absaroka formed the geography of his life.

He nearly died in an accident a few years ago on the Trident Plateau just east of Yellowstone Park. He still limps from the massive injuries. In his head, he carries around the map of a four-year-long search for his son Kirk, a wildlife biologist whose plane went down in the Absaroka in 1991.

Inberg has another life. He runs his own surveying company and is president of the Riverton Lions Club. But he says he is most comfortable in the mountains. He travels by himself most of the time, though he admits he has become cautious, maybe even a bit superstitious. He wears a belt and suspenders. He coddles his mules, slathering them with liniment at the slightest sign of abraded skin. When he packs them, he uses customized pack straps he made out of trampoline cloth that won't pinch the delicate flesh behind their forelegs. On steep descents, he dismounts and leads his animals. It's easier on them and safer. He rarely travels more than fifteen miles a day. There are places he won't return to. The Trident Plateau is one.

By firelight that evening in Turpin Meadows, he unfolds an oilskin map and goes over the route we will take.

"From right here, we'll go up the north fork of the Buffalo, past Soda Fork, up North Fork Meadows to Trail Creek." He pronounces it "crick." "Probably, we'll spend tomorrow night at Trail Creek, ya. There's good grass for the mules and we won't have to push all that hard to get there. Then we'll follow Pacific Creek to Two Ocean Pass and try to make our way up over the plateau."

If there's snow on the trail or a storm is threatening, we'll have to skirt the plateau's high, exposed crown and settle for a longer, less adventurous course around the southern flank. We wouldn't be the first travelers foiled by Two Ocean Plateau. Jim Bridger, the famous mountain man and scout, was leading a U.S. Army surveying party to the park in the early summer of 1860, when deep snow forced him to detour around it. A "bird wouldn't fly over there without taking a supply of grub along," Bridger told the party's commanding officer, Captain W. F. Raynolds. The setback delayed the first official survey of Yellowstone Park for ten years.

Inberg believes we will have better luck. Besides, if we were to get stuck up there, we have a pannier full of grub—steaks, chops, sausages, beef stew—and a stove to cook it on.

"If we don't get lost, I figure we'll come off the plateau at Phelps Pass and camp over on Mink Creek," he says. "There's a good spot on Mink Creek where I stashed some firewood a couple of years ago. Then the next day we'll drop down into Fox Park. It's a real pretty place, and we might just have it to ourselves. The fishing isn't so hot, and the outfitters don't tend to take many tourists in there. We'll lay over in Fox Park a day or two, and maybe do some day riding into Yellowstone. After that, hell, I don't know. Maybe, come back down around Enos Lake to Clear Creek. We'll figure it out when the time comes."

Altogether, we plan to cover a 100-plus leisurely miles. We'll be following a network of trails blazed by Shoshone Indians who came north on hunting trips into the Yellowstone region. Crossing over Two Ocean Pass, we'll intersect the trail many historians believe John Colter took in 1808 when he became, in all likelihood, the first white man to lay eyes on Yellowstone's fuming wonders. He returned with stories of smoking pits, noxious streams, brimstone odors, and a fifty-foot-long petrified fish. Some people wondered if Colter's account wasn't all one big fish story. Real or imagined, it sounded like a fearful place, and the Yellowstone country came to be known as "Colter's Hell." It wasn't designated a national park for another sixty-four years.

In the morning Inberg and I saddle up after a hot breakfast fixed by Judy.

"Aren't you going to kiss me goodbye?" she asks her husband.

But Inberg, mounted on Trouble, has already developed a case of the 100-mile stare. His mind's eye is fixed way out there on an aspen grove near the juncture of Trail Creek and Pacific Creek where he hopes to find a two-year-old cache of firewood and tepee poles, if he can only recall the hiding place.

"Goodbye." Judy Inberg waves. "Be careful."

The best thing about Turpin Meadows is how fast it disappears once you're on the trail. You round a bend, and a curtain parts on a world not unlike the one Colter and Bridger saw. You are on a sliver of trail grooved into a steep, forested mountainside that falls away to the North Fork of the Buffalo, a shining ribbon of water 500 feet below.

"Come on, you lazy bugger," Inberg says.

He is talking not to me but to Trouble, the mule he raised from a rubber-legged colt. Trouble's pace is set by his own internal metronome, and some mornings the beat is barely perceptible. But no amount of cursing or flogging will change it. Nor is Trouble always in a traveling mood. He may stop at the first stream, turn around, and head for home. But he ran the race of his life once, saving Inberg's life in the process, and the two of them are bonded now like bickering brothers.

"That way is Soda Fork," Inberg says, pointing to a trail that splits off to the east. "That's where they found Kirk's plane."

For most of the morning, we travel in silence, listening to the *clink* and groan of tack, to muffled hoofbeats on soft earth, the screech of jays, and the tattoo of woodpeckers on hollow trees. The sounds aren't unique to wild places. We aren't hearing howler monkeys or jaguars. You can hear jays and woodpeckers in your backyard, but the sounds usually aren't as true. Wilderness is the great clarifier.

After an hour, the forest gradually gives way to North Fork Meadows, a ten-mile-long dogleg of open country. It is the main access route for fishermen and hunters into the game-rich Thorofare region thirty miles northeast of here. Thousands of people, horses, and mules come through every year, and the trail they have cut, actually a dozen parallel ruts, is twenty-five feet across. In wet weather it becomes a muddy slough. Grooved like a giant storm drain, the trail captures moisture that might otherwise feed trees and grass and sluices it away to creeks and rivers. Much of the native vegetation has been lost, replaced by hardier invader plants that offer little nourishment to wildlife.

Yet, it remains a lovely scene. Nature has a way of camouflaging its wounds. In the perverse way that graffiti can masquerade as art, a scarred landscape can seem as arresting as an unblemished one. To an ecologist, the spare, geometrical contours of a steeply down-cut river channel slicing through bald earth are the classic signs of desertification. Yet, such a damaged place is often startlingly beautiful. Erosion created the Grand Canyon. Travel magazines refer to the close cropped meadows of Yellowstone Park as America's Serengeti, neglecting to point out that the veldlike beauty is the result of overgrazing by wildlife. The Trail Creek campsite where Inberg and I stop for the night has a welcoming spaciousness that belies its sorry condition. The ground where we pitch our tents has been cleared of bushes, rocks, and nettles. The trees have been stripped of low-hanging branches, their trunks burled, and their delicate roots exposed. For years, people have been tying their mounts to the trees. The horses have eaten all the grass and pawed away at the earth, damaging the roots and girdling the tree trunks as they pulled against their halter ropes. Now the ground is barren and the trees are dying.

"It's bad like this in a lot of places," Inberg says. "We all did it in the old days. Didn't know better. You still have to educate some people. Don't tie your horses overnight to the trees, even though your grandpa did it and your pa did it and you did it all of your life. You can learn to use the place without using it up."

He points to other signs of slovenly camping. The fire pit is still smoldering and there are horse pellets, spilled from a feed sack, strewn about. This is grizzly bear country and leaving out food of any kind is like dangling your hand in a shark tank.

Inberg quickly scoops up the pellets. We tie up the mules just long enough to unload the packs. Then we move them to a nearby meadow where we hobble the front feet of Stuart and Apollo and picket Trouble and Hay Boy to a pair of short stakes we pound into the ground.

In the morning we will tie all four to the trees again for the few minutes it takes to saddle and repack them. Inberg says if his wife were along, she wouldn't permit even that.

"I'm married to a tree hugger. Good thing, too. Ya."

For a long time, Inberg's attitudes toward wild country were rooted in the workaday values of the farming and logging community where he grew up. He had a trap line by the time he was eight. With his mother's help, he skinned the muskrat and mink he caught and boxed the furs off to a Montgomery Ward store in Chicago. "I'd make two dollars per rat and twenty dollars per mink. I might make two hundred dollars in a winter. Not bad for a kid in them days. Many a grown-up was making under a buck an hour in wages."

There was also a $100 bounty on wolves. "Us kids would chase 'em behind hounds, on snowshoes. Killed all the wolves off in two years. I was part of it. I shot my first wolf when I was nine. Back then, we had the bright idea that if we killed off the wolves, the deer population would bounce back. It didn't. No one stopped to think that, maybe, the reason the deer were disappearing was because we were logging the hell out of the forests. But that would have meant blaming ourselves, and why do that when you can have a good time shooting a bunch of ornery wolves and make some money to boot?"

Inberg doesn't usually bring a gun into the Wyoming wilderness, even though going without a pistol into grizzly country strikes many people as foolhardy. Inberg thinks the pistoleros are the fools. "Christ, they look like Pancho Villa with their big revolvers and ammo belts. But you tell me how good a handgun is going to be up against a bear storming into camp and coming at you."

He goes into a crouch, hands outstretched and trembling as he grips an imaginary pistol. "There they are, scared out of their wits, trying to put a bullet into a bear's brain about this big." He holds up a fist. "They're lucky to hit anything. If they do, they usually just wound the bear and make him more dangerous."

It was just such a chain of events that led to the death of his son.

Kirk Inberg was a bear expert with the Wyoming Department of Game and Fish. He was searching for a wounded grizzly when his plane went down in the Teton Wilderness on a windy October day eight years ago.

It was Kirk's job to deal with injured or troublesome grizzlies. He had to decide whether to kill them, move them, or leave them be. The bears have been protected under the Endangered Species Act since the mid-1970s when any grizzly that wandered outside the park was fair game and the Yellowstone population was sliding toward extinction.

Once shielded by the law, the bears slowly recovered, and by the early 1990s, local sentiment was growing to cancel their protected status. Increasingly, wildlife agencies, like the one Kirk Inberg worked for, came under fire for coddling grizzlies that were killing livestock or menacing hunters.

Just twenty-eight, Kirk Inberg was a rarity, a champion of grizzly bears who was widely admired by people who did not share his love for the animals.

The search for his downed plane was the most extensive in Wyoming history. It involved nearly forty airplanes and helicopters and hundreds of people on the ground. Dick Inberg spent the first weeks coordinating the search from a command post set up by the Teton County sheriff's office. But when the searchers failed to turn up the lost plane, Inberg set off on his own. Riding Trouble, his supplies lashed to Hay Boy or Apollo, he spent much of the next four years crisscrossing the Continental Divide, heading up one drainage after another in the 900-square-mile Teton Wilderness and well beyond it. Sometimes he had company. Much of the time he was alone.

"I STARTED OUT in the Grouse Mountain area where the wounded bear was first reported. Then I went way up Pacific Creek, but it was already pretty late in the year and I got snowed out before I could do much looking around.

"The next summer I went to Yellowstone Point up near Hawk's Rest, then way north on Mountain Creek. I spent a lot of time over in the Dunoir, by Murray Lake and up the East Fork of the Wind River. Next year I went back into the Grouse Mountain country up Tripod Creek and into Squaw Basin. Then I came back into this country that we're in now.

"I got a report someone had heard a radio collar signal near Terrace Mountain. I knew they had a radio collar on the plane. I got up on some of the high peaks and listened but didn't hear nothing. In '93, if I remember right, a group of us went back to Yellowstone Point to check out another report that someone had heard a plane about the time Kirk's disappeared. Then we got a report from a guy who said he thought he'd come across some plane parts up on Two Ocean

Mountain. I think that was in '94 or '95. So I made my way up there, but I didn't find anything.

"In a deal like that, you check out every report and every hunch. I'd think to myself, 'Well, he might have been flying over there, so I better go over there next.' I'd stop everybody on the trail. I'd ask if they'd seen anything glinting, the way a metal plane part does if the sun were shining on it. I always went somewhere I thought he might possibly be."

In the fall of 1995, a hunter found the wreckage of a small plane on a heavily forested hillside near an old spring a few miles north of the Soda Fork of the Buffalo. The area had been searched at least twice. Inberg had flown over it in 1991 and seen nothing.

The plane and most everything in it burned up on impact. The only traces of his son to be found were Kirk's rifle, his nametag, and some bones.

"I hoped finding him would finally bring some closure. It did, but it didn't give us much relief.

"Losing him was the toughest thing in my life. Still is. Every time I come back to one of these places he and I went, like through here, I'll remember the certain ways he would do things. Different from me. We'd argue. Kirk was stubborn. Not mean, like me. But real stubborn.

"I guess his death affected the way I think about things, like these grizzly bears. They frighten some people from coming out here. My wife worries about them. But God I like going down the trail and seeing a big grizzly track. These mountains wouldn't be the same without them. I've even had one around my camp at night while I was asleep. Stepped out of the tent to take a piss and saw the prints in the snow. Made me feel good knowing one had come around."

THE NEXT MORNING we gear up for the haul over Two Ocean Plateau. The weather is sunny and mild. There doesn't appear to be a speck of snow on the great gray battlements of the plateau, which rises in plain sight to the north, about an hour's ride from our camp.

Fully loaded, each pack mule carries about 150 pounds. Inberg uses a hand scale to make sure the weight is evenly distributed across both flanks.

"Only one good thing ever came out of California that I know of," Inberg says, muscling one of the big, double-sided packs onto Apollo's broad back. "That's the Sierra Box hitch."

Horse and mule packers prefer different methods for roping heavy loads onto pack animals. The Sierra Box hitch may or may not be the most secure method, but it seems to cause the least wear and tear on mule flesh by slightly elevating the loads off the sides of the animals.

"See, if you don't take care of your mules, they won't take care of you. They'll bide their time, wait years, maybe. Then, when you're riding along daydreaming about the big ram you're going to shoot, they'll get their revenge."

The trail we take is muddy from the dew, and we are not a half-mile from camp when Inberg leans to one side of Trouble and points at the ground. "Grizzly. Came through last night, heading our way."

Mother Nature leaves few calling cards as splendidly nerve-rattling as fresh grizzly bear tracks. The wide tread and the grooves of its distended claw conjure up an ancient world and arouse primal fears. Tracks like these caused people to retreat to caves and pile up rocks behind them.

"He's a big one," Inberg says cheerily.

There is a comforting rule of thumb for mountain travelers. No need to be nervous if the guide isn't nervous. Of course, guides don't get nervous. Not the ones I've known. But the mules don't act skittish, and that's reassuring. Stuart walks on, unflappable as ever, though I'm not sure if he has a nervous system. I can imagine him plodding impassively through a gauntlet of grizzly bears.

We turn up Pacific Creek toward Two Ocean Pass and one of the planet's small but instructive wonders. Just ahead, in a forest glade, a bubbling stream splits merrily in two, one channel becoming Pacific Creek, the other Atlantic Creek. Nowhere on Earth is the principle of a divide more simply or graphically displayed. A divide functions like the crown of a road, causing water to flow to either side. There may be numerous small divides in one square mile of land. America has thousands of nameless divides. What distinguishes the Continental Divide is its awesome dominion, separating not just streams and rivers but oceans. Ultimately, the waters of Atlantic and Pacific creeks flow into their namesake oceans on opposite sides of the continent. Anyone who has ever struggled with the concept of the Continental Divide should come here and behold. It's nature for dummies.

Inberg says he was a skeptic until a few years ago.

"I'd heard about this place for years. I'd ridden by any number of times without bothering to come over and take a look. I'd heard about the stream that divides in two, but I thought it was a bunch of bullshit. Then I finally came over and seen it for myself."

The trail up Two Ocean Plateau is dry and only moderately steep, and we have no trouble. On top, it does disappear for a while. Inberg has not been up here before, but he is relaxed and we follow his own internal compass northwest toward what we expect to be Phelps Pass and the back door to Yellowstone that Raynolds never reached. After a while, we find ourselves following a procession of rock cairns, a good sign that we are headed in the right direction. The Continental Divide Trail, which Inberg helps maintain, meanders as much as fifty miles from the geographical Divide on its way from Canada to Mexico. But here the trail clings to the Divide.

Spit on one side of your mule, they say, and it will end up in the Pacific, on the other, the Atlantic. Up here, most likely, it will just end up in one of the landlocked ponds that dot the plateau and go nowhere.

We stop and dismount on top. At our backs the steeples of the Tetons float above the clouds. In front of us, moored to the northern horizon, is the Trident Plateau, the fortresslike promontory where Inberg came to grief a few years ago.

He was hunting bighorn sheep with his younger son, Eric.

"I was riding a molly mule [a female] I had bought that spring. I had been riding her all summer. She could really move, go anywhere, up anything. She was the most athletic animal I ever rode. What I didn't know was that she'd stored up a grudge. I learned later she'd been mistreated by a guy who used to own her.

"We were up near Mountain Creek, coming down a real steep trail, when she got me. I wasn't paying attention. When you're sheep hunting, you're always doing a lot of looking around. We'd spotted a ram earlier, and we were on the big sneak. I had the binoculars in one hand. All of sudden I was being catapulted out of the saddle. I did a somersault in the air and landed on my back twenty-five feet down the hill.

"Eric come over and asked me if I was hurt. I says, 'I think I am hurt pretty bad.' I didn't want to get up. But I knew I was on the edge of a shock situation, so I made a push to get back to camp while I still could walk. By the time I got back, I was having a hard time breathing. I got to coughing and saw flecks of blood flying all over the side of the tent. Then I started getting cold and knew I was going into shock. That's when Eric said he was going for help."

Eric saddled Trouble and headed for Yellowstone Park and the ranger cabin at Howell Creek. He would have to ride eight twisting miles in the dark, and a lot further if no one was at the cabin. He lashed Trouble into a gallop and for once the mule did not disappoint.

"Trouble knew something was wrong. He may be a pain in the ass most of the time, but he knows when you're in trouble. He saved my life. He and Eric did."

The Howell Creek ranger was home, and Eric used his radio to call in his father's location. They got back just in time to signal the helicopter that was hovering high overhead, searching for Inberg's camp. "The medics threw me inside, sleeping bag and all, and gave me a shot of morphine."

Inberg had broken nine ribs and punctured a lung. He had also fractured a collarbone and one shoulder blade. Transferred to an ambulance and driven sixty miles to a hospital in Cody, his lung filling up with fluid, Inberg was too broken up to be operated on. But after he made it through the first night, and his lung began to clear, the doctors decided he probably was hardy enough to heal on his own. The hospital discharged him after three days.

"I laid around home for about a week, then went back to work half-days. Pretty soon, it was full days. After about a month of that, I got to thinking, 'I still have my sheep license.' If I could get a sheep and eat him all winter, I figured I would get all my strength back. So I called up Eric and says to him, 'Let's go sheep hunting.'

"It was kind of a dicey proposition. My arm was in a sling. I couldn't ride at all. But I could walk pretty good as long as I could lie down whenever I got tired. That's what I did. I just lay down in the snow every now and then and rested.

"We had gotten to a place called Elk Fork and were looking around, when I looked up in the rocks and saw a little white spot. I says to Eric, 'You know, there just might be a sheep up there.' It was a long way off and neither of us thought we had much of a shot. We sat there and watched it and watched it while we tried to figure out what the hell to do. After a while, the light started to fade and it looked like a storm was coming in. It was pretty much now or never. I thought if Eric could boost me to some rocks above us, and I could brace myself, I might be able to get a shot off. He helped me up, and I lay my rifle over my wool cap on a rock. I says to Eric, 'I'm going to try to shoot him in the back of the head.' The rifle jumped off the rock, *boom!* and, by God, that sheep tumbled off the ledge. We watched it go end over end, all the way down to the bottom of the cliff. The next morning Eric went down and got him. We took him home, and I ate that sheep all winter long and got my strength back."

The story of Inberg's near-fatal accident and his triumphant return to the field of battle soon made the rounds of hunting camps, taverns, and lodges and assured him a place of honor in local lore. A newspaper columnist wrote that it was his brand of to-hell-and-back bravado that the artist had in mind when he designed the bronc rider on Wyoming's license plate.

"Ya, like they said, I'm tough and I'm mean. I tell my wife I'm two hundred pounds of sex appeal and cold, rolled steel. She says, 'Ah bullshit.' "

On Two Ocean Plateau, Inberg and I eat a lunch of cheese sandwiches and pass a pair of binoculars back and forth, scanning the hills opposite us for elk. We don't see any.

He says he hasn't shot anything since he got that ram.

"Ya, could be my hunting days are winding down. I'm pretty much content just to get a look at 'em. Last time I went elk hunting I had a five-point bull walk right in front of me and I didn't do anything. I just got to thinking, 'Why the hell do I want to shoot one of these things?' I had my gun right there. 'Bang!' I said out loud. The elk took off.

"The days of the Wyoming hunter packing into this country are pretty much over, anyway. Except for the outfitters and their out-of-state clients. The Wyoming hunter of today wants to climb into the pickup, go down Horse Creek Road, and shoot something without moving his ass off the seat. He'll get a tag in his wife's name, and bring the fat old lady along in the truck, so he can shoot two elk."

Behind us the clouds are forming up. It is raining in the Tetons, and the weather appears to be moving our way. We remount and slowly make our way off the plateau, down a series of natural terraces, and into a burned-out forest where the blackened tree trunks are thronged by purple fireweed.

"What kind of flowers are those?" I ask, pointing at a cluster of blue stalks amid the sea of purple.

"Only three types of vegetation I can identify," Inberg replies. "Sagebrush, tickle grass, and sticky bush, and it ain't none of those three."

Inberg says he knows what he needs to know—where to find sheltered campsites, water, and good grass for his mules, and how to distinguish between a grizzly bear track and a black bear track.

In general, he seems to pride himself on traveling lightly through the Information Age. He doesn't use a computer, rarely watches television, and almost never goes to the movies. "The old lady got me out to see *Star Wars*. It was a dumb movie. When I'm home, I read the Casper paper, the Riverton paper, the *National Geographic*, and my mule magazine. Then I go to bed.

"You want to know about flowers, better talk to my daughter, Lee Ann. She knows the name of everything that grows out here."

Inberg began bringing his children out here when they were toddlers.

"The main thing you learn back here is that when you get in trouble, there's no one else to blame. It's all on you, Bud. I think it's a good lesson for any kid. Kirk knew that. He and I talked a lot about it the summer before he died. He understood the risks. He said he knew the work was dangerous, going up in small planes, flying low and slow over the mountains, looking for bears. But he loved his work, and he thought he was doing some good with the bears."

AT FOX PARK, where we plan to lay over for a couple of days, we camp on a tree-covered island in the midst of a sprawling complex of creeks and wet meadows. Our neighbors include deer, coyote, moose, and a family of raucous sandhill cranes. We also have human visitors, long-distance hikers who are making their way south, down the Continental Divide. Inberg is delighted that people are actually using a trail he has helped create. He invites the hikers back to camp for "hors d'oeuvres," canned oysters and soda crackers, while he queries them on what they've seen and how much trouble they've had finding their way.

One young woman, a high school counselor, has been compiling a list of the ten most frequently heard comments from people she has met along the way.

"Number one is they tell me I'm lucky I can be out here and don't have to work," she says. "I spent two years saving up to do this."

Inberg snorts. "Ya, that's what people say to me, too. They tell me I'm lucky to be able to afford a mule so I can come back here. Usually, the guy that's saying it has got a couple of ATVs in his garage that cost a lot more than my mules. It's bullshit, this idea that wilderness is for rich people."

On this issue, history is not so cut and dried. There is precious little wilderness in the lower forty-eight states. Less than 5 percent of Wyoming is set aside. But the effort to save it often has pitted one class against another. The twenty-year-long quest to establish Grand Teton National Park, about thirty miles southwest of where Inberg and I are camped, is a good example. As National Park Service historian William C. Everhart has written, preservation of the majestic Teton country would not have been possible without the help of John D. Rockefeller, Jr. During a two-week trip to Jackson Hole in 1926, Rockefeller was awed by the scenery but concerned that only a tiny piece of it was protected as a park. He was not impressed with the human community, a clutter of tacky tourist cabins, gas stations, hot dog stands, and dance halls that had grown up nearby. That was not his only concern. Farmers wanted to build dams and turn the magnificent river valley at the base of the mountains into irrigated hay fields. In 1927 Rockefeller formed a dummy land corporation, the Snake River Land Company, and began buying up thousands of acres. When news of the tycoon's connection to the enterprise got out, local citizens were outraged. According to Everhart, one newspaper ran headlines that read: FEDERAL LAWS NOW IN FORCE IN JACKSON HOLE: ROCKEFELLER, JR., REQUIRES RENDITION OF FEUDAL SERVICE BEFORE GIVING GRANTS AND PRIVILEGES. Rockefeller was accused of cheating landowners, though he had not, having paid twice the assessed value of the real estate. Embedded in the resistance to the park was the idea that it would be a rich man's playground, and that it must be wiped clean of the commoners who had spilled their blood to settle the country. The opposition did not soften until well after the Second World War when the return of prosperity and the growth of tourism persuaded Jackson Hole civic leaders that an expanded park might be good for business. In 1950 President Harry Truman signed a bill incorporating the Rockefeller acreage into the park.

The wilderness of northwest Wyoming has been the province of royalty, celebrity, and the well-to-do for more than 100 years. The Earl of Dunraven was one of the first to enjoy it. The earl went on a hunting trip with Buffalo Bill in 1874 and wrote a book about his experiences. After the earl came Teddy Roosevelt, who hunted elk near Two Ocean Pass, and Ernest Hemingway, who shot a ram near Pilot Mountain in the Absaroka in the 1930s.

The Earl of Dunraven, in particular, faced serious danger. There were still hostile Indians around. He had to be a creditable shot and a decent horseman to survive. But his experience was still an expensive lark, a precursor of the paid wilderness vacation. Today, many if not most of the people who visit the Teton Wilderness do so in the company of a commercial outfitter. It is hard to find one who charges less than $200 a day.

. . .

THE NEXT DAY, as we ride north along the headwaters of the Snake River into Yellowstone Park, we encounter a cultural descendant of the Earl of Dunraven. He is Watts Wacker, corporate consultant, futurist, and volunteer wrangler.

Wacker, who is from Westport, Connecticut, is one of nine paying guests of Medicine Lake Outfitters on a ten-day pack trip and fly-fishing vacation. Each guest is paying $350 per day.

As we arrive, a lady outfitter is gently urging Wacker to cover up. He is dressed only in a pair of bathing trunks and his not inconsiderable torso is turning hot pink. Such is the life of a commercial outfitter, part nurse, cook, wrangler, and security guard. Earlier, she says, she had to speak to another guest about taking food into his tent. Grizzly bears will follow their noses pretty much anywhere, even into an operation as big as this one, which is spread out like a Bedouin encampment across a half acre of river valley.

Wacker and a few other guests are relaxing on camp stools in the kitchen area and sipping lemonade. They invite us to join them. The group includes a venture capitalist from New Jersey, a lawyer from Washington, and a surgeon's wife from Houston. They did not know each other before the trip, but all seem to belong to the same extended family of well-educated exurbanites. They dress alike, favoring the drab, layered, unisex look that has become the trademark of the affluent outdoor traveler. Their politics are a nervous hybrid of generous instincts and tightfisted beliefs. The subject of environmental protection can be problematic. Sitting in a place as magnificent as this, people flirt with Republican heresies, finding themselves sympathetic to arguments for government regulation. "Here in a national park, we don't have to worry about environmental protection, right?" one woman asks hopefully. "I mean, isn't the government already doing all it needs to?"

I am interested in what Wacker has to say about wilderness. He is a swami to the business world, a right-brain thinker hired by left-brain types, by executives who want to understand the inchoate forces shaping markets, who want to better position their companies for the future. Wacker has written a couple of books with catchy subtitles like *Ten Paradoxes That Will Shape the Future of Your Business* and *What Happens After What Comes Next*. He said he conceived of one of his books while he was on a pack trip. "It composed itself, more or less, while I was lying awake, looking at the stars one night. I don't usually sleep in a tent." Wacker doesn't talk about wilderness as such. He talks about it as a medium for revelation, like water is for electricity.

I ask him to do some prognosticating. He has spent a lot of time in this country. What does he think about the future of wilderness?

He nods thoughtfully. He'll oblige. But first, I need to understand the process he goes through to arrive at his conclusions. It is very experiential. "When I was hired to come up with a new corporate strategy for Krispy Kreme, I started by driving a doughnut truck." He takes the same approach to a pack trip in Yellowstone, not because he is being paid by anyone, but because he wants to. He explains that he is not a "dude" in the usual sense of the word. He is paying $350 per day, like the others, but he is a working guest—tending stock, repairing tack, leading pack animals, and clearing trail. He has been doing that and more every summer for at least a decade.

"Look, I'm a guy who has been paid twenty-five thousand dollars to sit down with a bunch of top executives for an hour and give them my ideas on the future. Some people think I might be the next Alvin Toffler. It's heady stuff. But I can assure you there is no experience in my business comparable to leading a string of pack mules through a forest fire."

About thirteen years ago, Wacker was invited by his local minister to join what was billed "as a gathering of men in God's country." "I know what it sounds like," Wacker says. "Like one of those sessions in the woods where you beat drums and cry about the relationship you didn't have with your father. It wasn't that, but it had its similarities.

"The outfitter took us on a sort of white man's vision quest. He led us to a pretty remote, pretty special place. It's called the Trident. It's a big, flat-topped mountain out that way." He waves his hand toward the northeast. "The outfitter took us up there and taught us the Indian ceremony of the Medicine Wheel."

I look over to see how Inberg is reacting to all this, but his expression shows nothing but polite interest.

Wacker says he got hooked on the country and signed up with the same outfitter the following summer. He kept coming back, volunteering to do more and more work, and one summer about ten years ago when a wrangler turned up sick, Wacker took his place.

"Now, when I go on a trip, I usually don't tell people who I am. I go by 'Mitch from Idaho.' That way there is no confusing my role." Being Mitch can have its drawbacks, he admits. Some people look at a hired hand, even one with a cowboy hat on, and see a servant. He tells a story about a teenager, still hungry after his noon sandwich, who requested that Wacker hand over his lunch. Wacker says he was about to tell the kid to fuck himself when it occurred to him that Mitch from Idaho would be more mellow. "I just told him no."

How does a business consultant calculate the future value of a place whose real worth can't be measured in dollars and cents?

"Wilderness is what I call a mythopolis," he says. "It's a place where people go to reconnect with their dreams.

"Wilderness is sort of like an old-fashioned Manhattan steak house with gas lanterns and sawdust on the floor. I go there to satisfy a longing. I need to pick up the bones with my hands and rip off the meat with my teeth. Wilderness is this hunter-gatherer sort of world full of things we can't control, and that's good. Where do you find magic anymore, except in places where you are not in control, and where the out of controlness forces you to be alive and alert, to be in the moment in ways that you rarely are anywhere else?"

Wacker tells a story of going to sleep one night under the stars and waking up to see a huge owl hovering a few feet over him.

"I suddenly knew what it was like to be prey, and, instinctively, I began shaking my head so he wouldn't mistake my nose for a mouse. The owl is one of the three animals in my totem along with the bear and the hummingbird."

In the future, Wacker believes, more people will be at ease with the language of magical allusion. In the future, he says, more people will come to appreciate the value of "out of controlness."

That night, our last in the Fox Park camp, Inberg unfolds his big oilskin map across a tree stump and looks for a route home that will give us a look at some different scenery. He proposes a southerly route along a series of trails he has not traveled for several years. At least one of them is not shown on the map.

"We'll head down Mink Creek, cross Ermine Creek and Pacific Creek, and spend tomorrow night at Enos Lake. After that, we'll be on our own. We'll just have to be a little more alert."

He warns it will be a long hot pull to Enos Lake, and he's right. After a couple of pretty easy days, the mules are in a lollygagging mood. Early on, the usually unflappable Stuart develops a case of nerves. He shies at a moose, and then treats every stump and boulder as a potential enemy. He stops, shudders, and gives each object a wide berth.

We ford Ermine Creek, only to find the opposite bank caved in and the trail erased. We tramp up and down the stream, looking for a break in the steep bank. Finding none, we dismount and start scrambling up the bank, holding reins in one hand while trying to grab a purchase in the sandy soil with the other. Trouble pulls free, then Stuart, and the two of them set off at a brisk trot back toward Fox Park.

I retrieve the runaways, recross Ermine Creek, and join Inberg where the trail picks up, high on the opposite bank. After a ferociously profane lecture by Inberg, Trouble seems to settle down. Stuart falls in line compliantly. His spirit may still be browsing in Fox Park, but his body seems to have gotten the message. Then the wreck happens.

Descending into a broad meadow north of Pacific Creek, we see a line of mules emerging from the woods at the far end of the clearing. We circle wide without incident, but the wrangler tells us there is much more to come—three more pack strings with seven or eight mules in each one. It's the Union Pacific of pack trains. One of the biggest outfitters in northwest Wyoming is setting up his hunting camps, and these are his mules ferrying supplies to the three camps.

Out in the open meadow, we circumnavigate all but the last of the pack strings. Once the trail reenters the woods, though, it becomes a narrow, twisting path with virtually no visibility. Nothing, except lightning, is more likely to stampede a line of pack animals than a sudden face-to-face encounter with a stranger. We are about to have one.

From the rear of our little caravan, I see Inberg stop. Then a big black dog appears and barks at Trouble. For a long moment, mule and dog eye each other. Then the dog leaps forward. I urge Stuart to keep his composure, but before the words are out of my mouth, Stuart hurls himself in the opposite direction and we gallop back toward the meadow. I jam on the brakes to no effect. We'll stop when Stuart wants to stop, which he does after about twenty-five yards. I look around at the rocky ground, remembering Dick's near-fatal fall from a mule. If Stuart had bucked as well as run . . . but I don't pursue that line of thought. Making your way around out here is supposed to acclimate you to risk. It can be good practice for life in the rest of the world these days—if it doesn't kill you. A dozen mules are scattered through the forest, ours and the outfitters'. Panniers are strewn everywhere, lead ropes are hanging from tree branches. But Inberg is smiling.

"We didn't lose a pack, not a one," he says.

"Hurray, for the Sierra Box hitch," I say.

"It ain't just the hitch. It's the hitcher," Inberg reminds me.

THE SITE OF our last campsite, Enos Lake, is a melancholy place. It is notched at the bottom of a forested amphitheater, but the trees have been reduced by wild fire to a million carbonized stilts. The ubiquitous fireweed is all around. Here, the clumps of purple flowers remind me of bouquets in a cemetery.

"I wouldn't get too interested in that lake," Inberg says, sensing my desire to cool off. "The shore is made of pretty boggy stuff."

The last time he was here, he found the carcass of a moose that had gotten stranded in the lake, unable to climb out of the ooze. The moose had retreated to a little silt island, eaten all of the grass on it, and eventually starved to death.

We circle down toward the lake and come upon a family of swans drifting serenely on the mirror smooth water. But this is not a happy place for them either. Every spring a pair or two fly in and hatch their young, only to have them marooned. The season isn't long enough for the offspring to gain enough strength to make the steep flight out. The lake freezes, and year after year, the swans die.

We make camp at the south end of the lake, near a Forest Service patrol cabin. Like the others we have seen, it is shuttered and pad-locked. Wood meant for a half-built outhouse lies in a heap, rotting.

It's nearly dark before we get the fire going and supper cooking. We're down to Dinty Moore, but out here, at the end of a long day, even canned stew will pacify the growling gut.

"So what did you think about old Wacker?" Inberg suddenly asks. "I couldn't tell you beans about the future," he goes on, not waiting for my answer. "But I'll say one thing. It's people like him from back east who are going to save this place. They appreciate what they're getting. If it was left to the people of Wyoming, it would have been destroyed a long time ago. We can thank our lucky stars for the likes of Wacker."

We go to bed to the yodeling of sandhill cranes and the yipping of coyotes across the lake. Before dawn, I hear one of the mules coming toward me, hefting its hobbled front legs in a plunging rocking horse gait. It's Stuart. He has decided to plant himself next to my tent. Apparently, the grass is greener. His relentless champing keeps me awake. I decide to walk down to the lake, watch the sun come up, and see if anything has come down for a drink.

Nothing stirs except one of the young swans, working on its flying technique. There's still a couple of months left to perfect the liftoff, time enough, I'd like to think. Maybe this is the way evolution works and a new and stronger strain of swans is poised to take wing and soar triumphantly over the lake. Over breakfast, I ask Inberg what he thinks about that possibility.

"I wouldn't count on it," he says.

DRIVING HOME LATE that afternoon from Turpin Meadows, I turn off the main road south of DuBois to see the memorial that was built by the state to honor Kirk Inberg. It's twenty miles up a bumpy dirt road in a game refuge that has been named for him and biologist Kevin Roy, who was also on the flight.

I asked Dick Inberg if he wanted to come along. But he declined. He is angry at the state Game and Fish Department, the agency that built the memorial, for allowing all-terrain vehicles in here. Sure enough, on the road in I pass three pickup trucks carrying the squat little motorized monsters.

But there is nothing around to disturb the memorial when I get there. It is set at the head of a pretty river valley, framed by a ruffle of gray-green sagebrush and rimmed by sandstone bluffs. Standing here, the thought occurs to me that one day there ought to be something to remember the old man by, a memorial to him and his kind, the vanishing breed that showed the rest of us how to reconnect with our dreams. I imagine a plaque carved with the images of Inberg riding Trouble and leading Apollo and Hay Boy, heading up the trail to mythopolis.

Hanging Tree Ranch

Art weems won't speak to me. He only glares when I try to make conversation. I have done him wrong in his own home. The least painful course of action would be to throw my duffel in the back of my car and leave. The nearest motel is in Silver City, New Mexico, four hours away, though I can always pull over and sleep in the back of the car.

I decide to dig in my heels, reminding myself that for many people life out here involves staring down failure most every day. It fills the air like the odor from a dead cow or the yapping of the coyotes that killed it. I came out here to learn how people have stuck it out. Stubbornness is high on their list of survival skills.

I can't say I wasn't warned.

"You're going to see Art Weems?" asked the turkey hunter, slightly incredulous. I had stopped him to ask directions the day before. "You'll be lucky if he opens the door to you."

The hunter said I wouldn't have any trouble finding the Weems place. Keep driving and look for the sign that says HANGING TREE RANCH and the hand-lettered warning: VISITORS NOT WELCOME. TRESPASSERS WILL BE SHOT.

Out here, such messages should be taken seriously. Western kitsch has not caught on in the piney recesses of the Tularosa Mountains, Catron County, New Mexico. Catron County was the birthplace of Geronimo, an early hideout for Billy the Kid and Butch Cassidy, and a haven for outlaws, hermits, and misfits. The county remains in thrall of its past and does not quickly embrace change or newcomers. A recent ordinance encouraged the wearing of sidearms. Roughly the size of Massachusetts, the county has fewer than 3,000 inhabitants.

I learned of Art Weems from a local forest ranger I had interviewed occasionally about Catron County's combustible politics. The ranger had grown up in the mountains and felt a kinship with people still trying to make a living from the land. If I was looking for a recluse, he said, Weems fit the bill. He might not talk to me. On the other hand, he had married recently, and his wife was trying to socialize him. I called her. She said she'd speak to Weems and get back to me. She did and told me to come.

I rent a car in Albuquerque and drive west, watching tongues of dry lightning flicker on the horizon. I am drawn to the edgy weather, to the unraveling emptiness, and to the old ranches that rear up out of the prairie like derelict ships, their rusty windmills leaning like mizzenmasts over a sagging cluster of cabins and sheds. I carry a used cowboy hat with me that I bought in a second-hand Western wear store in Los Angeles. I don't wear it often and doubt I will grow into it. It is sweat-stained and frayed. The crown is properly dented and the brim is furled at a jaunty angle. It conjures up the sort of person I am looking for, someone whose clothes bear the imprint of a hard, simple life, gracefully lived, someone who doesn't crowd his speech with words like "like" or "cool," who doesn't put gel in his hair. I am reminded of a sweatshirt worn by a woman I passed in a café in Magdalena. The slogan on her front, COWBOY UP, means bear up come what may, broken bones or broken heart, winterkill, wolves, or foreclosure.

Environmentalists look at the Western scene with a clinical gaze and what they see often flunks their inspection. Fuel oil from old tractors draining into the ground water. Hungry cows stripping out the sparse vegetation, helping transform grassy meadows into sandy-bottomed thickets of piñon and juniper. They regard someone like me as a case of arrested development, stuck on the myth of the Marlboro Man. I suppose I am something of a sucker for it. I'm not blind to the damage that has been done. Yet, I'm still drawn to this reprobate culture. I take refuge in the wisdom of F. Scott Fitzgerald, who wrote that "the test of a first-rate intelligence is the ability to hold two opposed ideas in the mind at the same time, and still retain the ability to function." I grew up on John Ford movies and went to school on John Muir's writing. Muir's nature was a window opening into heaven, while Ford's outdoors was the glorious backdrop for epic human struggle. Their views aren't necessarily irreconcilable. While he was a young forest ranger assigned to these mountains in the early 1900s, Aldo Leopold began working out a secular theory of conservation that valued nature as an integral part of the American experience. The preservation of wild country would allow future generations to taste the sense of unbounded opportunity that drew the pioneers westward. "I am glad I shall never be young without wild country to be young in," Leopold wrote. "Of what avail are forty freedoms without a blank spot on the map?"

I left the pavement behind fifty miles east of Art Weems's place. On the way, the road traverses the Plains of St. Augustine, an oceanic expanse of umber short grass that seems peculiarly un-Western, almost steppelike, treeless and empty except for the wind. The only sign of human presence is a couple of boarded-up adobe buildings marking the crossroads at Horse Springs.

A pioneer ranch woman, Agnes Morley Cleaveland crossed over the Continental Divide and onto the plains in a covered wagon in 1886. Her description still provides an accurate picture of what the traveler sees today. It is also a sad reminder of what you don't see anymore.

"The road unrolled in a long straight thread across the San Augustine Plains, an irregular ancient lake bed, fifty to seventy miles in cross directions. Rimmed by the Magdalenas, the San Mateos, the Datils, and the Gallinas, the plains form a vast saucer."

To Cleaveland's astonishment, the barren ground seemed to move.

"Off to the left where the San Mateo Mountains formed the southern rim of the plains, the dry earth appeared magically to have changed to tawny water, which rose and fell in long undulating swells . . . The whole foreground seemed to be one mass of living creatures galloping flank against flank . . ."

The mysterious tide turned out to be thousands of antelope whose high, cottoned rumps broke like white caps as the herd suddenly changed direction.

"While we stared, the waves that had been rolling steadily onward appeared to break into foam against an invisible shoreline."

The antelope are long gone. Many perished in a horrific blizzard just two years after Cleaveland first saw them. The rest were hunted to extinction.

The only wildlife I see are six Rocky Mountain elk, which are themselves immigrants, imported at the behest of big game hunters a half-century ago. The elk are thriving, edging out the native deer population, and competing with domestic livestock for the best forage.

Like so much of the contemporary West, the transplanted elk offer an illusion of naturalness. No matter. They are a lovely sight as they trot daintily across the road in front of me. A restocked, reseeded Eden is probably the best we can hope for. We fish mountain lakes full of trout released from hatchery trucks and hike through wilderness areas crosshatched with logging roads and bedecked with flowering plants whose seed stock made its way here from Europe and Asia clinging to the hems and cuffs of the pioneers.

But I am looking for the real thing, a living remnant of the endangered past.

THE WEEMS PLACE occupies a small clearing set among stately ponderosa pines a few miles west of the Continental Divide on the edge of the Tularosa Mountains. The homestead consists of a three-room house, a corral, a couple of sheds, and an outhouse. The Continental Divide Trail, not yet complete through Catron County, would come down an old logging road through Barrel Canyon within sight of the Weems place. I was curious to learn how a recluse like Weems greeted the prospect of a nationally publicized recreational right-of-way less than a quarter of a mile from his house. I get there just before sundown.

A quartet of mongrels rushes out to greet me. They are raucous and friendly. So is Weems, who disarms me with a shy smile and a warm greeting. Dressed in rumpled dungarees and striped cotton shirt worn near to transparency, Weems is pushing seventy. He ushers me inside and introduces me to his wife, Elsie. She is younger than he is by several years and more outgoing. She has a country woman's sturdy good looks, more handsome than pretty, and a figure that has not been blurred by age. She takes me in with a searching, friendly gaze, asks me if I would like a drink. By that she means lemonade. She extracts a glass from a cardboard box full of dishes she has brought with her from town, where she spends winters, cut off from her husband by unplowed mountain roads.

Weems stays in the mountains year around with the four dogs, three mules, and 100 cattle that graze the canyons and meadows of the Gila National Forest. At least ninety miles from the nearest hardware store, supermarket, or hospital, Weems gets along without a well or a hot water heater. He has a balky generator for electricity and gets his drinking water from a homemade system that captures snow melt and rain on the tin roof of his house and sluices it into a cistern. He heats his house with the same ancient wood stove that he cooks his meals on. The only concession to comfort is the La-Z-Boy recliner Weems sinks into after he has put the mules out to pasture each evening.

His small house is a monument to plain style. Every room is a storeroom. The pine rafters and plank walls sprout hooks and bent nails draped with lariats, saddle blankets, stiff leather chaps and tools, horse shoeing knives, and shark-toothed crosscut saws. Unpainted shelves bulge with veterinary supplies, worming medicine for cattle, drops for ear mites in cats and dogs, iodine wound wash, liniment and salve for the mules. One wall is taken up by a row of boots. Two rifles are propped in a corner. The only decorations are framed pictures of the American flag, the face of Jesus, a view of a mountain stream, and a scene of cowboys at work on the range.

Behind Weems's recliner is a waist-high bookcase full of hardbacks. They include a World Book set of encyclopedias, several Zane Grey and Louis L'Amour novels, a history of the Tularosa Mountains, a book by Rush Limbaugh, and Wayne Hage's *Storm Over Rangeland*. A manifesto of Western property rights, Hage's book argues that ranchers have legal ownership of public lands and should not have to pay a fee, as Weems does, to graze their cattle.

The largest of the three rooms in Weems's house serves as kitchen, dining room, and parlor. Meals are taken in bunkhouse buffet-style. There is no tablecloth or place mats. Iron pots and skillets are plopped on the center of the table. The coffee is left warming on the wood stove. Weems urges me to grab a dipper full of beans and dig in. Besides the beans, supper consists of Elsie Weems's sweet corn bread and a bottle of nine-year-old preserves, opened in my honor.

Mrs. Weems apologizes for the crudeness of the setup. Weems has heard it before and shushes her. "This is a pretty good cow camp, and that's all I need. I don't know anything else. I've slept in tents and bathed in stock tanks all my life. My wife don't like it. She wants to modernize."

Weems looks at his wife, who just this week has returned from her winter apartment, nearly two hours away, even in the best of weather.

Weems would like to have her here more of the time. But if she is to live here year around, changes will have to be made. She wants room for her books and furniture. She wants a dependable supply of electricity for a computer and she wants a well with filtered water so they don't have to drink from the cistern with its sour aftertaste of soot and algae.

"I do like having her here and not in town, where I have to check up on her, make sure she is not entertaining the troops."

His wife reddens.

"Shame on you," she says.

She sounds genuinely hurt and reproachful. But no amount of old-fashioned wifely deportment can negate the fact that Elsie Weems, though somewhere in her fifties, is a woman whom men still like to look at who chooses to spend half the year away from her husband. In the world that Art Weems inhabits, there are no bicoastal marriages, only good ones and bad ones, only men who can control their wives and those who can't.

Weems is well beyond retirement age, but there is nothing re-signed about him. He is short, around 5' 8", with a horseman's bandy-legged grace and the viselike wrist strength that comes from years of cinching leather and stretching wire fence. His face is slightly lopsided, like a bruised melon, and the flesh of one nostril has been torn away as if a horse had dragged him through the barbed wire.

It is only when he doffs his cowboy hat, dons his reading glasses, and takes to his easy chair that he looks like the little old man he is becoming. He has the bad luck to be an outdoorsman with a soft pink visage. After a day in the sun, he can look less like a cowboy than a Rotarian on a bender.

After a lifetime as an itinerant cowhand, Weems moved to the mountains of southwestern New Mexico about a decade ago. He had been living on the edge of suburban expansion in central Washington and was looking for a place that reminded him of the way the West used to look.

About that time, Catron County was being promoted as a kind of Celtic homeland where the spiritual descendants of nineteenth-century Scotch-Irish pioneers could still fort up, get off the grid, and live blessedly free of government regulation. Weems says politics had nothing to do with his decision to move to Catron County in 1989. "I was looking for a piece of land I could own free and clear, where I could run a small herd of cows in the [national] forest," Weems says. But relying, as he does, on public lands for most of his pasture, he can't afford to ignore the acrimonious debate over the use and mis-use of federal land. Lawsuits by environmental groups have forced the U.S. Forest Service to keep livestock out of areas that have been overgrazed in the past. Until recently, Weems was not affected. His cattle roam the high, pine-studded plateaus of the Gila, up and away from the river canyons where most of the livestock damage has oc-curred. But a drought has prompted the Forest Service to look more closely at the condition of his leased ground and forced him to cut back on the size of his herd.

Like Wayne Hage, Weems believes the rancher has earned a stake in the public lands, by importing water and making other improvements that both livestock and wildlife benefit from. But he isn't inclined to pick a fight with the Forest Service.

"I'm the radical one," his wife says. "Art thinks I mouth off too much, and maybe I do. But I just can't be silent in the face of what's been going on. A bunch of government bureaucrats telling people they don't know how to take care of the land, when they have been doing it all their lives, and it looks better today than it ever has. It's no wonder that people in this county finally rebelled."

She is speaking of Catron County's starring role in a short-lived county supremacy movement that swept across parts of the rural West in the early 1990s. It was a reaction to efforts by the federal government to protect wildlife, efforts that led to new costs and restrictions on logging and grazing. In Catron County, the Forest Service, after decades of neglect, began adopting regulations to save the Mexican spotted owl from extinction. After a local sawmill closed down, the owners blamed the new regulations, even though the mill's closure was already in the works. The county commission passed a series of defiant ordinances challenging the authority of the federal government to police the public domain, which makes up about 65 percent of the county's land base. Without local consent, the commissioners decreed, Washington could not arbitrarily impose regulations that resulted in economic hardship on ranchers or loggers. Ignore the laws and risk arrest, the commissioners warned the federals in one of the ordinances. The county then elected a new sheriff, a former state policeman named Bob "Scarface" Wellborn, who assured the commissioners that with a valid warrant he was prepared to arrest anyone, including a federal officer.

The leaders of the revolt were in a minority. Their representation of Catron as a cow county was largely fanciful. The rebels were also reacting to a painful fact of life, their own obsolescence. Typical of

rural Western counties, Catron's economy by 1990 was far more dependent on retirement income, government salaries, and the tourist
trade than on cattle ranching, logging or mining. Still, the rebellion
had a lot of support. The idea that one's destiny is intertwined with
the land is a powerful conceit. Whether you were a motel owner or a
real estate agent, voting for the ordinances was a good way to express
solidarity with the salt of the Earth. The revolt was also an expression
of the upstart county's penchant for theatrical nonconformity. Dave
Foreman helped found Earth First! in Glenwood, a leafy hamlet along
the San Francisco River. Hippie expatriates from a Colorado commune founded a "stress retreat" for corporate executives near
Reserve, the county seat, during the 1980s. Stephen Kaufman, relocated from New England where he had trained as a Jungian analyst,
changed his name to Uncle River and wrote a food column for a local
newspaper, extolling recipes for tofu fried in bacon grease, goat ribs,
and burro jerky. Uncle River became the most thoughtful apologist
for the county and its politics during a stint as a commentator for
National Public Radio. River's Catron County was a libertarian arcadia of rednecks and bohemians united in a fierce commitment to the
principle of live and let live. When I met him, River was railing
against the Forest Service for imposing a $10 collection fee on firewood gathered from the national forest. Someone was always resisting something. In Glenwood, the operator of the only gas station in
town threatened to shut it down if the oil company that owned the
franchise didn't drop its demand for the removal of the elk head that
was mounted over the gas station door. The standoff ended only after
someone stole the elk head.

The atmosphere of dotty anarchism grew more menacing as the
county supremacy ordinances began attracting militia buffs and professional xenophobes. The pastor of a white separatist church in
Idaho staged a United Nations flag burning in front of the county
courthouse in Reserve. A government biologist in town to consult

with ranchers about the Endangered Species Act was told he'd be murdered if he ever came back. Local forest rangers turned up pipe bombs and plastic explosives hidden in several places around the woods.

The county's legal blustering was contagious. By 1995, more than thirty counties across the country had adopted their own local sovereignty measures. Nye County, Nevada, went the furthest, enacting a law that purported to transfer authority over all federal land in the county to local hands. The ordinances did not survive court challenges. Judges told the locals they couldn't trump federal law on federal land.

A RT AND ELSIE Weems are sorry the antifederalist fight fizzled. Grazing restrictions have already put a few small ranchers out of business, and the Weems fear they too are vulnerable. The drought in the Gila National Forest has already forced Art to reduce his cattle herd by 25 percent, bringing it down to about one seventh the number most livestock experts say is necessary for a ranching family to make a living. Aside from a $500 monthly Social Security check, Weems has no supplementary income and no other way to stretch the meager natural resources of this high, dry homestead.

"We have too short a growing season to have much of a garden. We can't grow tomatoes or hardly any corn. We do real good with cabbage and turnips," he chuckles.

For Weems, the challenge of living where he does isn't so much to outwit nature as to accommodate himself to its limits. The economizing is evident in his frugality of speech and movement—in the offhand way he has of coaxing a long, hot fire out of a stick of last night's charred firewood. It is not hard to imagine Weems surviving hard times by walling off that part of his system that requires corn and tomatoes.

This year, with the drought, he figures he will have to get by on less than $20,000. "I don't have many expenses out here, not much beyond fuel for the generator, the telephone, and gas for the car. I can usually find a way to cut back a little more. It's all according to how you want to live. I'm a hermit, myself, and I have always lived plain, doing this kind of outdoor work. I don't necessarily like it all the time. But I come by it naturally, and you can adapt to just about anything, except people. I don't deal with people very good."

I BRUSH MY teeth in the kitchen sink and retire to a comfortable bed in the low-ceilinged spare room. Somewhere in the forest, an owl hoots and it sounds like the moan of a distant train. A pack rat scuffles in the rafters. Out on the porch, the dogs murmur and fret briefly before settling in for the night. Then there is silence.

An hour before daylight I hear Weems's boots scuffing in the kitchen, where he is heating a basin of wash water along with a bowl of porridge. Before I am dressed, he is out the door, rounding up his three mules for the day's work. We will be hauling protein blocks to cattle that are scattered across miles of forested canyon and mountainside. We will also be checking his string of coyote traps and shooting any who cross our path.

"Eat these," Mrs. Weems says, pushing two eggs and a rasher of fat, greasy, tasty bacon in front of me.

I am embarrassed at being served a breakfast no one else is eating.

"It will be a while before you eat again," she says. "Art goes pretty hard. And take some water. He never does."

Outside, Lotty, the tamest of the three mules, is saddled and waiting for me.

"So you're up," Weems chortles. "I thought for a while there we were going to have to call the coroner."

His wife hands him his rifle.

"You forgot this."

Lotty is a laggard, constantly falling behind Weems. I kick her into a crotch-mashing trot every few minutes. I try to coax her into the long striding walk Weems says she is quite capable of.

"Use your whip," he says.

T HE ROUTE IS a roller coaster, up one drainage and down another. The trail has been beaten down to a limestone cobble. The streams are all dry. Dust wells up with every footfall. There is no sign of life, except for the occasional lowing of one of Weems's gaunt cows.

One by one, he finds his traps are sprung and empty. The coyotes have thwarted him. The rifle stays in its scabbard. But Weems isn't fazed. An old hand at the varmint wars, he expects to come up empty more often than not, though he thinks he may have caught one, up ahead. He has booby-trapped the carcass of a mule that was shot last fall. Weems thinks the shooting was done on purpose by hunters who were angry that he wouldn't let them on his land.

The bad blood between ranchers and recreational hunters is another symptom of the festering discord over Western land.

"Used to be hunters were sportsmen," Weems says. "You were glad to have them around. They would let you know if they came across something, a dead calf or a cow that was in trouble. Those were the days when you left the cabin unlocked in case someone got hurt and needed a place to rest. But my Good Samaritan days are over. Too many people out here trying to take advantage of your good will."

Recreational hunting has changed over the years. It's mostly a trophy sport now. The antlers are what matter. Dehorned elk carcasses litter the woods, much to the disgust of people like Weems who can feed their families for the winter with a single elk.

For their part, the weekend hunters regard ranchers as freeloaders on the public land, who are allowed to graze cattle in national forests at low lease rates that do not cover what it costs to replenish grass that rightfully belongs to deer, elk, and other game animals. The hunters vent their displeasure by leaving pasture gates open, dumping trash, and, now and then, shooting a cow or a mule.

There was a time when hunters and ranchers got along better, when they had the country pretty much to themselves. That was before backpacking and mountain biking became popular pastimes, before the Japanese auto industry began promoting the recreational uses of off-road utility vehicles and before the ski industry decided to extend its dominion by building high country condos. All of this activity has spawned interest groups and lobbies and triggered competitive animosities as well as placing new stresses on game animals and livestock. Like a pair of aging guard dogs, overwhelmed by threats to their charges, sport hunters and ranchers have turned on each other.

Weems rises in his saddle and squints at the dead mule, now more skeleton than carcass, looming beside the trail just ahead. The traps are empty.

"I thought we might get one. Right here is where I caught five over the winter."

Trapping may be a bygone profession in most places, but a skilled predator killer is still highly employable in these mountains. The exploits of bounty hunters like Ben Lilly and Shorty Lyon are the stuff of legend, their colorful careers celebrated in books of cowboy poetry, on roadside monuments, and on the backs of restaurant menus.

Shorty Lyon was one of the most accomplished exterminators. A trapper for the New Mexico Department of Game and Fish, Lyon took credit for killing 56 adult coyotes and 112 unborn pups in the course of one month's work in 1962. By the time Shorty was retired and enshrined in New Mexico's Trappers Hall of Fame, grizzly bears, wolves, and jaguars were extinct in New Mexico.

Weems believes the government has backed away from its responsibility to rid the public lands of the remaining predators—coyotes, mountain lions, and black bears—because of protests by animal rights activists. But the official tally of predator kills tells a different story. As recently as 1997, the U.S. Department of Agriculture spent more than $2 million to exterminate troublesome wildlife in New Mexico while livestock losses amounted to less than $200,000.

Weems shrugs at the figures. He says he lost 30 percent of his calves last year to coyotes and says he won't be able to stay in business if he continues to suffer such high losses.

"Survival is a year-to-year proposition. I'm still on top of the food chain, but barely," he laughs dryly. "Out here, you're always trying to make things work better, trying to figure an angle. Right now, I need to come up with a way to make my cows meaner. It seems to me they're just giving their babies away."

Recently, the federal government raised the odds against ranchers like Weems by reintroducing Mexican gray wolves into the region. So far, there have been no livestock attacks blamed on the wolves, but that hasn't softened opposition to the reintroduction. Bumper stickers and signs on gun shop windows encourage armed resistance. On roadside fences ranchers have taken to hanging up the carcasses of coyotes they've shot to let the public know how they feel about canine predators in general. During the first year of wolf reintroduction, nearly half of the original twelve wolves set free to roam the wilds of the Gila and nearby Apache National Forest were shot to death.

"Want to see the eighth wonder of the world?" Weems asks. He points up at a cliff face high above us. Getting up there requires a steep ascent on a narrow trail littered with loose shale. At first, the mules balk. Weems lashes his forward. I dismount and decide to lead mine.

"There was bear sign back there," Weems says. "It spooked the mules." Weems gestures at the scarred trunk of a pine tree. Wisps of fur are stuck to it where a black bear has rubbed against it.

"Look at this," Weems says when we get to the top. He rolls away a small boulder from the cliff wall to reveal what looks like a secret passage leading to a deep pool of water. We are at least 100 feet above the canyon floor, and it is indeed a wonder how the water managed to collect in such volume so high up.

"An old man who used to roam these mountains showed it to me. I guess the Indians must have shown him. It's a useful thing to know about in a dry year like we're having now."

Lapsing into a dude's reverie, I wonder aloud about the wildlife you might see coming for a drink, if you left the rock cover ajar and came back to watch at dawn or dusk.

"I'm not much of a wildlife watcher," he replies. "I like to look at a deer. But I don't care much for the bear or the coyote. You ever see a hungry coyote around a pregnant mother cow? He'll start eating that baby calf before the mother has even dropped it."

By the middle of the afternoon, we are done and back at the house. "We made pretty good time, considering," Weems says to his wife with a glance in my direction. I take it as a compliment.

We sit down to a meal of beefsteak, beans, and homemade cake. I eat myself groggy. So does Weems. He retreats to the La-Z-Boy, and turns on the radio. It's Rush Limbaugh. The old crank seems to have a clear channel to every nook and cranny of the Western outback. Weems appears more comforted than stimulated as he sinks into his nap. The whining radio voice propels me toward the door. I can't think of anything less cowboylike than to take a walk, but it is the only excuse I can think of that will get me out of earshot of the radio.

"Want to join me?" I say, looking in the direction of Weems's wife. I assume she will turn me down. She has mentioned soreness in her leg, but I figure it's the polite thing to do to ask her. I'm curious about what she might say, away from her husband, about life out here.

She accepts my invitation. Outside, I am struck by her appearance. She is wearing an ankle-length dress and the kind of stiff leather shoes that the department stores used to advertise as comfortable ladies' footwear. I am reminded of an old family photo of my grand-mother and her sister at a picnic in 1913. The attire underscores Elsie Weems's own discomfiture. It is a subject she is eager to talk about to a city dweller, someone who can surely empathize and who won't in-terpret her misgivings as disloyalty to her husband.

"You can't imagine what it's like to move from a three-bedroom house with all the goodies to a place like this where you don't see a soul for six months. I can't have my books, and I'm always shuffling things around to make room for the bare necessities. I feel dirty. Art doesn't mind because he's used to making do with practically noth-ing, to washing in tanks. It's the only life he knows. God bless him. But I'm not like that.

"I'm afraid out here now," she says. "And I didn't used to be. When Art first moved out here, we never locked the doors. You left your house open in case friends drove out from town or for travelers who might be in trouble and need to use the phone. But it's not the way it was. A lot of the hunters are still good people, but more and more of them couldn't care less how they leave things, beer cans, toilet paper, you name it. Drunk, they'll shoot anything, like Art's mule. Last year, someone broke in and used our phone. They ran up a huge bill. There were calls to New York and the Dominican Republic. Can you imagine anyone out here wanting to call the Dominican Republic? Makes me nervous just wondering who they are."

Stories of vandalism and robbery are commonplace now among outlanders. There have also been seven unsolved murders in Catron County in the past two years. Among the victims was a family of three executed in their isolated cabin near Mangas, an hour's drive north of the Weems place.

"When I'm by myself and Art is out all day with the cows, I carry a pistol with me, even if I'm just going to work in the garden."

The crime wave has followed a rash of mine and mill closures. They put dozens of people out of work and contributed to a surge of alcohol and drug abuse.

Stopping several days earlier in Reserve at Uncle Bill's, the town's only bar and a popular hangout, I could taste the anger. "You make people feel that they don't count for anything, anymore, don't be surprised if they lash back in ways that aren't very civilized," a forest ranger, who shares some of his neighbors' antipathy toward the environmental movement, remarked to me over a beer.

Catron County's woes can't be blamed entirely on the environmental movement. The global economy has little room for men like Art Weems. Copper and cattle prices have been plunging. And though there is still plenty of valuable timber in the Gila National Forest, it is hard to get at. Most of the accessible big trees, along roads and rivers, have been cut. The cost of harvesting timber from steep slopes in roadless terrain tends to eat up a logger's profits.

In some ways, Catron County is a victim of its own politics. The county's strident rejection of land regulation has invited the propagation of rural slums. Former ranchland north of the Plains of San Augustine, the area homesteaded by Agnes Morley Cleaveland, who wrote of the vast herds of antelope there, is today strewn with the trailers and shacks of the nomadic poor. They are the threadbare abodes of families lured to isolated, waterless tracts by newspaper flyers promising a piece of the Wild West for $90 down and $90 a month.

It is only after the new pioneers settle in that they discover how expensive it can be—many thousands of dollars—to drill a well. Without one, they can't grow food or raise livestock. The dream of frontier self-sufficiency deteriorates into the squalid reality of food stamps and welfare, of hauling jugs of drinking water for miles every day, and of scrounging to make the monthly land payments by selling firewood or peddling elk horns to tourists.

Five miles south of Art Weems's place, a 200-acre ranch has recently been split into forty-five parcels. The plots sell for $3,000 an acre. The developer refers to the land as a "recreational subdivision." It is local real estate parlance for property without water, electricity, or telephone service. Straddling the Continental Divide, it is a lovely expanse of meadow framed by rows of aspen and pine.

The agent for the property says it works best as a weekend getaway. He says it is the perfect spot for hunters or outdoorsmen from the city to park their campers while enjoying their own private corner of wilderness. The beauty of it, says the salesman, is there's no one around to tell you how to live. He means there is no one to tell you where to throw your trash or bury your waste.

I ask Elsie Weems if the subdivision worries her. It does, she says. But it is private property, after all, and the owners have the right to do anything they want with it. "I don't quarrel with the American way," she says.

She is more concerned about the proposed Continental Divide Trail. "It's an invasion of our privacy," she says. "Strangers will be able to look right down on us."

Most of the people who use the trail are going to be environmentalists, she says, who will complain about the cows. Or they will be rich people who could care less about the likes of Art and Elsie Weems.

"Who else is going to have the time to walk on a trail that goes all the way from Mexico to Canada?"

WEEMS IS SEETHING.

I have abused his hospitality. I, a stranger, have brazenly asked my host's wife to take a walk with me. I remembered his grim little joke about Elsie "entertaining the troops." It was fair warning, and I ignored it. The hurt is not going to go away until I do.

His wordless fury reduces me to a state of mute passivity. I am like an addled teenager too undone by parental anger to recall the exact nature of my offense. Had I specifically asked his wife to take a walk or had I merely asked if anyone wished to join me on a walk? But so what if I had asked her? Are we not all grown-ups here, aging grown-ups at that? It was, after all, just a walk. We didn't go on a picnic or slip off to the swimming hole.

Elsie Weems is also dismayed by her husband's reaction. She tries to jolly him out of it. Sitting on the armrest of the recliner, she holds his hand, kisses his bald pate, and clucks girlishly at him. But the storm will not pass.

I can remember being in this position only once before, years ago, and knowing there was no way to undo the damage. One summer during college I worked as a volunteer in a French forestry camp headed by a taciturn ex-Army officer who had served in the French Army in Algeria during that country's war for independence.

I stayed in the officer's house and ate at his table until what seemed to me a perfectly harmless question caused him to throw me out without out a word of explanation. I had asked him his opinion about the accusations of torture brought against the French military in Algeria. "Get out," he said with a wave of his hand.

Once again, it appears, I am in a foreign country violating taboos I could not foresee or even comprehend. But if I am going to understand his world, I am going to have to see it through Weems's eyes. I decide to stay one more night.

It isn't going to be pleasant. As night falls, the old Zenith is switched on again, fiendishly loud. This time Limbaugh is just the warm-up act to an evening of moral shellacking by the Druids of talk radio and Y2K pitchmen hawking gold bullion, solar-powered generators, cook stoves, and water filters.

They are addressing a rural audience for whom Y2K is merely a metaphor for the real endtimes. The listeners are aging cowboys, lumberjacks, miners, and roustabouts whose way of life is coming to an end. Society has handed them the millennial pink slip, and they are staring at a time clock that can't be retrofitted like a home computer.

"I'll stay out here as long as they let me," Weems had said the night before. "I'll stay until the government cuts my cattle numbers down to where it doesn't make sense to be out here any longer. They could do that. They're threatening to do it now."

Poor Weems. He is frazzled enough without having to worry about a stranger slipping off to the woods with his wife.

The radio finally off, I close myself in the spare room and try to imagine a way to put things right with my host. But I fall asleep without having come up with a plan. Sometime in the night a pack of coyotes starts howling. They are close by, and the noise riles the dogs. I hear Weems shush them, then shuffle back to his bed.

I wonder what he is thinking—that come morning the rude stranger would be gone and he would be back to his blessedly solitary routine—checking traps and looking for stray calves. Things will be back to normal then, with no one around to remind him that he is an old man with a younger wife and that his world, his custom and culture, his antique sense of propriety is so obsolete that other people don't even know when they are offending him.

The radio bombardment starts up again before dawn. I don't need any encouragement to get going. Duffel bag in hand, I am confronted by a downcast Elsie as I make my way to the front door.

"I am sorry about this," she says. "My husband is a jealous man. We shouldn't have taken that walk. I shouldn't have. I tried to tell him it was my fault. But it didn't do any good. I hope you can understand. He is the way he is."

She continues to stand in the doorway as if she is not through wanting to talk. Weems is out feeding stock and gathering his mules, so I ask her a question that has been on my mind since I got here.

"How did your husband's face get so disfigured?"

It was cancer, she says.

Sandy-haired and fair-skinned, Weems has been working outside since he was six years old, when his father, a ranch caretaker for a wealthy Texan, put the boy on a tractor and ordered him to disc the hay field. "It was an all-day job, and his father would tie him on the tractor so he wouldn't tumble off if he fell asleep."

After sixty years in cow camps from New Mexico to central Washington, growths began to sprout on his ruddy face. "Art has never put much stock in doctors, and neither have I. He probably hasn't gone to one in ten years."

Instead, the Weems put their trust in home remedies—in this case, a toxic concoction of bloodroot and other herbs, sometimes referred to as black salve—which can kill skin cancer by destroying the surrounding tissue. "It causes gangrene and flushes the bad tissue out. That's how Art lost that bit of his nose," she says. She says her first husband refused to use the potion and died of melanoma. Weems has treated two cancers with the salve. It arrested a malignant growth behind one ear, but the cure made him deaf on that side. "It is not a gentle cure. It causes a fever and the pain is so bad at first you want to die."

Elsie Weems knows this from personal experience. She has a scar over an eyebrow where she treated a malignancy of her own.

"Art doesn't let these things bother him. Right after the first treatment, he saddled his mule and headed off for the day to clean stock tanks. He told me if he died out there, just wrap him in a canvas and bury him with his dog."

I thank her for her hospitality and head for my car. Weems is still nowhere in sight, and I'm relieved not to have to face him.

Five minutes later, turning onto the main road, I realize I have left my hat behind. No doubt, Weems is back in the house and I will have to confront him if I return. But I'm not about to go hatless, not after the story I've just heard, and I turn around.

On the way to the door, I hit upon a scheme to make things right. I will restate the offer I made when I first arrived. I will insist on paying for my bed and board.

"We don't take handouts," Weems all but sneers. His wife titters behind him.

I am momentarily seized by the impulse to match his unpleasantness. Instead, I thank him for putting me up and offer my hand. He gives it a quick jerk, mumbles something in reply but doesn't look at me.

Heading out the driveway, stopping to unlatch the gate, I get a last look at the sign for HANGING TREE RANCH and remember Weems's brief explanation of the name. In 1890 a man was hung here after he'd shot somebody in a dispute over a woman. Perfect.

As I bump down a dirt road at dawn, the mountain scenery begins to work on my dour mood. A line of elk ghosts by at the far end of a foggy meadow. By a small lake in Houghton Canyon, a great blue heron preens on the mirror smooth water.

Down the road a mile, I come upon a young man and woman dressed in form-fitting Day-Glo Lycra laboring over a broken bicycle. They were making their way north from the Mexican border along the Continental Divide when a bolt sheared off the seat of one bicycle.

I give them a ride to the nearby Beaverhead Forest Service station, where they can get the bike fixed. They say they have ridden 200 miles, much of it through glorious countryside. People have been very friendly, they say, except for some of the ranchers they have encountered.

"You're in Catron County," I say.

But that means nothing to them.

"Is that like saying we're in Dodge City?"

"Sort of."

The woman asks me why ranchers hang the bodies of dead coyotes out on roadside fences for people to see. "Is it, like, they're trying to tell us this is the Old West and here's what can happen to you if you make trouble?"

I tell her I think it's more like they are saying, "This is the Old West and get used to it."

"Well, that's kind of dumb," she says.

I wonder what the two bicyclists will think if they run into Art Weems. Their route will take them right by his place.

I drop them off at the ranger station and go on my way.

Bending south from Beaverhead toward the old mining towns of Kingston and Hillsboro, I catch crackling snippets of Catron County news. It's all about an eighty-four-year-old ranch widow who is being hauled off to jail for putting up a fence that has blocked access to a new subdivision next door to her ranch.

The woman says her cows are being run over and won't move the fence.

"Good for her," I say. Gliding along in the air-conditioned comfort of my rental car, I'll take cows over cars any time.

Outside of Nutt, New Mexico, I pick up a hitchhiker. I need a distraction. I can't get Weems out of my head. My thoughts keep straying back to his ranch like coyotes pawing at a shallow grave.

The hitchhiker is an elderly, out-of-work cowboy carrying a knapsack and a bedroll. The cowboy calls himself a drifter, but his crisply laundered pale blue shirt, the formality of his speech, and the relaxed, cheerful gaze are not the hallmarks of a hobo. His name is Lou Belisles, and he is on his way east and north, eventually to Montana, with stops planned along the way in Vaughn, New Mexico, and Scotts Bluff, Nebraska, where he is counting on finding old pals and odd jobs to support him on his journey.

Belisles has been living this way for the past few years, he says. Hitching to Montana in the spring and wintering in southern Arizona, where he has built a crude shelter out of found lumber in a vacant lot between a Price Club and the edge of the Sonoran Desert.

"I rely on Providence and what I call the Dumpster from heaven to supply my needs," he says, referring to the Price Club's bountiful disposal unit. "I do odd jobs for the neighbors, or look out for their property when they are away. They pay me what they feel it's worth. It doesn't amount to much. Pocket change. But it gets me by. I stay away from missions. They make you pray before they feed you, and that doesn't sit right with me."

We talk about cowboying. He says he made a living at it for twenty years.

"When they came up with a way to suppress the screwworm fly, that pretty much ended my career. They didn't need guys like me, after that, cutting out the infected cows and treating them." The screwworm got under a cow's skin, turning the flesh into a gangrenous pulp, he explains.

"People always blaming somebody else for their failures. Hell, a lot of these outfits went out of business because the owner drank up the profits. But I quit drinking, and I'm fine now. Wouldn't trade my life for the old one, even if I could get a job on one of the ranches around here."

I ask him the same question about the dead coyotes hanging from ranch fences that the bicyclists asked me.

"No need to kill a coyote," he says. "I think it's stupid. It's the lazy rancher who leaves his dead calves out that gives a coyote a taste for beef. The coyote will get by fine on mice and gophers. But the average rancher, you know, he has to shoot anything that moves just to show he's the boss. I always got along with nature. Seeing the wildlife was part of the pleasure of working outdoors."

We are both hungry, and Belisles points us to a cafe south of Truth or Consequences. It is a no-name place where cigarette smoke curls over thin coffee.

"They know the secret of good Mexican food," he says, "and I don't mean chili."

"Lard," I say.

"That's it," he says. "I knew we were soul mates."

Our paths diverge in Socorro. I let Belisles off at a Gambel's store where he intends to buy fuel for his camp stove. I ask him if he has everything else he needs.

"I got a bedroll, a pressed denim shirt, a spare pair of shoes, two pairs of socks, a slicker, a stove, a plate, a knife, and fork. And when I get done paying for the Sterno, I'll still have a $1.75. What more could an old cowboy want?"

We wish each other good luck and I take off, heading north toward Colorado.

I can tell by a widening spiral of dust on the horizon that the afternoon wind is building up its usual head of steam. Overhead, a cloud bank the size of Texas swells with the promise of badly needed rainfall. The sky is an incorrigible trickster out here, but this time it's not kidding. I can smell the rain on the wind before I see the drops on the windshield.

THE SHEPHERD

I T IS HAPPY hour in the mountains high above Vail. The sheep are bedded down for the night. The dogs are fed. The people are gone. The jeep tour to Ptarmigan Pass is over. The backpackers have retreated to their camps below timberline. In this gray interval, after the hot pink Alpenglow has bled from the summer sky, you can almost see things as they once were. The houses recede into the hillsides. The highways shimmer like rivers and the ski runs and golf courses blend into the remnant hay fields and elk meadows. From where Sam Robinson and I sit, about 11,000 feet high on an aspen-fringed knoll just south of Vail Pass, the Colorado countryside looks almost as unblemished as it must have when the explorer Zebulon Pike first spied it through a telescope in 1806.

· · ·

"You want a drink?" Sam asks, pushing a bottle of Everclear, 190 proof grain alcohol, in my direction. Everclear is tonic for sheepherders and sheep alike. Sam is a Mormon and doesn't drink. He uses the Everclear to anesthetize ewes that have expelled their wombs while giving birth. He injects a centimeter or two above the hip flange, waits for the alcohol to take effect, and pushes the organs back inside.

"You want to drink it straight or do you want to put some pop in it?" Sam asks.

I pass.

I learned of Sam from the Colorado Wool Growers Association. The director told me that if I wanted a dose of culture shock, I should visit Sam's tumbledown sheep camp just above one of the toniest resorts in America. Sam is Vail's last sheepherder, the only remaining link to the area's pastoral roots. He is part of the twilight mirage, a throwback to the time when recreation and real estate were not the twin turbines of the Rocky Mountain economy, before the developers bought out the ranches and the environmental movement launched its campaign to run livestock off the Western range.

Sam is forty-five with deep-set eyes and a boyish smile. He is short and compact, thick through the wrists and shoulders. He is built like a wrestler, which he was. He has a wrestler's penchant for seeking avenues of least resistance, for leverage over force. He avoids run-ins with tourists where he can, though he will shoot a loose dog if it attacks one of his sheep. When a hiker angrily accuses him of overgrazing a mountain meadow, Sam gestures at the lush growth of clover and timothy grass where his sheep have been feeding and asks the hiker to point out the damage. When a passerby sees him butcher a sheep and demands that he be prosecuted for animal cruelty, Sam has the sheriff explain that stock growers are entitled to harvest their own food.

For the past twenty years, Sam has grazed his herd of Rambouillet sheep across 25,000 acres of the surrounding White River National Forest, most of it above timberline, that he leases from the U.S. Forest Service. Every summer he moves the sheep from one mountaintop to the next, dodging lightning, doctoring injured lambs, and battling coyotes and bears. He raised his three children in sheep camps and clung fast to a city-bred wife who swore she could not survive two years of herding life, let alone twenty.

I met his wife, Cheri, a few weeks ago at the Robinson's small ranch near Meeker, Colorado, northwest of Vail. She would be visiting an ailing grandmother while I was with Sam, and she wanted to counsel me on how to survive the rigors of sheep camp. Don't consume any alcohol or caffeine until you get used to the altitude. Drink water only from the spring, not from the creek like Sam does. Be prepared for coffee pot showers and meals of stale bread, beans, and boiled mutton. Stay away from Buddy, the yellow horse. He is a killer. Watch your step. Mountain meadows may look pretty, but they conceal booby traps, abandoned mine shafts, old Indian graves, and willow bogs that can swallow a horse.

"I should warn you," she said. "We're poor. You'll notice we have crap for equipment. We can't afford the trappings you might be expecting, like cowboy hats and boots. The power steering is out in the truck. The carburetor is screwed up and the brakes are almost gone. There were times, when the kids were little, when we looked for stuff to sell to buy milk."

Cheri apologized for the downbeat introduction but thought I ought to know what I would be in for. "I don't know what your expectations are coming from Southern California," she said. "But I'm from there, and this was a shock to me. When Sam talked about sheep camp, the image that came to my mind was a Girl Scouts' camp with log cabins, a barn, and indoor potties. I had no idea of the reality of it. I didn't foresee the frozen, scared, dirty, poor-as-church-mice part. I didn't foresee living in a trailer and having people come by, making ugly comments about my kids. 'Stay away from them, Baby Doll, they look like they have lice.' "

Sam and Cheri married in the early 1970s while they were under-graduates at Utah State University. She was a professor's daughter from the Los Angeles suburbs and a dance major. He was an animal science major and a member of a family that had been raising sheep since the 1850s. Sam worked summers for the Forest Service while he was still in college, hired on as a mechanic at a vanadium mine, and eventually saved up enough money to buy a herd of sheep. For the next seven years, Sam and Cheri were landless nomads, following the sheep from one leased pasture to another, living in a one-room trailer like the one Sam is in now. They moved every few months from winter range in eastern Utah to spring lambing grounds near Rio Blanco in the canyon country of west central Colorado to their sum-mer allotment above Vail. They braved forty-below-zero days when Cheri kept the babies warm by sandwiching them in bed between her and the dogs, while Sam lit a fire under the frozen truck so he could get to town and buy more propane to heat the trailer. In the evenings they read to the kids from the *Book of Mormon*, from *Little House on the Prairie*, and from *The Lord of the Rings*. They kept up with current events by listening to National Public Radio, to Rush Limbaugh, and to a Denver call-in-show host named Alan Berg, who talked about the Beatles (overrated), women's fashions (unflattering), and about hate groups whom he baited and ridiculed. "He had a dead honest way about him that was kind of irresistible," Sam said. "He didn't take any crap." A gang of neo-Nazis murdered Berg outside his home in 1984.

The Robinsons eventually bought the ranch outside Meeker where they could live in the winter while the three children were enrolled in school. Their son, Cullen, now in his early twenties, was the valedic-torian of his high school class and won a scholarship to Utah State. Their eighteen-year-old, Samantha, was chosen homecoming queen at Meeker High and also won a scholarship to her parents' alma mater. Their youngest, fifteen-year-old Sierra, finished her freshman year in high school ranked second in her class.

Sam's camp is 100 miles west of Denver, a two-hour drive on the interstate through Colorado's "urban-wild land interface," Western geographers' jargon for sprawl. Gone is the bucolic interlude of farms and fields where you could count the red cows on one side of the road and black ones on the other. Instead, you pass a string of stand-alone suburbs with deceptively exotic-sounding names like Silverthorne and Frisco, their storefront karate parlors, video rental stores, and auto detailers butting up against the mountains.

The road in to Sam's camp is an unmarked dirt track that peels off the highway to Leadville. The dirt road is high-centered, pitted, and muddy. It can rip out the undercarriage of a sport utility vehicle, but it doesn't stop nearly as many of them as Sam would like. After six miles, you plow through a shallow stream, climb one last rise, and there it is. A clutch of horses and dogs, saddles, propane tanks, jerrycans of motor oil and fifty-pound bags of grain and kibble encircle a one-room silver and white trailer Sam bought used in 1974 for $2,500. A green Ford pickup truck of the same vintage is parked next to the trailer. Designed for weekend getaways, Sam's trailer overflows with household possessions. The tiny kitchen counter is a jumble of metal pots, toilet paper rolls, cans of tuna and potato chips, biscuit batter, shampoo, plastic drinking mugs, and bottles of fungicide for treating foot rot in sheep. Shelves overflow with ledgers, old newspapers, and cartridge boxes. There is a Bible, a dictionary, a leather-bound volume of Robinson family history, and paperback novels by John Grisham, Tom Clancy, and Michael Crichton. What floor space there is appears largely taken up by bushel bags of pears and tomatoes, several propane lanterns, and a couple of ten-gallon jugs of drinking water. A Weatherby 270 hunting rifle leans against the doorjamb.

Before supper my first evening in camp, Sam clears away space on the table in the breakfast nook, putting away the Everclear and moving a holstered .44 pistol.

He has butchered a ewe and left the carcass to cure on the roof of the trailer, out of reach of dogs and varmints, if not the rain.

He hands me a plate of mutton.

"I boiled the heck out of it, but some of it still might be rank," he says. "Just smell it before you eat and cut off the taint. You'll be OK." For dessert, there is a carton of peaches, more than half-full and also on the far side of ripe. We won't need to buy groceries until the ewe has been consumed, Sam says. It appears we will be eating like Romulus and Remus for days. "Don't worry," he adds, catching the look on my face. "The dogs will eat a lot of it."

Sam has good reason to stint on groceries. The sheep operation has lost money two of the last three years, nearly $30,000 one year. If it were not for Cheri's new job teaching high school mathematics, the Robinsons might have had to sell everything, including the ranch it took them seven years of scrimping to acquire. Cheri's salary covers all family expenses except for gas, telephone bills, and insurance.

Sheep raising has always been a dicey enterprise, at the mercy of weather, wild animals, trade policies, and environmental pressures, but it has been in a free fall since the early 1990s. The crisis is due partly to the vagaries of fashion and partly to politics. Nylon, polyester, and other synthetics are cheaper than wool, easier to care for, and, stylistically, more popular in this era of dress-down Fridays. The heaviest blow to wool growers came in 1993, when the Clinton Administration terminated a thirty-year-old program of price supports. About the same time, the Australian government began releasing a huge domestic stockpile, over a billion pounds, on the world market. By 1999, the average price of wool in the United States was the lowest in history. Growers were paying more to shear a sheep than they were getting for the wool that came off the animal. The industry hemorrhaged. In Colorado and neighboring states, sheep permits on federal grazing land declined by 40 percent. Sam Robinson saw his annual wool profits evaporate.

"I'm sitting here on the ragged edge," he says.

In the distance we can hear the faint murmuring of sheep. They are bedded down nearly a mile from camp in a snow-specked cirque just below the Continental Divide, but on nights when the wind carries their plaintive voices down off the Divide, they seem much closer. The nocturnal bleating sounds like a plea for help. It may be nothing more than lambs calling for their mothers or it may be a predator alert. A black bear ambled through camp the night before I arrived, riling the dogs and knocking over the privy.

More likely, Sam thinks, the sheep are reacting to a coyote. Sam has had years when he hasn't lost a lamb to coyotes, bears, or mountain lions and years when they have killed 200. Whatever is unsettling the herd at the moment, there is nothing he can do about it.

Until this year, Sam used a "boom gun," a propane cannon that blasts harmlessly at random intervals, to frighten away nocturnal predators. But campers complained about the noise. Sam stowed the gun in the back of his truck and went shopping for a guard dog. His first choice was an Akbash, a formidable breed imported from Turkey. But Akbash have not always distinguished between predators and hikers. Wary of being sued, Sam acquired Big Dog, a cross between an Akbash and a Great Pyrenees. Big Dog is a happy-go-lucky fellow, less in the tradition of Rin Tin Tin than of Nana, the canine nursemaid in *Peter Pan* who barked nervously at Tinker Bell. In the spring, at their ranch, Big Dog showed more interest in playing with newborn lambs than in guarding them. But Sam had to bring him to the mountains. He had no other line of defense. Tonight Big Dog stands between Sam's net worth, about 2,700 white-faced sheep, and whatever carnivore might be out there. From time to time in the darkness, a stentorian woof interrupts the nervous blatting of the sheep.

"Sounds like Big Boy is on the case," I say.

"You can only hope," Sam says.

Before dawn the next morning, we saddle two horses and go looking for the herd. Sam's been up for an hour, baking sourdough pancakes for Big Dog. We won't be eating breakfast. Sam's muscular yellow gelding, Buddy, the horse Cheri warned me about, is draped with sacks of salt supplement for the sheep, Big Dog's pancakes, and a duffel full of veterinary supplies: splints, antibiotics, disinfectants, and antifungals. Sam slips his rifle into the scabbard beside his right leg and swings onto Buddy. We jog uphill, accompanied by three black-and-white border collies, Rush, Fly, and Jeff, who scuttle ahead like a family of merry skunks. The trail climbs over a series of benches that step up to the Continental Divide. We ride past the iron bones of old mining operations. Silver, gold, lead, zinc, and molybdenum, a mineral used to harden steel, were extracted from the mountains here for over a century. Abandoned mine portals stare out from the hills like empty eye sockets. I recall Cheri's admonition about the shafts you don't see, holes in the ground that are often camouflaged by willow thickets.

"Cheri worries too much," Sam snorts. "She ought to thank her lucky stars we're not in Wyoming, where the wind blows all the time."

The trail leads through fifty-year-old sheep camps, where the names of itinerant herders are scratched in the bark of aspen trees like the ones in front of us. E.T. GALLINA, N.M. 1927, EDWIN CH., LIMA, PERU. The herders came from Mexico, Spain, and Greece as well. They still come, recruited by a guest worker program that is exempt from minimum wage laws and pays between $600 and $700 a month. The herders stay for three years, work from four in the morning until eight at night, and live in cramped tin-roofed wagons. They work for bosses who can barely afford to hire them and who labor alongside them. Their employment can be a form of indenture. Some are forbidden to go to town for fear they will fall prey to women, drink, or more civilized employment. Yet, many keep returning to their herds after their three-year terms are over.

Sam has never been able to afford herders, but he has an explanation for why they are drawn back to such low-paying, arduous work. "It feels right, living out with the sheep, the same way people did in biblical times. You take care of the sheep, they'll take care of you. At least, that's the way it used to be."

He raises a hand and cocks it to his ear.

"Whistle pig. Hear it?"

A marmot is piping in intermittent, high-pitched notes. It's not unlike the shrill peeps a smoke alarm emits when the battery is low. In marmot country the peeping is often a sign that a coyote is close by.

We crest a hill and see a big white dog loping up Chicago Ridge, a steep, half-mile-long rim that bisects the Divide and tops out at 12,500 feet in a cornice of snow. It's Big Dog, and he's chasing a coyote. Once the coyote disappears over the top, Big Dog stops and trots back toward us, refusing to be lured too far from his charges.

"Attaboy, Big," Sam yells, then gallops after the coyote. The steep ridge appears almost vertical where it meets the snow line. Sam kicks the yellow horse through the snow and over the top, unsheathes the rifle, and settles himself in a sitting position. The coyote, 100 yards away, makes the mistake of stopping and looking back. Sam fires and the animal falls. The three border collies race after it. Sam follows on foot, unclasping a pocketknife. He is not happy with the shot he made. He had aimed for the heart and hit somewhere in the midsection. Badly hurt but far from dead, the coyote lashes out at the dogs. They retreat a few feet, noses streaming blood, and charge a second time. Sam shoos them away, holds the coyote's mouth shut, and cuts its throat.

"I hate it when it's not a clean kill," he says. "I wouldn't shoot them if I didn't have to. They're about my only neighbors. There have been times when they were my sole source of entertainment. I've laughed myself silly watching them throw pocket squirrels high in the air and try to catch them. They're clowns. And they're smarter than me."

Sam guesses he shoots ten to twenty-five coyotes a year, about one for every two sheep they kill. He says he is hearing and seeing fewer pups this year and wonders if he may have finally put a dent in the population of breeding females. It is probably wishful thinking, given the extraordinary resilience of the species. We humans have murdered about four million coyotes during the past 100 years. We machine-gunned them from helicopters and gassed them in their dens. We lured them to sodium cyanide charges that were baited and stuck in the ground like land mines. We poisoned them with sodium fluoroacetate until the outcry over unintended victims, including dogs and a few children, led to its banning. Yet, there are probably more coyotes, more widely dispersed and more trouble than ever.

When a pack of coyotes is targeted, the females compensate for the losses by breeding at a younger age. They produce more pups that require more food. As the adult population is thinned out, the survivors learn to be more efficient in their own hunting methods. They start looking for larger prey that are easier to run down and have more meat on them than rabbits or marmots. Sheep fit the bill.

So why keep killing them? I ask Sam.

He shrugs. He has heard it all before and doesn't disagree. He shoots coyotes as reflexively as someone else sprays a line of ants marching toward a bowl of sugar, knowing full well that more of the little pests will be back in a day or two.

"Here are the options," he says. "We can do it my way, and let me shoot the ones that come near my herd. Or I can feed your predator. You can pay me to run my sheep and I'll feed the coyote, the bear or the mountain lion. Give me $30,000 a year. Hell, that's not much money. Everybody makes more than that these days. I'll put up with the lifestyle, the hikers and mountain bikers and jeepsters and everyone else, and I'll just sit and let the coyote eat and eat. At the end of the summer, I'll ship off my little pickup truck full of lambs, because that's all that will be left. But what happens when the lambs are gone? You don't think the coyote will be down the mountain in people's yards, looking for dinner? You don't think somebody will ask, 'Whatever happened to old Sam and his gun?' "

We come off the ridge and back down to the herd. Sam wants to move the sheep off the high ground where they spent the night into a shallow basin where they haven't yet fed. On a day like this one, warm with only the hint of a breeze, the sheep seem to ooze like tar, slowing to a halt at the bottom of draws, in clumps of spruce trees, or in low willow thickets. I ride in among them, yelling and slapping their butts with a willow switch to get them going again. Sam, I notice, is more patient. He sits for long minutes on a hill, looking over the sheep and the terrain, not unlike a pool player studying the lay of the table, figuring out his next five moves. Sam is also looking for gimps, and there are quite a number. A few have dislocated legs that need to be splinted. Most are afflicted with foot rot. There are also a half dozen rams that have avoided castration. Sam must get to them before they get to his ewes. A lamb conceived in the summer will be born in the dead of winter when its survival chances are lowest. Sam sets the dogs to work. He wants them to corral groups of sheep and hold them while he does the necessary doctoring. The dogs are eager, but they are young and still learning how to gather and hold a band of sheep in a tight circle.

"Push 'em up, Fly," Sam yells at his youngest and quickest border collie. "Now, get behind 'em . . . Good boy, Macfly," he says acknowledging the dog's Highland pedigree . . . "Now, lay down. I said, 'LAY DOWN.' " Instead, the dog circles crazily, turning the band of sheep like a merry-go-round. In a moment the circle will break and the sheep will bolt in all directions. "What the hell are you doing, you knucklehead," Sam yells. "Get behind me, Fly. GET BEHIND." Head down, Fly creeps behind Sam and lies down. Order is restored. Sam gets off his horse and takes Fly's head in his hands. "You're a good boy, a fine boy. You have quite a life ahead of you, MacFly, if I don't go broke."

Then he reaches into the circle with his eight-foot-long sheep hook and snares a fat ewe out of the band and flips her on her back. She struggles at first, then relaxes completely. Her head lolling between Sam's knees, her legs in the air, she is a picture of plump matronly lassitude. Sam smells the ewe's front right foot and wrinkles his nose. Rot. He unclasps his knife and cuts the tainted tissue down to the bloody quick, his dexterity unimpeded by a missing ring finger. It was torn off during a moment of inattention while he was operating a mechanical sheep loader several years ago. Sam puts away the knife. "Remind me not to use this on dinner," he says. He slathers the ewe's foot with a sulfa solution. gives her a shot of penicillin, marks her back with a green crayon to indicate that she has been doctored, and sends her back to the herd with a smack on the rump.

"Let's find us a buck," he says.

There does not appear to be a consensus on the best way to castrate a ram in the wilds. Some herders use rubber bands that pinch off the blood supply and cause the testicles to wither and eventually fall off. Others say this method takes too painfully long and prefer the knife. Like his father and grandfather before him, Sam does it with his teeth. He is quick about it. Flipping the ram on his back, he first slits the scrotum with his knife, then sucks the testicles out, pulling them away from the animal until they are connected by a slim strand of tissue and slowly biting them off. Sam believes doing it this way runs the least risk of infection to the sheep, since almost all of the contact is with the parts that are being amputated. But this little fellow isn't going to have an easy time of it. He is three months old and well developed. "That's got to hurt him some," Sam says, watching the mutilated animal stagger back to the herd. "It will slow him for a week." Later that day, we see the sheep struggling to keep up with the herd, dripping blood from his wound, still unsteady on his feet. Sam doesn't seem especially worried. He'll probably make it, he says, if a coyote doesn't get him.

Sam stays with his sheep nine to ten hours a day, nursing them, moving them at least once, or waiting for them to settle down after he has moved them. The countryside has benefited from his attentiveness. It is hard to see where his herd has been feeding. The meadows where the sheep have been grazing for the past two weeks are still thick with clover and laced with wildflowers. There are no bare spots or signs of erosion. The sheep have only topped the plants.

Left to their own devices, sheep are notorious for cropping plants down to the ground and destroying the roots with their sharp feet. The naturalist John Muir described sheep as "hoofed locusts." In the later 1800s Muir called for military guards to patrol the national forests and put a stop to the damage sheep were causing. As the flocks advance, he wrote: "flowers, vegetation, grass, soil, plenty, and poetry vanish." He was not exaggerating. By the 1930s, when the federal government finally began regulating grazing on public lands, a Congressional study concluded that overgrazing by sheep and cattle had severely eroded virtually all of the public range then accessible to livestock.

In Muir's day there were eight million sheep foraging in the Western national forests. Today, there aren't that many in the entire country. In the White River National Forest, where Sam Robinson summers his herd, the sheep count is down more than 60 percent since 1940. Yet, Western lands in general have recovered slowly. Nature works that way, replenishing topsoil inch by inch over centuries. Droughts and floods complicate the mending process. So do politics. Influential livestock associations have resisted regulation and kept grazing fees low. According to a recent study by the U.S. Forest Service, the government pays three times as much to supervise sheep and cattle in the national forests as it receives in grazing fees. Meanwhile, environmental groups have been going to court to force the federal government to close fragile public lands to grazing. Their efforts have been most successful in Arizona and New Mexico, where the arid countryside is especially fragile. The mountains of central Colorado, on the other hand, get forty inches of rain or more a year, making them much less prone to erosion. That hasn't made them totally immune to damage, however, or to antigrazing pressure. Sam's leasehold takes up a small fraction of the 2.3-million-acre White River National Forest. But it is one of the most scenic fractions and one of the most heavily visited. If people complain about getting manure on their shoes, and many do, there is a good chance it came from Sam's sheep.

The White River Conservation Coalition, a group representing several Colorado environmental groups, wants the Forest Service to bar sheep from steep slopes and to keep them away from busy hiking trails and river valleys popular with fishermen and rafters. If adopted by the Forest Service, the recommendations would amount to an eviction notice to Sam and other herders in the White River high country. It would be a victory for recreation over agriculture. But what would it do for the environment?

Rocky Smith, who drafted the recommendations for the coalition, told me he didn't know Sam and had never visited his allotment. He seemed willing to accept my opinion that Sam is a responsible steward, easy on the land. I brought up the coyotes, but Smith said he didn't blame a fellow like Sam for shooting coyotes that maraud his herd. Sam needed to be able to protect his investment. Precisely. So why kick him out? Which is the greater menace: a few thousand sheep or eight million humans? That's the number of recreational visitors the forest gets every year, trudging across the soft tundra, riding their bicycles or their jeeps, turning their dogs loose, scattering deer and elk.

It was a fruitless line of questions. The answer was the same as it has always been. Even if you can trust Sam, you can't trust Sam's kind. Livestock still do damage, Smith said, and the regulations governing it are not strict enough. The ancient enmity between conservationist and cowboy seems impervious to mediation. For over fifty years, ever since the first range reform laws were passed, environmentalists seethed while the grazing boards and good old boys used politics and intimidation to protect their turf, no matter how beat up it was. Eventually, the environmental movement came up with an effective counterstrategy. It grew out of the Vietnam era when the destruction of peasant villages and pristine jungle was often portrayed as an expression of America's cowboy culture. The Old West was recast as the great American abattoir, where we first became proficient at slaughtering primitive people and ravaging nature. Environmentalists began raising money on the backs of the cowboys and continue to do so. It hardly matters that the cowboy himself is an endangered species or that someone like Sam doesn't fit the part of the villain. He and his ilk are much too valuable as enemies. Sam may not look like a cowboy in his construction boots and baseball cap with the faded logo of a mining company on it. But he rides to work every morning on horseback. He carries a loaded rifle at his side, and he shoots coyotes. Sam goofs on the role that has been assigned to him. He named one of his border collies Rush for Rush Limbaugh, the right-wing blunderbuss. Another is Jeff, for Jeffrey Dahmer, the serial killer. "Society sees me as the bad guy. I see myself more as the Indian. Either way, history says I'm screwed."

Sam says there probably are irreconcilable differences between him and the environmentalists.

"It boils down to aesthetics," he says. "My great-great grandfather saw this country and wanted to make something beneficial out of it. I'm the same way. It tickles me to think I am producing fiber and food. These environmentalists see it and say, 'My God, it's a wilderness. Leave it be.' But this is not a wilderness anymore and getting rid of my sheep isn't going to turn it back into one."

He points to a pile of brightly colored bamboo poles on the ground. They are guideposts, stuck in the snow, to mark a snowmobile route across Chicago Ridge and down the Continental Divide. The snowmobile clubs that put them up are supposed to remove them in the summer, but they don't. Strewn among the poles are discarded plastic water bottles and cast-off articles of clothing. Sam picks up the trash and puts it in an empty sack he carries for that purpose. He also finds live artillery rounds occasionally. They are fired by cannons that ski resorts use to trigger avalanches before the snow can pose a threat to skiers. When Sam's son was a little boy, he picked up one of the unexploded shells and carried it down the mountain to his mother, wanting to know what it was.

In the heart of Colorado's ski country Sam's allotment is ringed by three of the state's busiest resorts, Vail, Breckenridge, and Copper Mountain. Vail was the first. Its founders bought out a 500-acre sheep ranch and opened for business in 1962. Vail became the largest ski resort in the country and the first to realize its future lay in four-season recreation. When it couldn't acquire all the land it wanted, Vail leased it from the federal government. Today, 70 percent of Colorado's downhill skiing takes place on mountainsides in the White River National Forest. Thousands of trees have been cut to make room for ski runs. Dozens of permanent shelters have been constructed for cross country skiers and snowmobilers. Vail and its imitators begot a real estate boom that, in turn, spawned a frenzy of summertime recreation. Rafting on the rivers that wind through the forest draws 100,000 people every summer. Since 1995, the number of mountain bike riders and all-terrain-vehicle users in the forest has risen by 200 percent. Three of the state's most popular recreation corridors, the Colorado and Continental Divide Trails and the Peak's Trail, a particular favorite of mountain bikers, were dug out of the forest's alpine tundra. All three run through Sam's grazing allotment. Before the trails were completed, he would see a dozen hikers all summer. Now he encounters 1,000.

The environmental movement is in a difficult position. It owes many of its victories to alliances with commercial tourism. Beginning with Yellowstone National Park in 1872, crucial support for creation of the national parks came from the railroad industry, which wanted to promote the parks as destinations for train travel. Over the years, groups like the Sierra Club introduced thousands of people to Western wilderness areas on rafting and hiking trips run by commercial guides, outfitters, and dude ranches. In this way, the environmental movement became an important catalyst for one of the region's most robust growth industries. Call it wilderness adventure, inc. Conservationists argued that an economy based on enjoying the outdoors would be more vibrant than one devoted to exploiting nature. Turn a mining camp into a tourist village. Promote its scenic and recreational value, and nature will pay dividends far in excess of what a finite ore body will yield. The environmentalists couldn't have been more right. The combined forces of recreation and real estate turned rural economies on their heads. Suddenly, a cowboy or a lumberjack could earn at least twice as much building houses. Realtors discovered that people were willing to pay premium prices for mountain views, nearby ski runs, hiking trails, and trout streams. Throughout the 1980s and '90s, much of the rural West grew faster than the rest of the nation. Unfortunately, much of the growth was haphazard and ugly in the time-honored tradition of Western boom towns. Laws governing air pollution, water quality, and open space were permissive, where there were laws at all.

"See for yourself," Sam says to me when he learns that I have never been to Vail. "Go on down there. Vail's a treat if you can afford it. My wife and I used to eat dinner there occasionally when she was working for the Burger King."

I go looking for a land use expert and find Brad Udall. Brad is a member of the West's first family of conservation. His father was Arizona Congressman Morris Udall, the architect of the nation's most far-reaching wilderness protection legislation: the 1980 Alaskan lands act that created ten new national parks and protected 100 million acres of forest, mountain, and tundra. Brad's uncle, Stewart Udall, was Secretary of the Interior under Presidents Kennedy and Johnson and probably did more than any politician of his era to rally public support for wilderness protection.

Tall and lanky with the formidable Udall chin, Brad rowed tourists through the Grand Canyon in wooden dories before moving to Vail and becoming the director of the nonprofit Eagle County Land Trust. The trust works to save undeveloped land from the bulldozer either by buying it or by persuading property owners to dedicate a portion of their land to open space and wildlife habitat in return for tax breaks. Brad offers to take me on a tour of Vail's changing landscape.

Looking at the growth on paper, it is hard to see what all the fuss is about. Eagle County, of which Vail is a part, is a little larger than Rhode Island. Although the population has nearly quadrupled since 1970, when Vail was still content to be a mock Bavarian village, there are still only 30,000 residents, many of them part-time. What worries Brad about Vail's growth is the way it leapfrogs from one valley to the next, pulling roads, utilities, and services behind it, pinching off wildlife corridors, blocking views, and steadily colonizing the mountains. The federal government owns 80 percent of the land. Most of the remaining undeveloped private land belongs to isolated ranches. With spectacular views and easy access to the high country, a Colorado ranch can be the perfect template for an expensive subdivision. The state's lax land use laws abet the process. Legislation enacted in the 1970s allows developers to subdivide ranches into parcels thirty-five acres or larger without government approval.

We head for Cordillera Mountain Ranch, a massive complex of million-dollar homes that winds its way 8,000 feet up to a monolithic resort and spa. On the way, Brad talks optimistically about the trust's future. He says more and more local residents are becoming supportive of his efforts. Even Vail Resorts, the company that started it all, is having second thoughts about the growth it has spawned. The company has become the trust's biggest contributor, good for one quarter of the organization's annual budget. "It is a sign that they do recognize the value and the uniqueness of the place," Brad says. "They understand that part of the experience of buying into Colorado high country are having the meadows out there, of seeing the West out your window and not suburbia."

Near the top of the Cordillera development, Brad and I stop at an open house celebrating the grand opening of Kensington Green, an English-cottage-style tract of split-level stucco houses trimmed in dark wood, each selling for just over $1 million. The houses overlook the narrow fairways of a golf course scooped out of the mountainside. The open house is a festive affair with a Mardi Gras motif. The house is abuzz with the chatter of a score of real estate agents; men and women, costumed in necklaces strung with glass beads and cardboard masks. The listing agent for the house is Tom Stone, a tall, genial fellow wearing one of the necklaces. Stone is also a member of the Eagle County Commission.

I go outside to the edge of the golf course, next to a kiosk marked RESTROOM AND LIGHTNING SHELTER, to take in the view. This is one of nineteen golf courses in various stages of completion in Vail Valley. Several others are visible below.

The word "Fore" is spoken sharply from somewhere close by. A golf ball is bouncing in my direction. A blonde, middle-aged woman with long, tan legs has just whacked her tee shot perfectly sideways.

She is mortified. Her companion, a young man wearing a turned around baseball cap and low-riding baggy pants, has her adjust her hands on the club. She fires another foul ball and hangs her head. Grimly, she keeps at it, hitting one skittering slice after another. "God, I am so embarrassed," I hear her say. Her permed yellow curls flash in the sun as she shakes her head. Looking bored, her teenage handler stands off, waiting for the woman to compose herself. She is one of those people for whom sport is drudgery. No golfer myself, I feel for her. What a fate to live here in duffer's heaven, hopelessly flailing about like an angel without wings.

Riding out to the sheep the next day, I tell Sam I think his best hope is to get political. I tell him what Brad Udall related to me about a pending ballot initiative in Colorado that would require rural communities like Vail to protect open space and make it harder for developers to arbitrarily cut up ranches into thirty-five-acre parcels. Sam knows about it and might vote for it, if he weren't handcuffed by his libertarian ideals.

"I just don't think it's a good idea when government gets so involved in business decisions. People should be more *restraintive* on their own," he says, as if by adding another syllable he might restore a little respect for the idea.

"How can you expect capitalism to restrain itself?" I ask. "A businessman believes he either grows or dies."

"I know," he says. "That's always seemed to me like a flaw in the capitalist system. I've sat here and stagnated for twenty years, and it's been pretty pleasant."

IT's TIME TO move to Sheep Mountain. We push the herd north from Chicago Ridge, through Eagle Basin, over the east fork of Eagle Creek and past Robinson Lake, named for a nineteenth-century mining town that no longer exists. We follow a dirt road around a huge tailings pond, a reservoir full of water as toxic and chemically blue as toilet bowl cleanser, then head up the flank of Sheep Mountain. From there to Ptarmigan Pass is Sam's best grazing ground, where his sheep should put on the most weight. For him to make any kind of profit, Sam's lambs need to average 100 pounds apiece. It's not an unreasonable goal, but it will require deft management and good luck. The trick is to be in the right meadow at the right time—for the lupine on Sheep Mountain, the willow at Cataract Creek, and the mountain vetch and cow parsnip above Ptarmigan Pass.

The country is also the busiest segment of Sam's allotment, where the Colorado and Continental Divide Trails come together. In such heavily traveled terrain, restraining a herd is often harder than moving it. Sheep are flighty. Rain unsettles them. So do people and dogs. Hikers walking through a herd of sheep often cause the animals to pick up and go, abandoning a rich patch of clover after just a few bites. "A group of ten hikers will come through the middle of 'em and try to pet one of 'em. They don't want to be petted. They're not pets." They lose weight when they move too much, especially in the mountains. Sam estimates that the summer foot traffic costs him $2,000 each year in lost weight. Every pound counts when he goes to sell his crop of lambs in the fall each year. His profit is the margin between annual expenses and the price he can get for his lambs. The leaner the lambs, the thinner the margin.

It is easy to see why the country has become so popular. This is the Colorado that John Denver sang about, but up close the clichés of song and postcard don't begin to capture the scenery. The mountaintops are not so much soaring peaks as unfinished sculpture gardens erupting in bizarre hoodoos and pinnacles. North of Sheep Mountain two withered sandstone columns spring from a boulder field. Inclining toward each other but not quite touching, they have endured eons of wind and snow that has reduced everything around them to rubble. Engaged in their solitary struggle against the elements, the gaunt figures are more evocative of the twentieth-century English sculptor Henry Moore than the nineteenth-century American Thomas Moran whose lushly reverential paintings did so much to put the Colorado Rockies on the tourist maps.

The sandstone figures are called "The Dancers," Sam says.

Beyond the dancers, in a rocky strait known as Searle Pass, a coyote saunters across our path. Sam is affronted. "Hold the horses," he says. "That bugger is just a tad too cocky." The coyote accelerates up hill in long, loping strides. Then he stops, fifty yards away, and looks back at us, as if to invite pursuit. Sam, stretched out across a boulder, his arms braced, fires. The coyote topples over, dead, shot in the heart.

He picks the animal up by its tail. Its lips are peeled back, revealing several missing teeth.

"He's an old campaigner. Like me, I guess. Taken his knocks."

We breach the pass and ride on a bit, looking northwest toward Battle Mountain and Vail. The mountain got its name from the Ute and Arapaho Indians who fought each other for the right to hunt the game that flourished here.

For the past five years, a team of biologists from Colorado State University has been studying the reaction of elk to people in the mountains around Vail. The researchers have found that when a herd is repeatedly disturbed, its birth rate begins to drop, because the cows don't eat as much as they should. The elk abandon a meadow, regardless of how much feed there is in it. A herd that is interrupted seven or eight times during the summer, may have 40 percent fewer calves the following spring. Displaced ten times or more and the birth rate may drop to zero.

Ahead of us, its roof peeking out of the pines, is the reason, Sam believes, the elk have fled the area.

"There's Janet's Cabin."

The cabin is one of a lengthening string of "huts" built to shelter cross-country skiers. The huts can save the lives of skiers during a blizzard, but they also help to civilize the mountains. Gradually, the huts are being opened for summer use, too. The term "hut" doesn't do justice to Janet's Cabin, a soaring chalet that can accommodate thirty overnight visitors. Still, a log cabin in the pines can be an alluring sight and I say as much.

"Pretty as a picture," Sam replies. "Every time I pass it, I wish I had a Stinger Missile."

We pick our way down the mountain at dusk, riding past collapsed mining cabins and across iron rails, old ore car tracks that disappear into a hole in the mountain. We come upon a large tent, the size of a two-car garage. It is a winter shelter for snowmobilers, a portable version of Janet's Cabin that has become a year-round fixture.

"My dad predicted this country would look like Disneyland. I wasn't listening. I wanted the same life he'd had. I wanted the freedom to raise my family the way I saw fit. I'd seen the way kids were raised up in town, turned loose in the summer, and I didn't like the way it affected them. It was 'my old man' this and 'my old lady' that. I wanted my kids to feel they were a vital part of their family. I wanted to make them into humans. But Cheri is the story there. I couldn't have done it alone. I don't think she realizes the debt I owe her. I have to sit back in my saddle sometimes and ponder the cultural leap she's had to make. Lord knows why she still loves me. Maybe she doesn't. She says she doesn't sometimes. She says I'm addicted to living on the edge. That may be true. But I'm not apologizing for it, anymore than I'm apologizing to the animal rights crowd for pulling oysters with my teeth. It's what got me to this point. Living on the edge keeps you sharp. I don't see any of these old sheep men, the few that are left, dying of Alzheimer's. The ones that retire are the ones that start dwelling in the past. I don't plan to quit unless I'm forced to."

A half-mile farther down the mountain Sam shows me where he

buried the best sheep herding dog he ever owned, a border collie named Lassie.

"There's a day coming when a dog like Lassie won't have anything to do except catch Frisbees. I don't think you'll find any sheep on this mountain after I'm gone."

Sam's mood doesn't match his words. If anything, he sounds cheerful. He is like a doctor who draws professional satisfaction from diagnosing his own terminal condition.

He points at the sky.

"You might see the meteors tonight."

He is talking about the annual Perseids meteor shower which up to now has been obscured by moonlight and hazy skies. The meteors are fiery exhaust from a comet that astronomers believe was first sighted over China around A.D. 200. Sam says he has counted more than 100 meteors on clear nights. It is a little early on this evening to see anything so dramatic. But the curtain has parted. The stage lights are twinkling, and we have orchestra seats. The show seems just an arm's length away.

THE BADGER

ADOZEN BLACKFEET Indians and I sit in an aspen grove up against the backbone of the world, watching a horse die. We sit on stumps, averting our eyes from the terrible hole in the horse's flank, and wait for someone to get back from camp with a gun. Accidents in remote country can bring people closer together or they can revive old doubts and stereotypes and reinforce the distance between us. This accident shouldn't have happened. It was avoidable. A teenage girl cries quietly. The rest of us sit in gloomy silence.

Plains Indians once occupied virtually all of the Continental Divide. The Ute and Arapaho fought for control of Battle Mountain along the Divide in Colorado where I have recently come from. Today, only a handful of tribes lay claim to land along the Divide—the Navajo and Jicarilla Apache in New Mexico, the Shoshone in Wyoming, and the Blackfeet in Montana and southern Canada. The Montana Blackfeet no longer own any of this mountain land, and I could have come here on my own, without their consent. But the Blackfeet still have strong feelings about this place, and, to the extent I could, I wanted to see it through their eyes.

The backbone of the world runs along the Divide from the Canadian border through Montana's Glacier National Park to a place known as the Badger-Two Medicine. The Blackfeet call it the Badger, 130,000 acres of crags and peaks girdled by narrow, winding river valleys. To the Indians, it is not only a sanctuary for vanishing wildlife but one of those rare places where the world of their ancestors is still intact and vibrant, where the old spirits still inhabit the spring torrents and the winter winds.

Today, the land is part of the Lewis and Clark National Forest, but 100 years ago it was the last high ground of a tribal empire and a place that figured prominently in Blackfeet creation stories. It was one of the tribe's holiest places, where people stole away to practice their faith in secret after the U.S. Government outlawed native observances in the 1880s. The mountaintops bear the names of deities and heroes: Feather Woman, Scarface, Poia, and Morning Star. Things that happen here can take on a heightened significance. The slow agonizing death of an injured packhorse is not a sign to be ignored. The Thunder God is supposed to live in a cave up here, and he is known to have little patience with blasphemers. I wonder if the Indians still worry about such things, and if they now think bringing in a white man was a big mistake.

White people have their own superstitions about Indians. The word "savage," from the French "sauvage," referred to someone living in a state of nature. Our own creation stories look nostalgically to the ancient world of the noble sauvage, to Arcadia and Elysium. The discovery of America and its native inhabitants gave a powerful new impetus to the old longings. Arcadia came to life in the New World with its indigenous population of gentle, peace-loving primitives. In time, the term "savage" acquired a much darker connotation as in savage Blackfeet warriors. But the old nostalgia died hard. After the Indian ceased to be an obstacle to westward expansion, he again became a symbol of the nation's lost innocence, a role model for the Boy Scouts, and an icon of the environmental movement.

I grew up in Minnesota, where people hired Indian guides to take them hunting and fishing because it was believed that Indians were better at such work than white folk. I thought of Indians as perishable exotics who could only thrive in the soil of pre-industrial America. A girl I knew became infatuated with a boy who was part Indian who did yard work in the neighborhood. He could water ski barefoot and once I saw him dip his hand into the lake and pull out a sleek sunfish. He lived with relatives nearby but would disappear for long periods of time. He once told us he went off to live in an abandoned bear cave to fast and pray. His cousins scoffed at the story and said the cave was more likely his parents' squalid house on the reservation. He probably went back there for the annual fair to pick up girls and gamble. My girlfriend thought he was deep and mysterious and preferred to believe his story about going on a vision quest. I accused her of girlish idolatry, but I was also in his thrall.

I first became aware of the Badger-Two Medicine in the early 1990s when it figured prominently in a struggle between the environmental movement and the energy industry, which wanted to drill for oil and gas in the wilderness. The environmentalists said that all of the blasting, road building, construction, traffic, and people that drilling entails would destroy the natural character of the place. The Badger was a sanctuary for grizzly bears, wolves, deer, elk, and eagles. An analysis by the U.S. Forest Service concluded that just two oil wells would play havoc, displacing animals and fouling the air with dust and toxins. An oil spill or a pipeline rupture would likely contaminate mountain streams that are the main source of clean water for the Blackfeet Reservation. Blackfeet elders said drilling would be an act of desecration.

Interviewed for a documentary about the Badger-Two Medicine in 1996, Buster Yellow Kidney, a Blackfeet spiritual leader, compared it to Mount Sinai. G. G. Kipp, another tribal elder, told the energy companies that developing the Badger would be like destroying all of the Bibles in the world. Without Bibles, Kipp asked, how long would the true Christian beliefs exist? John Muir likened wilderness to a church. But only the Indians could say it was their church. The oilmen asked if the Badger-Two Medicine was so sacred, why did the Blackfeet decide to sell it to the federal government in 1896? It seemed a fair question. The first Bush Administration gave the Fina Oil and Chemical Company the go-ahead to begin drilling just days before the President was leaving office in 1992. But the decision was soon reversed by President Clinton in one of his first bows to environmentalists. With the project on indefinite hold, the energy industry walked away from the Badger, although they did not surrender the mineral rights they had purchased from the government for about $1 per acre.

I was drawn to the Badger less by the din of wilderness politics than by my own vivid imaginings. I assumed a place that was so important to the Blackfeet must somehow be deeper and more mysterious than other wilderness areas I had visited. There must be something different about it to have caused its oldest human residents to credit the birds, animals, trees, rocks, and rivers with sentient, even supernatural powers. The Creator, Napi, said if you went into the mountains alone, fasted, and slept, one of the more powerful beings, a spirit bear or an eagle, would come to you in a vision and confer upon you some of its power or wisdom. Tribal mythology abounds with stories of injured or demoralized warriors who take refuge in bears' dens and awake healed and newly emboldened. The mountains are dotted with the crumbling remnants of stone altars and shrines erected by the faithful who still come here in search of courage and enlightenment.

My first glimpse of the Badger was in the summer of 1999. I drove to the end of a dirt road and stood in a light rainfall at the edge of Badger Canyon, a magnificent rock-walled passage to the wilderness beyond. The view of fog-shrouded, emerald mountains through the aperture of the canyon walls was all the encouragement I needed. While I stood there, a young man who had been following a small herd of cows in a pickup truck walked up to me. He pointed at the ground, to a fresh set of grizzly bear tracks, and said it probably wasn't a good idea to be alone out here. I agreed and walked with him back to his truck. He was friendly, talkative, and remarkably dashing-looking, his rich black hair swept up under a new felt cowboy hat, his creased jeans tucked into a pair of pretty, hand-stitched boots. He caught me looking at him and laughed. "I'm an urban cowboy," he said, explaining he didn't live on the reservation anymore but came back on weekends to help his brother with the cattle. He nodded at another handsome young man who sat silently in the pickup. I asked him where he lived and what he did when he wasn't here. He hesitated for a moment before replying that he lived 200 miles away in Missoula, where he went to college and paid for his tuition by working in a dance club as a female impersonator. He smiled at my double take and asked me what I was doing here. I told him I'd come to explore the Badger-Two Medicine and hoped to learn something about its secrets from the Blackfeet. Why is it such a special place? I asked him. "Good grass for the cows, I guess," he shrugged. "Isn't that right?" He looked at his brother.

"That's about it," his brother replied. "The cows do real well out here if you can keep the bears away from them."

When I arrived in the Badger, the moratorium on drilling was still in effect. But the wilderness was facing new pressures. The strip of mountains had become an important link in the Continental Divide Trail connecting Glacier National Park to the north with the Bob Marshall Wilderness to the south. The route ran east of the Divide, well within the Badger, and had been opened to all-terrain vehicles and snowmobiles. Traditionalists like G. G. Kipp and Buster Yellow Kidney deplored the Forest's Service decision to allow mechanized travel. But the machines made it possible for hunters and fishermen to reach places in hours that used to take two or three days, and many Indians were happy to join the motorized throng. Nor were the Blackfeet speaking with one voice about the subject of oil and gas. In 1998 the tribal council leased thousands of acres of reservation land bordering the Badger-Two Medicine to a Canadian energy company. Some members of the tribe said they would reconsider drilling in the Badger if royalties were offered to the tribe. Meanwhile, friendly relations with white environmentalists had broken down. "Who are you, and what right do you have to comment on matters that are really none of your business?" asked the tribal land board chairman in a letter to the Montana Wilderness Association. The group had worked with the Blackfeet in the campaign against oil drilling in the Badger but was now raising questions about the wisdom of drilling on the reservation. The letter said that environmentalists had little support from the tribe. "It is the constant unwanted meddling of bleeding heart organizations like yours that do not have any endorsement from ninety-nine-point-nine percent of the people whose day to day lives you are interfering with." I asked Lou Bruno, a member of the Montana Wilderness Association who lived on the reservation and taught school there, if he thought the vast majority of Blackfeet were as hostile to white environmentalists as the letter writer. "Hostile or indifferent," Bruno said. "But talk to G. G. Kipp or Buster Yellow Kidney. They've been on good terms with us. They'll know better than I do where things stand."

Kipp told me he would be happy to take me into the Badger when I called him long distance and introduced myself. "Just bring your sleeping bag and a mess kit, and I'll saddle a tame horse for you." We set a date. It seemed too easy, cementing arrangements for a trip into the backcountry with a total stranger during the course of one five-minute phone call. I called him back to confirm two weeks later and got a slightly distracted "Who's this? . . . Oh, yeah. Sure thing. No problem." A week later, I flew to Great Falls, rented a car, and drove to the reservation. I called Kipp from a convenience store in Browning, the commercial hub of the reservation. Kipp's phone was out of order. I drove to his small ranch fifteen miles south of Browning and found no signs of life. A neighbor said he was out of town.

I went looking for Buster Yellow Kidney. His house was perched on a treeless knoll that protruded like a pimple on the wind-lashed northern plains. He stepped outside when I drove up and greeted me as if I were an old friend, although we had not met before. He took my hand in both of his and invited me in. Somewhere in his seventies, tall and stooped, with mottled skin and a weary, beaked visage, Yellow Kidney did not look well. He spoke with a husky, congested voice. "So you want to go into the Badger? I've taken guys like you in before. We'd go back to a tepee I had up there. I told them they better be ready to fast because that's what I did when I went back. Fasting makes you complete. You feel that you are part of the natural world. I used to hunt when I went back there. But I don't anymore. I shot a bear by mistake. I didn't mean to kill him, only to scare him." He pointed to a large black hide hanging on the wall. "That's him, there. I hope he forgave me. I believe he did. The bear is really sacred to us. His power is in the medicine pipe that has always brought health to the tribe. I'll tell you the story behind it. One day this guy with an arrow wound in his leg fell into a bear's den up near Goat Mountain in the Badger. The bear took him in, set his leg, fed him, and took care of him until he was well. Before he left, the bear gave him the medicine pipe. Today, people kill bears without thinking what they are doing. Our people do it now because they are lost and ignorant."

Yellow Kidney's wife, a white woman several years his junior, entered the room and introduced herself.

"Time for your nap."

Yellow Kidney nodded, rose, and extended his hand to me. "Maybe, next time you come, I'll be feeling better, and we can take a little trip into the Badger."

I had wanted to ask him why the Blackfeet had agreed to sell the Badger Two-Medicine, back in 1896, but that question, too, would have to wait for another time.

I found lodging at Darrell Norman's Lodge Pole Gallery, a combination Indian arts emporium and beauty salon with a cluster of tepees out back for tourists. Norman's daughter, Tina, a pretty, plump beautician, led me to my tepee. "You're going to need to have a fire in here tonight. It's going to be cold," she said and showed me how to adjust the flap at the top of the tepee to let the smoke out. She pointed at several holes in the ground and said it would be a good idea to plug them up with rocks. "The badgers like warm tepees, too," she said.

"Do they bite?

"I have no idea."

"You've never stayed out here?"

"What, are you kidding?"

She told me not to miss dinner. "We're having fresh seafood, and my dad's a great cook."

She was right. Dinner consisted of fresh oysters and venison jerky, followed by clam broth, crab, and salmon filets. A bottle of wine was opened with each course. Dinner guests included Norman's German fiancée, Angelica; David Dragonfly, an artist whose work was on display in the gallery; Curly Bear Wagner, a tribal historian and tour guide; Larry Reevis, a local writer; and three other men who got wind of the feast and invited themselves to dinner.

"You're wanting to know how a bunch of landlocked Indians got their hands on a load of fresh salmon and shellfish," Norman said to me. "There's a guy with a truck, an Indian from British Columbia, whose family are all fishermen. I've known him for a long time, and I

buy whatever he's got when he shows up in town. The trick is knowing when he's going to be in town. He doesn't call ahead of time."

An artist, Norman had moved back to the reservation after living
twenty years in Seattle. He was short and stocky and wore his thin-
ning hair in a ponytail. He said little as he bustled back and forth
from the kitchen, refilling glasses and presenting each new course.
His guests were dressed in workingmen's garb, blue jeans and flan-
nel shirts. They ate ravenously and chided Norman good-naturedly
whenever they wanted something.

"Where's the white wine? Jesus Christ, Darrell, you expect us to
drink this red stuff with crabmeat?"

I was seated next to Norman's German fiancée and asked how she
thought she would like living on the reservation. She replied that she
was an environmentalist, appalled by the gluttony and waste of
American consumerism, and could only feel at home in this country
if she were living on an Indian reservation. "I want to be in a place
where nature is respected."

I asked her what she thought about the oil and gas drilling that was
scheduled to begin soon. She looked at me uncomprehendingly.

"Don't go there," Norman said to me.

After dinner, as I prepared to go to my tepee, Norman said I might
prefer the empty bedroom on the second floor of his gallery.

"You don't have to sleep with the rodents."

In the morning, he said, he would tell me how to find someone
willing to take me into the Badger, a man named Terry Tatsey, an ad-
ministrator at the Blackfeet Community College.

Tatsey lives along Badger Creek, where it flows out of the mountains, and has been leading friends and family members into the
Badger-Two Medicine for many years. I found him in his office on
the second story of a prefabricated metal building at one end of the
college's muddy parking lot. Tatsey ushered me in with a wave of his
hand. He was in his mid-forties, tall, and meaty with a serious face

and dark circles under his eyes. He sat in a semisprawl, his big frame pinning a swivel chair against the wall while he tapped a pencil softly on the blotter and listened to me talk about my search for a Blackfeet guide. He was not surprised that I'd had a hard time finding someone. "People think because we are Blackfeet we must know our way around the mountains. The truth is most people on the reservation have never been back in these mountains. But no one likes to admit that. The Blackfeet can be pretty good liars.

"My grandfather used to take me and my brothers back there several times a year. He showed us how to live off the plants and animals the way our ancestors did during the starvation times. We take people into the Badger at least once a year. This year we're going to have a Learning Lodge back there. It's an old-style camp where we try to educate people about what's back there and why it's so much a part of our culture and religion. Maybe you could help us by writing something up."

But camping in the Badger isn't for everybody, he said. Last year a grizzly bear ambled through the gathering and caused such pandemonium that half the people packed up and went home. Each year fewer people seem interested in joining the camp. "There are just a handful of us primitives left."

He asked what I hoped to learn by coming along. I told him that I wanted to experience what it is that pulls him back to the mountains every year.

"It sounds like you are hoping for a vision," Tatsey replied. "Will you understand it if the vision comes to you in Blackfeet? It's the Creator's chosen language." He smiled. "Don't worry. I don't speak it either, and I don't understand it when people speak it to me." Then he cautioned me not to expect too much from the trip. "A lot of people go back there and say, 'What's the big deal? It's just a lot of rocks and trees and bugs.' "

The gathering was planned in six weeks, but he said I should be flexible. He would be spending much of the summer driving back and forth to Seattle, where his wife was being treated for leukemia and waiting for a bone marrow transplant. "You don't know how something like that is going to go."

THE LEARNING LODGE consists of about a dozen tepees erected in a big meadow by Mittens Lake on the edge of the Badger about twelve miles east of the Continental Divide. As I arrive, several women are fixing dinner under a tarpaulin the size of a circus tent. They are cooking game on a huge cast-iron grill. Nearby is a green 400-gallon military surplus drinking water wagon. Tatsey's twelve-year-old daughter and a couple of friends lope their fathers' horses, expertly wending their way through parked cars and tepees. They ride bareback, whooping it up, their long black hair flaring behind them like ravens' wings. A group of men carrying drums set up metal lawn chairs and seat themselves around a campfire. They begin to chant, low and halting at first, like any group of amateur backyard musicians unused to being performers. Along with the drumming, their voices grow stronger over the next several hours. They sing continuously, the men's high, insistent vibrato sounding alternately joyous and imploring. The gathering recalls a time, before the reservation, when the widely scattered bands of Blackfeet came together once a year to feast and dance, renew friendships and hold marriages. During the course of the next few days, there are to be lectures on Blackfeet history, talks by tribal elders on Blackfeet traditions, songs, and storytelling.

The encampment is smaller than Tatsey had hoped for. But he knows the Learning Lodge, with its overtones of summer school, can't compete with everything else happening on the reservation. Twenty miles away, in Browning, a track-and-field competition has attracted hundreds of young people. And in nearby Heart Butte, the annual summer powwow is under way with its dance contests and gambling games.

I spend the first evening sitting on a folding chair by a campfire, gorging on fresh venison and fried bread topped with powdered sugar, listening to tribal linguists reacquaint the Blackfeet with the language their grandparents spoke.

The handful of native speakers struggle to keep a quaintly pictorial language alive in an age of abstraction. Literally translated, a moose is "came into the clearing, black." Hungry is "a jumping in the chest." The newly coined phrase for a personal computer is "as you write, it prints." Beer is "when you open, it bubbles." In physical cultures where actions often spoke louder than words, there are no words of "thank you." The closest approximation to "I'm sorry" is "I've made a mistake." Many words and place-names have no English equivalent and have never been translated. As native speakers die, their knowledge dies with them. It is partly knowledge of native botany, of recipes for medicine prepared from ingredients found in places like the Badger-Two Medicine. "You often find very practical reasons why people valued certain places. But to gain that knowledge you need the language. The map to the treasure is not always written in English," says Darrell Kipp, a relative of G.G. who runs a school on the reservation that teaches only in the Blackfeet language. The language also provides an important clue to the tribe's worldview. The Blackfeet language has two genders, but rather than male and female, they are animate and inanimate. When a noun is used, its gender indicates whether or not the subject is regarded as a living entity. Trees and plants are classified as animate, as are the sun, the moon, and the stars.

I try to learn to count to five in Blackfeet and make a hash of the pronunciation. "Don't say it with your mouth," I'm told. "Speak with the upper part of your throat." Words teeming with consonants are shaped deep in the glottis and then uttered, ventriloquistlike, with-

out moving one's facial muscles. I don't get the knack. But then neither do most of my Blackfeet companions around the campfire.

The conversation reverts to English. Some of the men have been
invited to a conference in Spokane, and they are trying to figure out
how to drive from northwest Montana to northeast Washington
without going through Idaho, which they refer to as the "Aryan
Panhandle." One man turns to me. "It's a little like the anxiety you
guys must have felt when you tried to figure out how to cross Blackfeet
country without running into us guys."

The Blackfeet were known to be the most ferocious fighters of all
the tribes on the northwestern plains. For years, wagon trains heading across Montana detoured to avoid them. The eventual subjuga-
tion of the Blackfeet was due more to the white man's diseases than to
his military. Smallpox struck in 1781 and during the next 100 years
recurring epidemics reduced the tribe's population from 15,000 to
about 2,000. When the Sioux and Cheyenne were waging their epic
war of resistance in the 1870s, the Blackfeet had ceased to be a serious threat to westward expansion. Even in their weakened state, however, the Blackfeet were not exempt from military reprisal. During a
smallpox outbreak in 1870, soldiers out to avenge the killing of a
white rancher massacred 176 inhabitants of Chief Heavy Runner's
stricken band in their winter encampment on the Marias River.
Three fourths of those killed were women and children.

By the close of the nineteenth century, a series of treaties and cash
transactions had shrunk the tribe's domain to a reservation no more
than seventy-five miles across at its widest point. In the Rockies, the
ceded land amounted to 800,000 acres, much of which later would
become part of Glacier National Park. It also included the last of the
tribe's most sacred sites, the Badger-Two Medicine. At the time, the
Blackfeet didn't put up much of a fuss. They were a defeated, starving
people. The buffalo were gone, and the old prayers and ceremonies
did not bring them back. Forced to adapt to a new way of life, they

needed money for farm equipment and cattle. Tribal leaders bickered briefly over the price before agreeing to $1.5 million, half of what they had initially demanded.

ON MY SECOND morning in the Blackfeet camp we get up at dawn and prepare to move the camp farther into the mountains. Tatsey says we will ride about twenty miles following Badger Creek west to its junction with Lee Creek at a place called Ropes-Tie-Banks-Together, where the Blackfeet used to trap buffalo in the stream. The confluence has been a favorite camping spot of the Tatsey family for nearly a century. A sweat lodge has been built near the campsite where we are to spend our first night on the trail.

Before we leave, we get a lesson in horse packing from Tyson Running Wolf, a young man who has spent almost as much time as Tatsey in these mountains and who is supplying some of the horses and gear.

Tatsey warns that things may be a little rough at the start. He is going to be breaking in a new packhorse on the trail. The animal has never been ridden, never had anything tied to its back, and now it's going to be made to carry 150 pounds of camping equipment.

The three-year-old gelding stands quivering while Tatsey and his nephew, Joey, cinch up the packsaddle and strap on a set of heavy panniers. The moment the two men step clear, the horse bucks wildly and gallops off across the meadow, over a hill, and out of sight. Tatsey and his nephew mount up and take off in pursuit. They return a few minutes later with the runaway. The horse is repacked, only to bolt again. The scene is repeated until finally the horse seems to tire.

Tatsey rides out well ahead of us with the packhorse in tow. He wants to see how things go on the trail and thinks it prudent to keep some distance between the skittish horse and the rest of the livestock. The only time he lost an animal, he says, was once on a steep trail over Badger Canyon when nervous horses began to crowd each other, causing one to lose its footing and fall off a fifty-foot cliff. We are not taking that trail, which is both the quickest and most treacherous way in. But where we are going, over a pass known as "the Shoots," is perilous enough.

Leaving the Mittens Lake encampment, we enter a dense forest carpeted with blue and purple wildflowers. We are in one of those intersections of nature where the land is a mosaic of geologic features not usually found near each other. Here, the northern plains, dotted with glacial ponds and furrowed by rivers, roll up abruptly against steep mountains fringed with aspen, balsam, and cottonwood. Botanists call the complex an aspen parkland biome. It exists almost nowhere except along a fifty-mile corridor between the Blackfeet Reservation and the Rocky Mountain front. An abundance of food, water, and cover make for some of the best wildlife habitat in the northern Rockies. It also may harbor one of the largest untapped pools of natural gas in the Northwest.

I have traveled about a mile when word filters back that there had been an accident. The packhorse is down and hurt. "Fell on a beaver cutting," I hear someone say. Then "Oh Jesus." Ahead, two girls are standing on one side of the downed horse, sobbing.

The beaver cutting looks like a punji stake covered with blood. It is actually the butt of an aspen sapling that a beaver has chewed to a lethal point.

The packhorse, frantically trying to get free of its load, had been throwing itself from side to side, and had managed to impale itself on the aspen stake. Now the horse is lying on its side, its feet lashed to a tree, held down by four men as Tatsey attempts to sew up a gaping wound in its flank. He is not having much success. Every time he makes a little progress with the needle and thread, the horse thrashes violently and a slick, ghastly globe of intestine, the size of a soccer ball, pops out of the hole in its flank.

Again and again, Tatsey plunges both hands into the wound and tries to push the viscera back inside. This goes on for nearly a half an hour. Then the blob of horse gut deflates, a clear sign that the intestine itself has developed a puncture. The horse stops struggling. Its respiration changes from anguished heaving to a shallow rattle. It is going into shock.

Tatsey lays aside the needle and thread, looks for a long moment at the wounded horse, and turns to his cousin, one of the men holding the horse down.

"Better get the gun, Squee."

A tall heavyset man, Francis "Squee" Guardipe, gets to his feet and starts walking back toward Mittens Lake. Several minutes later, he returns carrying a holstered .44 Magnum pistol, which he places on the ground near Tatsey. The men here are all familiar with guns, but nobody wants to be one the one to pull the trigger, not Squee, not Tatsey, not Marlin Spoonhunter, Tatsey's Arapaho brother-in-law, not Tyson Running Wolf, not me. Finally, Joey Tatsey, Terry's nephew and the youngest man present, reaches for the gun. "OK," he said. "Let's get it over with."

Afterward, we pick up the panniers and lead the other horses back toward the trailhead. I grab up one end of a pack that Tyson Running Wolf is dragging down the trail. It is bulky and hard to get a grip on. Running Wolf, who has been struggling with his emotions, is walking fast and is hard to keep up with.

"Dumb Indians. Right? Always screwing up. That what you're thinking?" he says.

"I don't know how anybody could have handled that horse," I say. "That horse was out of control from the moment they put the saddle on him."

"There was nothing wrong with that horse. He was a good horse. He was green, that's all," Running Wolf says. "You don't bring a green horse like that, load him up and lead him into these mountains. This is no place to take an unbroke horse. You got to work with him first, get him used to the load. There is no excuse for this happening.

"I'm getting out," he says. "I'm pulling my horses. I don't want anything more to do with this outfit."

I help him load his horses into his trailer and watch him drive off. His anger and embarrassment have caught me by surprise. As I watch his horse trailer rattle off, I think about Indians and animals. I remember what a local environmentalist asked me when I mentioned I had just driven through the Blackfeet Reservation. "How many dead dogs did you see along the road?" On the reservation, people will say. Be careful you don't run over any dead dogs. "I always brace myself when I come to a household with a lot of unfed dogs around," a social worker told me. "It's often a sign I'll find neglected children inside."

Poverty is a well-worn excuse for the mistreatment of animals. John Steinbeck once wrote about watching his sick dog die because he couldn't afford to take it to a vet. But we have come to expect more of Indians. We have been taught to believe they lived in harmony with the natural world. One of the famous contemporary myths is the story of Chief Seattle, who became a symbol of the environmental movement as the result of words attributed to him in a film about pollution. "Every part of the Earth is sacred to my people. Whatever befalls the Earth befalls the sons of Earth." That noble sentiment was made up by a scriptwriter and never spoken by the chief. With the ad and others like it, Madison Avenue and the environmental movement used the necromancy of television to rehabilitate an old stereotype. The noble *sauvage* became the crying Indian. Real Indians, meanwhile, were killing whales, tracking down elk and caribou on snow machines, and shooting them at close range with automatic rifles.

I don't know how many Blackfeet share Buster Yellow Kidney's reverence for grizzly bears, but I meet several who would just as soon shoot them on sight and who bitterly resent the Endangered Species Act for making it a crime to kill grizzlies. The bears may hold a place of high esteem in the Blackfeet cosmology. But a lot of people on the reservation have come to regard them as a scary nuisance.

"I call them 'fuzzy pigs,' " Clyde LaBell said to me over a cup of convenience store coffee in Browning one morning before I joined Tatsey. LaBell, a Blackfeet, is a project manager for a local construction company and owns a small ranch. He said environmentalists distort traditional Blackfeet attitudes toward bears and other animals to fit their preservationist agenda. "Blackfeet always hunted bears. It was part of our culture. Now, thanks to the Endangered Species Act, all we're allowed to do is raise grizzly bears. And we've raised a ton of them on this reservation in the last twenty years. Every year in the spring they come prowling down the creek bottoms, looking for cows and sheep to eat, scaring the kids to death. Hell, I was playing golf the other day when I had one of 'em looking me over. Try concentrating on your golf game when a grizzly bear is peeking out of the woods at you."

It is early afternoon by the time Tatsey reappears from the woods, carrying the dead horse's halter and packsaddle. Word of the accident has spread around the camp.

"Hey, Terry, did you cut a steak off for me?" someone yells. Tatsey's daughter runs up to him and asks if he will cut the mane and the tail off for her. He brushes past, saying nothing to anyone. Losing the horse is just the latest setback in a long, unhappy summer.

Tatsey climbs into the cab of his pickup truck and beckons me to hop in.

"It was a bad thing that happened today. It's kind of put a cloud over everything we are trying to do here. I'm sure you feel it."

He goes on. "But I don't want you to feel too bad. So I thought I would tell you how we try to deal with the situation when an animal dies. Losing an animal is part of life. It helps you prepare for losing loved ones. We believe that when an animal dies, often, it is taking the place of a person, in other words, so that person doesn't have to die. We always try to be thankful that the death didn't happen to our immediate family or to a good friend. In our way of life, nothing really dies anyway. Spiritually, it's all still there. Like with that horse. We're going to burn up the remains later today because we don't want it attracting bears. But the spirit of the horse will be intact."

We sit there in the truck for a bit, neither of us saying anything.

"You been to Heart Butte, yet, to the powwow?" Tatsey asks after a while. There would be dances, food, and the old Blackfeet stick game, a highly popular form of gambling on a reservation where there is no casino yet. Heart Butte itself is worth visiting, Tatsey says.

"You might want to take it in now that you've got the time. Give us a day to think things over as far as the Badger is concerned."

Heart Butte is one of the more isolated communities on a pretty isolated reservation. If you are from around Heart Butte, as the Tatsey family is, you are considered a "southsider," which is reservation slang for hillbilly. People who live in Heart Butte have few of the conveniences of Browning, which though hardly a metropolis, is the center of government and commerce on the reservation. The tribal council meets there. The community college is there, as are most of the motels, restaurants, and stores.

The south end of the reservation was last to get houses, wells, and indoor plumbing. "People liked to think of us down here as kind of deprived and ignorant," Tatsey says. "I like to think the ghosts of our ancestors are more at home down here. The south side has always been kind of a refuge. It is easier to be an Indian here. People in Browning don't always want to be Indians. If a guy gets into trouble in Browning, people will say he is being an Indian. They don't say that down here."

A cluster of cinder block houses on green slopes that step down from the Badger-Two Medicine, Heart Butte is a fifteen-minute drive from the Mittens Lake camp. The powwow looks like an old-fashioned county fair. Acres of cars, campers, canvas tepees, and nylon tents fill in the perimeter of a weedy vacant lot the size of a football field. In the middle of the field, an open-air dance pavilion is ringed by an arbor for spectators and judges. Flanking the pavilion are aisles of walled tents and trailers where vendors sell food and an assortment of factory-made Indianesque goods—jewelry, beaded belts, rugs, and wall hangings. There is a row of card parlors, at the end of which is the biggest, noisiest tent on the premises. It houses the Blackfeet stick game, where thousands of dollars are won and lost each day of the powwow.

Inside, two sitting rows of people face each other. They are the hiders and the guessers. Both sides try to gin up the ante. They wave bills in the air, looking for someone on the other side to match their bets. The game begins with a fanfare of drumming and chanting on the hiders' side. It is meant to distract the guessers. One of the hiders takes two white bonelike objects, one with a black stripe on it, and passes them back and forth from one hand to the other. The point of the game seems childishly simple. Guess which hand the striped bone is in. But the hider is a wizard of distraction, and the transfer of bones from one hand to another is lost in a windmill of gestures by him and others on his side, who add to the confusion with their own elaborate pantomimes of hiding. The hider fools me. I remember Tatsey's comment about Blackfeet being pretty good liars. But on the guessers' side, an old woman in a Denver Broncos jacket grins a nearly toothless grin and points to the hider's right hand. The bones pass to the old woman's side, along with one of the five wooden sticks used to keep score. The first side to make five correct guesses is the winner.

The game has been around for ages. Walter McClintock, a forest ranger who lived with the Blackfeet at the end of the nineteenth century, wrote about the game of hiding antelope bones that were beautifully carved and decorated. According to Blackfeet legend, the game originated as a form of mortal combat in which the guessers fired arrows at the hiders. An arrow that missed its mark represented a wrong guess. A right guess killed. In one story, a warrior who has been unsuccessful in battle is ashamed to return home and face the ridicule of a tyrannical chief. He retreats to the mountains, where he falls asleep and is visited in a dream by a grizzly bear that bestows on him the power to withstand arrows. The warrior goes home, wins a lethal game of hide-the-bones, and becomes the new chief.

I try to follow the stick game from the sidelines, "guessing" silently to myself and being wrong again and again. Is there a lesson in this for me? Try as I might, I will not find what I'm looking for. The old world will remain hidden from people like me. That's probably as it should be. We worked too hard to destroy it. The stick game was banned along with other forms of native gambling, such as horse racing, by the Religious Crimes Code of the 1880s. The code was repealed a long time ago, but Christian clerics still rail against the stick game. It retains an aura of primitive ritual, of contraband pleasure. An old woman thumps me on the back. Give her my chair, she says, if I'm not going to play.

I arrive at the dance pavilion for the start of a dance contest offering $1,000 to the winner. The contestants are mostly young people whose costumes highlight lithe, muscular physiques. Knees lift high, torsos swoop, and shoulders dip in imitation of prairie chickens, ravens, wolves, foxes, and "brave dogs"—animals that the Blackfeet dancing societies are named after. But the dancers incorporate other movements, head-snapping, hip-flipping stuff that brings to mind the old rhythm and blues lyric "Shake a tail feather."

"What kind of dance is that?" I ask a man standing next to me. "Reservation rock and roll," he says wearily. He says that the high-priced contests have changed the nature of tribal dancing. A new, nomadic class of "professional" dancers travels the powwow circuit, improvising on and changing traditional routines. He says the dances no longer seem related to their original ceremonial purposes, the warding off of evil spirits, or the honoring of a deity. Yet what I am watching seems authentic to me. The young dancers embellish tradition, but they don't abandon it. They move to the rhythms of the old music, the high, fierce keening and drumming which has the same power to excite as it did 100 years ago when Walter McClintock was captivated by it. He said it was inspired by "mountains, forests and plains, their wild life of hunting and warfare, the Sun worship and those emotions and passions which are common to the human heart the world over."

I get back to camp just as Tatsey, his daughter, and brother-in-law, Marlin Spoonhunter, are walking toward the woods carrying a can of white gas. "Time to torch up the horse," Spoonhunter says. We march solemnly back to the site of the accident and pile branches and twigs on top of the horse, which is now lying stiff-legged under a cloud of flies. Tatsey lights the pyre and asks Spoonhunter to say a prayer.

"Grandfather, we ask your forgiveness for what happened here today, and we ask that you send this horse's spirit to watch over our horse herds. We ask your blessing on all our family members, old people, children, and infants. We ask your blessing on our people who are sick. We thank you, Grandfather, for all of the animate and inanimate things on Earth."

Then we have a "smudge," bathing our faces in the smoke from a burning tuft of vanilla grass. Tatsey's daughter wants assurance from the adults that some good has come from the horse's death. "Do you think he saved another life?" she asks. "Do you think he saved Mom's life."

"Maybe so, my girl," Tatsey says quietly.

The Tatseys invite me to spend the evening with them at their tepee. They've bought some steaks and have invited two tribal elders to come over. The elders are among the few Blackfeet who can speak the language and remember the protocol for all of the old ceremonies.

I do not know what to expect from the elders, but I do not look forward to an evening of formal speeches. Nor does Tatsey, who slips off after dinner to try his hand at a calf-roping competition in a community rodeo in Dupuyer about twenty-five miles away.

As darkness falls, I'm the only one left around the campfire. The fire spreads its warmth and I doze off. Sometime later, I'm slowly awakened by the voices of two old men talking and laughing nearby. They are reminiscing about long-ago adventures in the Badger-Two Medicine.

". . . had a case of whiskey . . . Too drunk to get out of the tent . . . When I woke up, there was two feet of snow on the ground. It covered up all our gear. Couldn't find a damn thing when, all of a sudden, a grizzly bear shows up. Old Joe Short was with me. He goes digging in the snow after his rifle. But all he can find is his pocketknife. He starts waving that little bitty knife at the bear and yelling he's going to rip him from asshole to top knot. I never seen a bear take off so fast. Afterward, Joe goes around telling people he killed that bear with his pocketknife. He was the worst liar."

Then the second man tells a story of a botched poaching expedition that led to fines and jail sentences.

"You'd think after all those centuries of raiding and stealing, we'd at least be able to get one damn elk without getting caught."

"Don't let that story get around. Ruin our reputation," the first man says, looking in my direction.

We pull our chairs closer to the fire, which is barely alive.

"Environmentalists are all hot and bothered about the oil. You think there's oil back there?" one of them asks.

"Oh, probably. But I don't want the environmentalists poking around back there any more than I want the oilmen."

He looks at me again.

"You an environmentalist?"

"I'm just a writer."

"A writer, eh."

I introduce myself and tell them how much I have been looking forward to their stories.

"I suppose you thought we were going to sit here and tell a bunch of the old, old stories about how Napi and them other gods traipsed around these mountains?" the first man asks. " 'Cause I don't know any of them stories."

I tell them I am not particular. Any story about the mountains will do fine.

"I got a lot of enjoyment from going into the mountains," the first man says. "Part of it was the beauty of the place and the peace and quiet. But part of it was just going someplace where you could relax and get away from the old lady."

"I got to know my boys back there," the second man says, "taking them on hunting trips, showing off my skills. That's how I won their respect. Of course, I threatened to leave the little buggers back there if they didn't show me respect."

Someone stokes the fire, warming us. After a while, I doze off again and stay asleep until a frenzy of coyote yipping and howling wakes me just before dawn. The coyotes are close by, probably fighting over the remains of the horse.

In the early light I see Tatsey moving about and hear the soft *clink* of metal and leather. A half-dozen horses have been saddled and tied to a grove of trees just behind me.

"Ready to take a little ride into the mountains?" he asks me.

"What changed your mind? You win some money at the rodeo?" I ask.

"No, I finished fourth, just out of the money. But I feel better today. I think our luck is changing."

He points to the sky.

"Marlin saw an eagle, and that's kind of like an all-clear signal from the Creator. At least, he says he saw one. You can never be sure with Marlin. He's an Arapaho, and they're pretty good liars. We'll just have to trust him."

ACTION JACKSON

AN AUTUMN WIND gusts up to fifty miles an hour. The trees come down along the trail at a rate of forty per mile. Often, they announce their fall with a crack as sharp and loud as a rifle shot. Just as often, they keel over noiselessly. Those are the potential killers. I stare out at the forest from atop my horse, as if by fixing my gaze on each passing tree, I can stop it from falling.

The day did not proclaim its evil intent. The three of us got up before dawn and saddled our horses under a starry sky. Not a breath of wind was stirring. The wind rose with the sun, more fickle at first than formidable. I didn't pay it any mind, but my companions, Meredith and Tory Taylor, took note. They have lived near these mountains for many years and have a mariner's feel for sinister vibrations. A wind like this one can get to "tunneling," as if moving in a horizontal cyclone. If that happens, they say you could expect the trees to fall like tenpins.

We are riding along the edge of a long meadow, with forests rising on both sides, when we hear the first one shatter and crash on the far ridge. My horse trembles slightly at the sound and cast a brief, side-long glance. Ten minutes later, we hear another tree go down, and another. Out in the open meadow, we are safe and will be for another several miles. But we have at least seven hours of riding ahead of us and much of it will be spent working our way through forest.

We eat a brief, nervous lunch. The wind is still sporadic and given to eerie calm spells. When it comes, it blows with powerful, lengthening exhalations. A mile to the northeast, where we are going, the meadow funnels into a river of grayness, a burned-out, long-dead forest where a gauntlet of rootless, teetering lodgepole pines await.

We are headed for the Thorofare district of Yellowstone Park in northwestern Wyoming. It is a land of humpbacked mountains and broad, lush valleys surrounding the confluence of Thorofare Creek and the upper Yellowstone River. If wilderness is gauged by its distance from the civilized world, the Thorofare is the archetype. Thirty miles from the nearest road, just east of the Continental Divide, it is as far from civilization as any place in the lower forty-eight states. Only one human being lives out here, the park ranger assigned to the Thorofare patrol cabin. For twenty years, the Thorofare ranger has been Bob Jackson, the man we are going to see.

None of us know much about Jackson and have no idea what we'll encounter once we got there. All we do know is that from the deepest recesses of a wilderness, this man who is rarely seen is creating a stir, and we want to find out what it is all about. Jackson is the last of his kind, a Western lawman who still chases down outlaws on horseback. Mounted on his high-spirited sorrel, armed with a handsome replica of an old army cavalry carbine, he tracks poachers through the forests and mountains of southeastern Yellowstone. He is known as "Action Jackson" among the park officials, game wardens, environmentalists, outfitters, and hunting guides who take an interest in what goes on in the backcountry. Some of them regard him as a bully with a badge, while others see Jackson as a modern version of the U.S. cavalrymen who patrolled on horseback and snowshoes and made the first organized effort to save the park's deer, elk, bison, and bear from profligate poaching in the 1880s and 1890s.

Lately, Jackson has been asking for help. He has reported that rogue hunting guides, operating just outside his jurisdiction in the adjacent Teton Wilderness, are illegally baiting elk and other animals out of the park. They have been dumping bags of salt, rich with nutrients that the animals crave. The hunters use the salt licks as ambush sites.

Now dozens of salt licks have turned the southern border of the park into a firing line for hunters who pay outfitters thousands of dollars for the opportunity to shoot a bull elk. Jackson is especially concerned about the fate of Yellowstone's endangered grizzly bears, which are also drawn to the salt licks. Inevitable conflicts with hunters lead to many bears getting shot. Such conflicts tend to arise most often in places like the Thorofare, where jurisdictions and policies collide. In the park all hunting is banned. South of the park, in the Teton Wilderness, elk hunting is legal. The boundary between the park and the wilderness, drawn without benefit of scientific study, makes no ecological sense. It separates the Yellowstone River from its headwaters, thus dividing a single watershed and its resident wildlife into two political subdivisions, subject to different policies and pressures.

Borders breed insurgency, especially in remote country like this. In the Thorofare poachers have been ignoring the boundary since Yellowstone, the nation's first national park, was created nearly 130 years ago. Hunters have been using salt licks to bait game across the line for almost as long. Except for Jackson, law enforcement is virtually nonexistent. For much of the past twenty years, he has been the only resident ranger in a region that encompasses about 100 square miles on both sides of the boundary line. If federal wilderness policies were strictly enforced, the salting would stop. So would other abuses. Outfitters would have to forgo some of the civilized comforts that allow their high-paying clients to live like pashas. The reluctance of government officials to take action, however, reflects America's ambivalence toward wilderness. Even those who like to be out in the wild have varying tolerances.

The wilderness, we should remember, is where Jesus went without food for forty days and met the devil. Not everyone is looking to repeat that experience. Many people prefer wilderness lite, where there is a floor between them and the ground and where the wild creatures step smartly into their gunsights and viewfinders.

On a stormy day like this, when nature toys indifferently with our safety and sanity, I recall the cautionary statements of two famous naturalists about wilderness. Edward Abbey called it an "austere . . . utterly worthless place." Of course, Abbey had his own sly motive in making it out to be so terrible—like Brer Rabbit exaggerating the torments of the briar patch, he preferred having the place to himself.

Henry David Thoreau, on the other hand, did not dissemble. America's first great outdoor writer was terrified and depressed by wilderness. After climbing Maine's Mount Katahdin during a violent wind, he wrote of being in the grip of a "vast, titanic, inhuman nature . . . [that] seems to say sternly, why came ye here before your time? I have never made this soil for thy feet, this air for thy breathing. I cannot pity nor fondle thee here, but forever relentlessly drive thee hence . . ." Thoreau retreated to Walden, where nature wore a kinder face.

For the three of us, riding to the Thorofare, there is no turning back. Crossing the Continental Divide at Atlantic Creek, we are fifteen miles from the road where our truck and horse trailer are parked and virtually the same distance from Jackson's cabin. As the wind reaches its peak, it is not tunneling so much as it is broadsiding the forest. This isn't a cyclone wind. But it is a very big blow. The temperature has dropped sharply since we started. The wind chill is aggravated by snow squalls, which come at us sideways and feel more like darts than flakes.

We ride along in silence, looking and listening. The woods may look dead, but they sound alive, creaking and groaning piteously, like old, fragile bones. Poor, tormented trees. I feel sorry for them, almost as much as I feel sorry for myself. I feel this way right up to the moment when I see something I have never seen before. A few paces in front of me, a large pine tree uproots itself and arcs noiselessly through the air in a glide path that will put it directly on top of where I will be in just one moment.

The horse and I come to our senses simultaneously. I've never heard a horse bellow before. He whirls, and we rocket away from the tree with the sound of its stupendous *crash* exploding in my ears.

The tree trunk lands just behind the rump of a packhorse that had been walking ahead of me. The branches tear the horse's pack straps to pieces, scattering its load on the ground. The other pack animals stampede. It's a full-blown wreck, but nobody and none of the horses are hurt.

"Anybody need to change their pants?" Tory asks.

The Taylors look at me quizzically, the way they might look at a flying cow during a tornado. "I thought you were a dead man, for sure," Meredith says.

I am hyperventilating and can't speak.

We regroup and plod on, but slower than before. The trail is barricaded by fallen logs. We go around where possible, Where it isn't, we labor to clear a path. We have forgotten to bring a saw.

All afternoon the wind continues to rise and fall in husky, irregular breaths as we move in and out of the ghost forest. My mood has become a prisoner of its own foul weather. From a state of slightly giddy apprehension, my fear has congealed into a cold, enervating mass. Is there such a thing as hypothermia of the spirit? I remember the drained feeling Thoreau experienced as he climbed the mountain, as if "some vital part of him had escaped from the loose grating of his ribs."

I remind myself that I've been in similar jams, lost in the woods after dark, swept down a river through rapids bigger than I could handle. I know what to do. Keep my wits about me. Put one foot in front of the other. Always be doing something. Prevent the spirit from curling into the fetal position. I'd hum if I could carry a tune. A lyric from the Gordon Lightfoot folk song *The Wreck of the Edmund Fitzgerald* comes to mind. It captures the exquisite torture of the sailors' vigil. "Does anyone know where the love of God goes when the waves turn the minutes to hours?"

You can feel almost as helpless in the mountains. There's not a lot more to do than hold the reins and watch the trees. Eye movement isn't much of an improvement over the enforced passivity of a sailor aboard a foundering freighter. Still, it's something.

So why do I keep coming to places like this? I am not a peril junkie. My wife blames it on an old-fashioned Catholic upbringing and its emphasis on suffering as a means of attaining salvation. Certain people, she believes, should not be exposed to that line of thinking any more than some Indians should be exposed to alcohol. It interacts with a natural tendency toward masochism, bidding some to lie down in the dark on reservation roads, luring others ever deeper into wild country where they have no business.

I know this much about myself. The dread will pass. I will remember the fear, but not the taste of fear. It won't be preserved in the sensory memory the way an adolescent romance is stored with all of the piquancy and pain well into middle age. Lucky thing, fear doesn't work that way or we'd be dodging trees in our dreams. A month from now, when I think about the forest path where I nearly came to grief, the mental picture will be like an Ansel Adams photograph, beautiful and benign, and I will want to come back.

Yet, it's not just the scenery that beckons. You can get that from the deck of a cruise ship or out the window of a Winnebago. Wilderness is a potent antidote to a life led too much on automatic pilot, where muscles are toned not in the field but the gym, where the work that once recruited our bodies is done by somebody or something else. The person we take into the woods is the old pal we laid off years ago when we hired someone else to do the heavy lifting. He is the alter ego in overalls. But it's also true that the old boy can be gainfully employed in ways that don't require donning a fifty-pound pack and trudging up a mountain. He can be happy building a summer cabin or planting a vegetable garden.

So what is it about the back of beyond that stirred Thoreau, even as he hustled off the wild mountain, and that appeals to city dwellers, though they must rely on dumb luck and smart horses to survive the day?

The wilderness is, indeed, the old country, Thoreau discovered. He said it was a place as ancient and raw as the surface of a distant planet, hostile to life but full of life, elemental and mysterious. "Nature was here something savage and awful, though beautiful . . . This was that earth of which we have heard, made of chaos and old night . . . Here was no man's garden, but the unhandselled globe . . . It was matter, vast, terrific.

"Talk of mysteries! Think of our life in nature—daily to be shown matter, to come in contact with it, rocks, trees, wind on our cheeks, the solid earth! the actual world! the common sense! Contact! Contact! . . ."

We arrive at Jackson's place just before dark, tie our horses to the hitching rail outside his two-room cabin, start pulling the packs and saddles off and looking for a spot well clear of any standing timber to pitch a tent. It takes a few minutes for us to get acclimated, to make sense of the human noises we are hearing, laughter, chairs scraping, beer cans opening. Suddenly the cabin door is thrust open by a stocky fellow, wearing a brown leather jacket and a rumpled ranger's shirt. He has a broad, fleshy face, a hank of hair curled over one eye, and a wide, slightly crooked smile. He has a beer in one hand and gestures at us to come in with the other. "What the hell took you so long?" Slowly, we come to. This may be the loneliest outpost of humanity in the continental United States, but there is a party going on inside. I can feel heat wafting out of the open door and smell food cooking on a stove. I don't know what the Wilderness Act says about all this, but it's all I can do not to yank the beer can out of his hand and inhale the contents.

"Hi," he says. "I'm Bob Jackson. You want beer or wine? I got some nice cold chardonnay down in the cellar."

The three of us look stupidly at each other, still trying to adjust. But we don't hang back.

Inside, we join Jackson's girlfriend, Sharon Magee, who lives with him here and works for the Park Service as a volunteer, and five other people who braved the storm and rode in a little ahead of us. They include the district ranger, who is Jackson's immediate supervisor; two field agents of the U.S. Fish and Wildlife Service; and two retired park officials. One of them is eighty-one-year-old Bob Murphy, who is something of a legend in the National Park Service. Murphy spent most of his career in Yellowstone, but he was also a superintendent of Death Valley National Monument. There, he headed the posse of rangers that caught Charles Manson in the California desert in 1969.

Murphy and the others have ridden in to see for themselves what Jackson has been raising such a ruckus about. It is soon clear that not all of his guests share his opinion of how bad conditions are out here. But that hardly matters. Jackson is glad for the company and enjoys an argument. His guests are happy to indulge him. After all, he has provided them with an excuse to sneak off to the legendary Thorofare, a place that for all of its remoteness, or perhaps because of it, has long been known as a bachelors' hideout, a toned-down version of the annual summer rendezvous where mountain men and Indians parlayed, gambled, drank, and debauched.

Liquor and women have always been part of the Thorofare scene. Fifty years ago, a certain Mrs. B. would ride back here each fall with a group of young women and a generous supply of spirits and set up camp at Bridger Lake, about a half-hour's ride from the park patrol cabin and from most of the hunting camps in the vicinity. Mrs. B.'s encampment came to be known as the Bridger Lake Lodge.

Mrs. B. was finally invited to depart the region in the early 1940s and the account of her eviction by a reluctant ranger is described in the Thorofare cabin logbook. But the Bridger Lake Lodge lives on in the fantasies of men whose notion of wilderness has less to do with the preservation of scenery and wildlife than it has with a free and easy life in the mountains. Today a moonlight trip to Bridger Lake is part of a young ranger's initiation to the Thorofare. After an evening of raunchy stories, he is encouraged to pay a visit to "the lodge." He is set on his horse and given a set of vague directions intended to keep him wandering around the marshy, mosquito-infested lakeshore most of the night. But Jackson insists the idea of the lodge isn't complete hokum. Occasionally, he says, he has come across an outfitter's camp with an unattached lady or two circulating among the male hunters. "The outfitter will try and make like they're cooks. But it's pretty obvious what they're doing there."

The Thorofare cabin has its own tradition of bare-naked hospitality. Over cocktails, Jackson brings out a photo album of nude bathers. A snapshot is the price of admission for the privilege of luxuriating in the wood-fired hot shower out back. Jackson's subjects stand rigidly, facing the camera in mock Grant Wood poses, cigars in their mouths and hats strategically held. "Any takers?" he asks, looking at our tired, dirty faces. "I can get the water heated up in no time after dinner."

We finish off a potluck dinner of lasagna and enchiladas prepared in a big barnacled skillet by Sharon. By now, I am half-expecting cigars and port, but that's a bit too much to ask for, even here. Instead, we clear the table and get ready for Jackson's presentation. He starts by flipping over a dozen color photographs of dead elk that he and Sharon have taken just outside the park. The carcasses are largely intact, except for the antlers. The animals lie where they were shot, in or near the salt craters that hunting guides use to bait the elk out of the park.

Jackson doesn't have to say anything. Everyone at the table knows that the salt traps are illegal in federal wilderness and that leaving behind edible portions of game animals violates Wyoming law. The state law was passed over 100 years ago when the citizenry recoiled at an orgy of killing by commercial hide and horn hunters.

Jackson's photographs are grotesque. They represent the sort of casual destruction that gives all hunting a bad name. To the people around the table, the pictures evince slovenliness repugnant to frugal country folk. Wanton waste like this is supposed to be an urban vice. It epitomizes the kind of moral squalor that rural dwellers point to when explaining why they chose not to live in the city.

"This is business as usual out here," Jackson says quietly.

Jackson is old-fashioned. Approaching his mid-fifties, he is a throwback to a time when hunters who came back here were willing to walk or ride over rough country for several days just to get a shot at an elk. They were people for whom the chase mattered as much as the kill, who did not evade the tiresome work of boning and dressing an elk carcass and hauling the meat out along with the antlers.

Today, hunters pay $4,000 to $5,000, excluding travel costs, for a chance to shoot a "trophy" elk, an animal with a handsome spread of horns. The meat is of no consequence. These well-heeled sportsmen didn't fly out here from New York and Atlanta to fill the larder. The wilderness experience is also of secondary importance. For many, the thirty-mile horseback ride is roughing it enough. Why trudge around for days in the October snow and freezing air when you can stand behind a tree for a couple of hours and wait for the game to come to you?

"Nobody has the incentive to do it right anymore, not the hunters and certainly not the outfitters," Jackson says. "Blame it on economics or greed, or what have you. The idea is get in, get your set of antlers to put in your den, and make way for the next guy."

It's a pretty accurate assessment. The business works like this: An outfitter pays $200,000 or more for a wilderness camp and thousands more in expenses—for horses, extra guides, food, and equipment. The outfitter has six to seven weeks every fall—the length of the hunting season—to meet his costs and make a profit. To succeed, he figures he must run a new batch of hunters through camp at least once a week. If a hunter is lucky enough to shoot an elk on his first day in camp, the outfitter can get him in and out in three days. The odds of that happening improve significantly if there's a place nearby where the elk are known to feed, especially if it is out in the open and an easy ride from camp. The salt licks fill the bill.

"The only way to end this bullshit," Jackson says, "is for the Forest Service to get back here on a full-time basis, keep order, and enforce the law."

His comments meet with glum assent. No one takes issues, no one, that is, until he starts talking about grizzly bears.

Jackson believes the bears are becoming collateral casualties of wilderness salting. The grizzles are drawn to the carcasses left in the salt pits by hunters interested primarily in taking home antlers. As the bears become habituated to a salt lick and its reliable cache of elk meat, the characteristically solitary grizzlies congregate, as if at a dump, and, as Jackson sees it, the chances of fatal encounters with heavily armed humans grow exponentially.

"The outfitters are bringing more hunters in here. I'm seeing more bears around, and we know more bears are getting killed during hunting season."

During the past twenty years, most of the 250 human-caused grizzly bear deaths in the Yellowstone region have occurred at the hands of hunters. Typically, bears are killed during surprise encounters with hunters who are after elk, bighorn sheep, or other legal prey. Although shooting a grizzly bear is illegal under the Endangered Species Act, exceptions are made in cases of self-defense. Hunters who claim self-defense are rarely charged with violating the act, even when they kill cubs.

Jackson suspects that only about half of the hunting-related bear deaths in the Thorofare country are being reported. But he lacks the authority to investigate bear deaths outside the park. And because no one else is investigating, the case he makes is largely circumstantial.

"I'd be over at one of the camps and hear people talking about a sow getting killed over by one of the salts. A few days later I'd see an orphaned cub or two wandering outside the cabin. You don't have to be Sherlock Holmes to figure out what's going on."

Dominic Domenici, a bear management expert with the U.S. Fish and Wildlife Service, is the first of several dissenters to weigh in. Salting is one thing, he agrees. It's clearly unethical, clearly wrong. But tying it to grizzly bear mortality is problematic, he says. There are just too many other ways these bears are getting in trouble.

Domenici makes the bears-will-be-bears argument, which says that there are too many grizzly bears, that they have lost their fear of humans, that they respond to the sound of a gunshot as if it were a dinner bell, and that they will try to scavenge an elk carcass whether it has been abandoned at a salt lick or properly dressed and hung from a tree limb in camp.

GRIZZLY BEARS ARE the *sine qua non* of Western wilderness if we think of wilderness in Thoreau's terms, as an ancient and alien world where we can learn something about our origins. Humans evolved with grizzly bears. Their remarkable memories and sensory powers may hold clues to survival skills we lost centuries ago. Their unpredictable behavior can remind us of human capriciousness. A bear in the wilds might bite you or he might nuzzle you. Before one bear was exiled from Yellowstone to a zoo last summer, the young male took to visiting park campgrounds for no apparent reason other than he liked to bounce off tents.

Jackson has a pretty simple prescription for dealing with grizzlies: Leave them alone. Don't remove their protection. Make sure they are safe in the most remote corners of the range, places like the Teton Wilderness. Get rid of the salt licks. Fine hunters who don't promptly dispose of game they shoot and require them to carry bear spray—a Macelike chemical repellent that wards off aggressive grizzlies without harming them.

"The trouble with the grizzly bear is he can be his own worst PR man," Bob Murphy says. Murphy has sat quietly for an hour, neither agreeing nor disagreeing, as Jackson and the others argue about salt baiting and its effect on grizzly bears. Now he has a bear story to tell.

Murphy's memories go back to the era prior to the 1970s, when Yellowstone was widely known as a sort of an outdoor circus, headlined by geysers and grizzlies. The most reliable bear acts took place at garbage dumps where the bears were encouraged to feed, and the public was invited to watch from bleachers set up behind metal fences.

"It was the middle of summer, and the place was crawling with kids wanting to see the bears," Murphy begins. "It was always a big hit when there were cubs around, and, here comes a pair of 'em, just as cute as can be, trailing behind their mama. She starts eating and so do the cubs. Everybody's loving it, snapping pictures. Everything seems pretty normal when, all of a sudden, this big male shows up. I get a little concerned because I know this bear, and I know he's not going to want to share the dump with any other bears. Sure enough, he and the sow get into it a little bit. Nothing serious, but enough to scare off the cubs. One of them heads back over the hill, and the sow follows him. The other cub heads over by the fence, near the people, and, of course, they just love that. Here's this cuddly little baby bear come over to say hello to the kids. I mean, you couldn't ask for more from Walt Disney. But I'm watching the big male because I know what can happen. He noses around the dump for a few minutes and then, wouldn't you know, he gets to noticing the little, lone cub over by the fence. 'Jesus Christ,' I'm thinking. 'Is there some way of at least getting the kids out of here before what I think is going to happen, happens.' But there's nothing to be done. This isn't some circus act you can control. This is nature, and it's about to get as raw and ugly as nature can get. Pretty soon, the male kind of ambles on over the way a bear does, acting like there's nothing special on his mind until he gets right up next to the cub, and takes a big bite out of the little fella's head.

"You can hear the crowd gasp. They can't believe what they are seeing. Then the big bear takes another bite and another. Now the kids are crying and screaming at their parents. 'Do something. Stop him,' and the parents are screaming at me to do something. 'Shoot him . . . Kill him.' Of course, there's nothing I can do, except give them a lecture on how wild bears behave, while the big male proceeds to make a meal of the cub. It was a goddamn disaster, and the people wanted to blame the park for what happened, you know, as if we were responsible. The lesson I learned from this is that a little wilderness goes a long way with the public."

There's no topping that story. Around the table heads nod in silent assent to Murphy's concluding comment. There are 150 years of wilderness experience represented in the five men seated here. They know why the public comes to places like this—to fulfill romantic expectations, to see Bambi or Smokey, to catch a twelve-inch cutthroat or bag a trophy elk. The satisfied customers are the ones who go home with a set of antlers. They store up images not of Thoreau's "chaos and old night" but of a wilderness pastoral, undisturbed by freak wind storms or cannibalistic grizzlies.

Outside Jackson's cabin, the wind continues to shriek.

Jackson points the way to a ratty-looking army tent he says will protect us from the wind, if not the cold, which is hovering around fifteen degrees. Inside, I feel no appreciable difference from the frigid outdoor air. So I erect my own backpacker's tent, burrow fully clothed into my sleeping bag, and mantle my head and shoulders with a second bag I find nearby. I gobble a handful of muscle relaxants to ease the cramps and spasms brought on by the ride and hope for dreams of a tropical beach. But neither the pills nor the extra sleeping bag around my ears can deafen me to the groaning branches of besieged pine trees. We are camped in a clearing, but we are within the trajectory of several tall lodgepoles. Any one of seven or eight could land on top of us. At times like this, I have found that efforts to lull the mind are generally futile. Unable to sleep, I find myself reexamining the genesis of my wilderness obsession.

It was born in the lake country of northern Minnesota and southern Ontario, years before the region became a popular destination for family vacations. Today, it is known as the Boundary Waters Canoe Area, an appropriately antiseptic name for a modern G-rated wilderness that minimizes risk and surprise. A web site allows people to chart the safest routes and reserve the choicest campsites. In my day a trip through the poorly mapped northern waters was more like a shakedown cruise up the Amazon of the male id. It was a place for smoking and swearing and authoritative conversation about sex by teenage boys who had never experienced it. On my first trip, five of us

pooled our lawn mowing money and hired a guide. He was a melodi-
cally foul-mouthed tree stump of a fellow in his sixties who had
learned to navigate the labyrinth of lakes at night during the
Depression as a bootlegger's helper. The bootlegger, half-Indian
himself, transported rotgut to remote reservations. Because it was an
illegal enterprise, it was best done after dark. Our guide was full of
stories about eluding the Mounties, about the wrath of reservation
missionaries, and the light-fingered passion of the bootlegger's
daughter.

Our trip was to travel a circular chain of lakes and rivers and be
back to our starting point in a month. But that single requirement
dictated a stern, inexorable routine, unaltered by bad weather or
rough water. Get up at dawn, start the fire, cook the food, break down
the camp, paddle for eight hours, set up camp, cut firewood, cook
dinner, and take turns every two hours keeping an all-night bear
watch. If a bear showed up, beat pots together or set off a firecracker.

I was the youngest and smallest boy on the trip, and by the third
day I was worn-out, soaked to the gills, and miserably homesick. We
stopped for lunch at the island cabin of a woman who turned out to be
a nurse. She made house calls via canoe and snowshoes and was more
accustomed to dealing with hemorrhaging lumberjacks and frostbit-
ten trappers than with waterlogged city kids. But she sized me up for
what I was, a shivering, potential patient, took me aside, and instructed me on how to take care of myself.

Take those wet clothes off and leave them off, she said. "Down to
the undies. Bareassed would be best."

"I'll freeze."

"You'll freeze if you set all day in those wet clothes. Paddle hard
buck-naked, or close to it, and you'll be fine."

I explained to her that because I was the smallest, the others
wouldn't let me paddle in the rough water.

She said she would take care of that problem for me and she did, lecturing the others on how they were to treat me in the future and following us down to the water's edge to make sure her orders were carried out.

At first, there was much grumbling. My companions didn't think I was strong enough to buck the wind and whitecaps. But I was, and after a while the big boys were letting me do most of the paddling and a lot of the other work. It slowly dawned on them that turning the tyke into a mule could make the trip considerably more enjoyable. Soon I was carrying a canoe that weighed half as much as I did across mile-long portages. I rarely wore my shirt again. By the time the month was over, I had learned the carnival trick of flipping a half-smoked butt backward in my mouth without singeing my tonsils. Best of all, I was accepted by the older boys. Their friendship seemed to confer the status I craved as a sort of apprentice hard case, nearly ready for the bootlegger's daughter.

In the thorofare the next morning we awaken to a blanket of snow. We are going to look at salt pits and visit a hunting camp where Jackson hopes to confront a guide he recently saw pouring fresh salt at one of the baiting stations.

On the way I ask Jackson how he ended up here. "I was running away, you might say." He was twenty-two, a farmer's son from Fort Dodge, Iowa, just out of college with a degree in wildlife biology from a small Midwestern college and a chance to play professional baseball. "I was a junkball pitcher and I had pretty good stuff." He was good enough to draw the attention of a scout for the Minnesota Twins, who told Jackson he thought he had a decent shot at making the big leagues. "I didn't take him seriously. I guess I looked at myself and didn't see major league material."

Jackson accepted a job as a seasonal ranger in Yellowstone in 1969. It meant spending each summer and fall in a cabin where he might not encounter another human being for weeks or even months at a time. "I don't naturally favor places where there aren't people around. But I needed to test myself, to push my own limits, and to do that I needed to get away from other people, from anyone that I could turn to for help."

During his first season, he was responsible for keeping the park's network of ranger cabins supplied with food and other essentials. Mule trains are the lifelines to these backcountry stations. Jackson found he had a knack for finding his way in roadless terrain where even the trails disappear. He could manage horses and mules in all kinds of conditions—in blizzards and blazing forests, around menacing grizzly bears and charging bison.

"There I was, this guy who likes people, likes baseball, likes going to the movies, who finds he is best-qualified to live in the nineteenth century, in some lonely outpost where his only companions are a bunch of crazy animals. I mean, look at my horse." He motions down at his big, feisty sorrel. "This horse is a sociopath. She is certifiable. No one in the park will ride her except me, and I've been riding her for twenty years. She's a maniac, but she's my girl.

"The way I look at it now, I was lucky. I found the one place where I could be a success at what I did. This is my little spot on Earth. I don't own it. I don't get paid very much to be here, and I don't get any benefits. But how many people can say they have found their spot?"

Jackson was assigned to the Thorofare district in 1979 and soon after began his long campaign against illegal hunting practices. "I came out here and found that I was in a place where laws weren't relevant, where the outfitters made their own rules. The law said that an outfitter's exclusive territory went out as far as it took for him to travel out and back in a day. That didn't mean you could hunt in the park. You were supposed to stop at the Yellowstone boundary. But back this far, a lot of guys figured no one was going to see them if they did cross the line."

Poaching was declared illegal in Yellowstone in 1883. Hunting pressure was threatening to wipe out the last remaining bison. A single buffalo head fetched $400. In 1881 the hides of nearly 80,000 elk, deer, and antelope were shipped down the Yellowstone River. Besides poaching, commercial hunters set fires in the park aimed at driving game outside where they could be legally killed. When poachers were caught, local judges refused to prosecute them. Park officials themselves trafficked in stolen artifacts and hides.

"When I got there, I don't think there had been a case brought against a poacher in the Thorofare since the thirties," Jackson says. "The policy was live and let live. A ranger would catch a poacher seventeen miles back in the park, the guy would say he was lost, and the ranger would believe him. It's pathetic, but that's the way things were done. You can read about it in the logbooks." Jackson's entries in the Thorofare station's log are telling in a different way. More than anything, they convey his keen enjoyment of the chase, of following a poacher's spoor for miles across rough terrain, down stream beds, or through falling snow.

". . . Skirted the upper reaches of the drainage. Saw a bunch of crows and three bald eagles. Found a mountain lion carcass about 400 yards in the park. Checked above on the rim rock and found Vibram prints. The lion had been skinned with the head and front paws chopped off. Ribs had been broken by a bullet. I figured it had to be J. B. Shotz because the tracks led in the direction of his camp."

Jackson followed footprints into Shotz's camp and confronted the outfitter. "He readily admitted killing it. Said he was lost. Didn't think he was in the park. He couldn't very well deny it. He'd recorded the deed with an ink marker on the wall of his tent. In big letters, it said 'J.B. gets pussy' with the date noted. I cited him for hunting in the park. It cost him $250 and his guiding permit."

Jackson quickly began to acquire a reputation. Richard Clark, director of the Professional Guide Institute at Western Montana College, says Jackson took to his work like someone obsessed with a jigsaw puzzle, building solid cases from disparate shards of evidence. "Where Bob is different, he doesn't give up just because he didn't catch a guy in the act of shooting. He'll take people to court on circumstantial evidence, footprints or spent cartridges, and get convictions. He's cost outfitters a lot of money in penalties, twenty thousand dollars to forty thousand dollars, and some of them don't forget."

During his first decade in the Thorofare, Jackson's pack animals were poisoned on two occasions, his cabin was vandalized, and his life periodically threatened.

His recent campaign against salting has been a stick in the eye to old antagonists. Harold Turner is one of the more outspoken critics. Turner is the dean of outfitters in the Teton Wilderness. He operates three hunting camps. His family has been in the business since 1938. His brother served in the first Bush Administration as the head of the U.S. Fish and Wildlife Service, the agency in charge of protecting grizzly bears and threatened species.

"Bob Jackson is a loose cannon," Turner says to me. "I've questioned his actions in the past, and I think some of the information he is putting out is self-serving and inaccurate." As for grizzly bears, he tells me, "they're eating themselves out of house and home. We're going to have to eradicate some of the aggressive ones."

Told of Turner's comments, Jackson asks. "Did Harold tell you about the time I caught one of his former employees three and a half miles inside the park with a dead elk? I figure that accounts for some of Harold's indigestion."

WE FIND THE first salt crater in a long narrow meadow called the Bowling Alley fifty yards from the edge of the park. The pit is three feet deep in the center and littered with the bone fragments of animals that have been shot here. In the new snow we can see fresh tracks of elk, grizzly bear, and several smaller animals leading from the park to the salt. Luring game animals with salt was first banned in east Africa in 1934 at the behest of professional hunters. Killing game at a salt lick, they said, was like shooting fish in a barrel. In the United States salting has been outlawed in a number of states and was prohibited in federal wilderness areas in 1990.

Jackson takes us to another lick twenty-five yards from a patrol cabin belonging to the Wyoming Department of Game and Fish. He says hunters have been using the cabin as a blind to shoot elk feeding in the salt lick. When we get there, Jackson is delighted to find two state game wardens at the normally vacant cabin. He describes what he has been seeing, including the most recent infraction—a guide freshening up the lick with salt from a box in his saddlebag.

The game wardens do not appear concerned.

"They've been salt baiting ever since they started packing in hunters," says one. "This lick out here was started back in the late sixties. I'd sure hate to see more regulation if that's what it's going to take to shut it down."

"Isn't baiting kind of like putting a worm on a hook?" the other warden asks, grinning at Jackson.

With tight smiles all around, we bid the two game wardens farewell and ride toward the outfitter camp, four miles away, where Jackson intends to confront the guide he saw throwing out the salt. Jackson can't cite the guide for an offense committed outside the park, but he plans to submit an affidavit to the Forest Service and he says he wants the guide to know his intentions. We know we are getting close to the camp when the outfitter's huge horse herd comes into view. I count seventy-five horses strung along both sides of the trail for a half mile. The camp resembles a fortified compound. Rows of big, brightly colored walled tents are fitted out with beds and stoves and ringed by corrals and electrified fences to keep out bears and other hungry wildlife.

Neither the outfitter who owns the camp nor the guide Jackson is looking for is around when we reach camp. We stop, anyway, and talk to a middle-aged hunter from New Jersey who is paying for his second season at this camp. He has been taking a nap, hoping the weather will improve before the evening hunt. The guides take their clients out twice a day, just before dawn and late in the afternoon, when the elk are likely to be feeding out in the open. The rest of the time is spent in the camp's comfortable confines. Here, the services include meals, hot baths, and heated tents.

We are introduced to the outfitter's son, a wiry boy, barely out of his teens, who is polite but standoffish. He has not met "Action Jackson" before, but one suspects from his manner that he has not heard good things about him. In a chatty, roundabout way, Jackson leaves the message he came to deliver. He says he is not going to stand by any longer while hunters shoot game in the salt pits. Besides being illegal, he says, it's dangerous.

"I'm getting tired of ducking bullets that come whizzing into the park," he says, adding that he is also concerned about the safety of people who hike or ride the park trails. The boy looks at Jackson levelly and says he hopes the ranger won't make trouble because all that outfitters like his dad are trying to do is offer their clients "a quality hunting experience."

Jackson scoffs. "If that's what you call quality hunting."

On the way back Jackson vents his lingering anger at the outfitter's son. "I'll show him a quality hunting experience. Maybe he'd like to come along while I go after some poacher back into the park on a day like this. Back up there." He points to the north toward Trident Mountain, now a great white hump barely visible against the white sky. "Up there where it can get so bad you can't see beyond your nose and it's so cold you want to slit your horse's belly and crawl inside. Hell, maybe we'd even catch his old man back there."

APPROACHING JACKSON'S CAMP, seeing the cabin, the corral, and the outbuildings, I am struck by the obvious similarities with the hunting camp we have just come from. It's not just that Jackson, the aficionado of pure wilderness, has built his own little bulwark of civilization, wine cellar and all. It is that he and the men he pursues are cut from the same cloth. They belong out here, getting about on horseback, following dim game trails, relying on firearms. Many of the guides and outfitters are as adept at sneaking around the park and poaching game as Jackson is at catching them. Jackson admits it. "Most of them get away, no matter how good I think I am. I catch them when they drop their guard, when they get sloppy and arrogant. Arrogance comes from their thinking all this belongs to them and not the public. But they beat me most of the time."

If anyone is out of place here, it is probably Jackson, the uniformed bureaucrat struggling to impose order on a place governed by forces no one can control, like wind and fire, where grizzly bears eat their young. Ecologists once believed that nature would advance toward a state of harmony and equilibrium, sort of like a new Eden, if only man didn't foul things up. Thoreau knew different after his trip to Mount Katahdin. Wilderness is chaos.

Jackson says he is here to uphold the public's interest. The public paid to have this land set aside and the wildlife protected, and he is here to ensure that happens. Maybe so. But the public includes the hunter from New Jersey we have just met, who this afternoon is probably standing twenty-five yards from a salt pit, waiting for an elk to come to the bait. The public includes the people who would repeal the law that prevents them from riding in on snowmobiles and all-terrain vehicles, who think it's undemocratic that only rich fellows with $4,000 to hire a horse and a guide can come back here. The public includes people who believe it ought to be legal to hunt grizzly bears.

So why do I find myself taking Jackson's side, as I lounge in his cabin over a glass of wine and listen to him denounce the outfitters and their allies in the Game and Fish Department as a bunch of vandals in cowboy hats?

For all of its sound and fury, wilderness is a fragile place. That was not so obvious in Thoreau's time when so much of the country was still wild. But today, less than 5 percent of the contiguous forty-eight states is classified as wilderness. Much of it is perishable. The proof is in the trails, wide as two-lane roads, in the scoured campsites and the meadows browsed to the bone by outfitters' horse herds. You look at men like Harold Turner coming down the trail, and they look as authentic as anything else out here. There's a hard-won gentility about these men who are unfailingly courteous, often chivalrous, and occasionally courageous. They know how to take care of themselves and others and act like they wouldn't be anywhere else for love or money. But the truth is they are hard on the country and always have been.

The West was changed by those who least wanted it changed. The late novelist A. B. Guthrie was among the first to capture the irony of it in *The Big Sky*, about the first white people to try to make a living from these mountains. In the last chapter two aging mountain men share a bottle and talk about how their world had changed for the worse and how they helped make it that way. They had trapped out the beaver, slain the varmints, and subdued all the Indians.

"It's all sp'iled, I reckon . . . The whole caboodle," says one.

"Everything we done it looks like we done against ourselves and couldn't do different if we'd knowed," says the other. ". . . It's like we heired money and had to spend it, and now it's nigh gone."

Harold Turner blames the damage on market pressures. You have to bring in more people more often just to make ends meet, he says. The growing customer load means more wear and tear on stock and equipment, which drives up the overhead.

"We are riding an upward spiral, and we're not getting rich."

So blame capitalism. The siren song of a global market in hides and hats drove the original mountain men to slaughter and plunder. Greed caused the Plains Indians to became accomplices in the extermination of beaver and buffalo in exchange for guns and other trade goods. Today, capitalism is bringing opportunities to the last frontiers of primitivism. No doubt, the planet will be better for it, except out here, where the ancient past is best left undisturbed, where we keep coming back, drawn like elephants to the boneyards of their ancestors.

On our last night in Jackson's camp the wind finally stops, but the temperature plummets. At dawn we look out at a crystal forest draped in swirls of steam where the frigid air collides with the Yellowstone's warmer water. A ghostly platoon of elk files two by two through the mist along the river's edge.

Jackson rides out with us as far as the river. I remember what he said earlier about the effect that splendid mornings like this could have on him. "I'll be out where nobody can hear me or see me and I'll put up my arms and let out a big cheer. Or, maybe, I'll gallop my horse like hell across the meadow. You can kill yourself doing that, if your horse steps in a hole. But what's life worth if you can't rip one off now and then?"

On this morning he has something else on his mind. "Poacher weather," he says. "They'll go hunting in the park, in weather like this, when they think the ranger is going to be huddled up in his warm cabin." Jackson puts his nose in the air like a bear. "Maybe I'll take a ride up on the Trident just to see what I can see."

It's so cold, only a few degrees above zero according to the thermometer on Jackson's cabin wall, that I get off my horse and walk briskly to warm up. When I look up again, the ranger has kicked his big red horse into a rolling lope across the sparkling meadow. He raises the back of his hand in a farewell gesture. "See you," he says. It's not exactly "Hi Ho Silver," but it will do.

Home on the Range

WE ARE HUNTING coyotes from Leo Larson's pickup truck, driving through a foot of freshly fallen snow down an unplowed dirt road about ten miles north of Jeffrey City, a dying speck of humanity near the center of Wyoming. We started out in the dark. Leo wanted to be in a good spot by sunrise. Earlier in the week he had seen coyotes hanging around a herd of cattle in the willow bottoms along the Sweetwater River. We headed in that direction, but other hunters got there first. We could see their headlights probing the bottoms. So we drove farther east on the highway to Muddy Gap, turned off on Agate Flat Road, and on to an unnamed track that winds around the back of Green Mountain. The road is buried in new snow. The tires of Leo's three-quarter-ton pickup make no sound as we nose along. It feels like we are gliding across the dark prairie.

Leo and I are among forty contestants in Jeffrey City's semiannual Coyote Round Up. I'd met Leo the previous spring. He was one of a handful of miners who still lived in this former uranium boom town. I'd come to write about them and the place, which like so much of the Divide, appeared to be teetering toward oblivion. Leo was doing odd jobs at the time, trapping beaver, delivering groceries, and cutting firewood. I bought one of his beaver pelts. Later, I learned about the coyote hunt from a flier in the Split Rock Bar and Café, the town's social center. Leo was interested in the prize money and invited me to come back for the hunt.

The two-day coyote hunt held the weekend before Thanksgiving draws hunters from across the state and offers $800 in cash prizes. There is no season on coyotes. They are classified as varmints in Wyoming and pursued year around by hunters in helicopters, snow machines, on all-terrain vehicles, and on horseback. The coyote may well be the last symbol of the unregenerate West, a thing a man can still feel good about shooting. "You need to be able to go out and kill something, and the coyote is something that you can kill in the winter when you can't kill anything else," says Ron Wilmes, who runs the Jeffrey City coyote hunt from the Split Rock Bar and Café, which he owns. For Leo Larson, the contest offers a chance to get a month or two ahead on his rent at a time when he can't make money doing anything else. The early snowfall has made it impossible for him to get back into the forest, and he can't fill his orders. Now he is worried that he won't have enough money to cover living his expenses, about $500 a month. "I'm going to have to watch my p's and q's if I'm going to avoid being winterkill," he says. Talking sends him into a fit of coughing and choking, his words drowning in a torrent of phlegm. He sounds like a flooded outboard motor. He leans his head out the truck window and spits, then lights a cigarette. Leo isn't sure what is wrong with him. He has no insurance and says he can't afford to see a doctor. Fainting spells forced him to quit his last mining job three years ago. Sawing and stacking firewood makes his heart race. He is almost sixty and tires quickly. "Moving them big logs around makes me dizzy. I'm getting too old to cut this wood. I don't know if I'm tough enough to do it for another year. I got forty-seven thousand dollars in Social Security coming to me, if I can live long enough."

Jeffrey City lies about ten miles north of the Continental Divide and almost 100 miles west of Casper, the nearest city. Wyoming was the fourth-largest supplier of uranium to the Atomic Energy Commission for the manufacture of nuclear weapons during the Cold War. Jeffrey City was the state's uranium mining capitol. The boom lasted for nearly twenty-five years. When the price of uranium collapsed in the early 1980s, the town folded. Today, it is little more than a cluster of foundations filling up with tumbleweeds. Most of the buildings have been torn down or trucked somewhere else. Leo is one of about fifty remaining residents, most of whom are ranchers living on the outskirts of town.

Leo's truck lurches and sideslips before regaining traction. We slow to a crawl, then stop. "Don't want to stick us," he says. "Where the road dips like this, you have to watch the drifts. There's four feet of snow piled up in some of them dips. You get stuck out here, you can't stay with your outfit. Ain't no one gonna help you. You gotta walk out. I think we can go another mile or two."

Leo doesn't carry a cellular phone as many hunters do.

Jeffrey City isn't on all the road maps of the United States, but it's in the Rolodex of obscure locations known for extreme temperatures. Radio weathermen call Ron at the Split Rock, who looks out the window at his thermometer. Yesterday, at minus thirty degrees, Jeffrey City was the coldest place in the nation. Today, it is only five below, but the wind is shrieking. I am thinking about the ten-mile walk back to town, wondering if I'd make it, when Leo seems to read my mind. "It probably wouldn't kill you, but they might have to fit you out with them plastic feet."

The worst catastrophe in the history of westward migration occurred not far from here in 1856. More than 200 people died, casualties of an early Wyoming winter. It is sometimes referred to as the Willie handcart disaster, although the storm waylaid at least one other group of pioneers besides James Willie's company. All were immigrants from Europe, converts to the new Church of the Latter-Day Saints on their way to Salt Lake City. Too poor to afford wagons and oxen, they walked across the prairie, pushing and pulling their belongings in two-wheeled carts. In late October they holed up at Devil's Gate, a deep chasm along the Sweetwater River about twenty-five miles from where Leo and I are parked. By then, there was a foot of snow on the ground and the pioneers were using frying pans and tin plates to shovel out tent sites. With the frozen ground too hard to dig graves, family members slept beside their dead loved ones. When a rescue party found them on November 16, people were surviving on a half-pound of flour a day and little else. Many were shoeless.

Dawn is breaking. "We can shoot now if we see one," Leo says.

The rising sun casts a rosy halo around the Sweetwater Rocks, a crusty, granite battlement northeast of us. Clouds swirl like wispy locks over the pink pate of Lanken Dome. "Nice little buckskin," says Leo, pointing at a set of antlers just visible over a snowy rise to our right. The rise conceals a herd of about fifty deer, mostly does. All we can see of them are their upright, twitching mouse ears. The snow is tattooed with tracks. Deer, antelope, bobcat, coyote, and rabbit. "You know how to tell a coyote from a cat?" Leo asks. "A cat walks more or less in a straight line. But a coyote makes a wavering track. See there." He points to a set of meandering paw prints. "Coyote's been here and not too long ago."

The morning light illuminates Leo's ravaged face. The lower half of it is heavy and distended, the corners of his mouth are pulled back in a permanent jack-o'-lantern grimace. His skin is a purple laminate, his lips raw and swollen. Like a swimmer emerging numb from cold water, he has trouble mouthing words with *b*'s, *m*'s, and *p*'s. He speaks out of the sides of his mouth, his voice a congested snarl.

The accident happened thirty years ago. Leo was going elk hunting in Antelope Flats near Jackson Hole. He was making a left turn into the hunting camp when he was broadsided by another car. His car exploded in flames. He suffered second- and third-degree burns over half of his body. His heart stopped briefly. He lost the end of his nose. He was in the hospital six months, getting skin grafts. "They told me I ought to have cosmetic surgery. But I was bullheaded and ignorant. I wanted to get back to making that good money in the mines. The doctors told me my appearance might hurt me later on in life. But I had to find that out on my own. Now I'm a fifty-nine-year-old guy with this complexion who can't get a job. I ain't gonna blame it all on that. But it's a factor. People don't come right out and say it, but you know by the looks they give you. Or they'll just shake their head and ask when did I get burned. Sometimes they want to know if I have any restrictions on the work I can do. I say there ain't, but they don't believe me. I got no references. The people that known me are either dead or gone."

After the mines closed, Leo took jobs no one else wanted. He worked for a while servicing gas wells in Bison Basin near Muddy Gap. It required a forty-two-mile-a-day commute on a snowmobile. Today, people around Jeffrey City call Leo when they want an extra body to help move cows or when they need someone to trap out beaver that have dammed up an irrigation pond. He delivers mail and groceries to outlying ranches. "The little dab of money I get back doesn't go very far. But sometimes they'll give me a deer or piece of elk for helping out." In 1998 the Kennecott Corp. briefly reopened the Jackpot, a uranium mine outside Jeffrey City, and Leo went back to work underground. That's when he realized he was sick. "I was getting goofy. I had bad dreams at night and hallucinations during the daytime. Later, I figured out it was probably hypothermia. I was wearing long handles, but I didn't have a hard hat liner. I was losing too much heat through my head. So it was probably my own fault. I sure didn't want to quit. I was making fifteen dollars an hour, and I hadn't seen that kind of money in a while. I just worked till I wore myself out. When I started blacking out, I knew I had to get out of there."

We sit, parked on the Green Mountain Road for a half hour, but no coyotes appear. Leo starts the truck and we make a U-turn in the snow and head back down Agate Flat Road toward a frozen pond where Leo thinks we might have some luck. This is the first time he has entered the contest, and he is handicapped by his meager resources. He can't afford the gas to cover as much territory as some of the other contestants, who will make a 100-mile sweep around Jeffrey City, delving deep into the wilds of the Great Divide Basin to the south. To save bullets, Leo has left his semiautomatic .22 at home and is relying on his single-shot Winchester .243. "I don't care if I win, but I'd like to be a contender."

While he's talking, a bushy black coyote lopes across the road in front of us and up the sage-covered hill to our right. Leo grabs the rifle and throws his shoulder against the driver's-side door. By the time he has forced it open and is braced over the hood of the truck, the coyote is nearly out of sight. Leo fires and misses.

Back inside the truck, Leo relives the shot, sighting down the barrel of an imaginary rifle. "He was a long ways off, but there was a time when I could have hit him. I don't know why, but I just don't hold the gun as steady as I used to."

I FIRST HEARD of Jeffrey City from the relatives of dying miners who were having trouble collecting compensation owed to them under federal law. A 1990 act of Congress authorized $100,000 payments to miners who had become terminally ill as a result of their work supplying uranium for the nation's nuclear arsenal. The miners had been exposed to radon gas, but they were not told how dangerous it was. Between 1955 and 1971, Wyoming mines employed as many as

5,000 people each year. However, only about sixty miners or their surviving relatives had received any money, according to the Justice Department office administering the compensation law. In the three other eligible states, Colorado, New Mexico, and Utah, payments had been made to nearly 3,600 miners. No one knew the overall mortality rate. Wyoming had not kept any records. One study of 4,100 miners on the Colorado Plateau found that 10 percent of them had died of respiratory disease. The 1990 compensation act was narrowly drawn to appease skeptics like Wyoming's influential Republican senator Alan Simpson. Only miners with lung cancer qualified for compensation, and only those who had worked underground were eligible. Men who had worked in processing mills or open pit mines could not qualify, no matter how sick they were. The rules limited the pool of potential recipients in Wyoming to less than 20 percent of the people who had worked for the mines. The law required documentation that in some cases was impossible to obtain. Many mining companies went out of business after the uranium boom fizzled. Employment records disappeared along with them. Moreover, the 1990 act made it especially difficult for smokers to receive compensation, and most miners were smokers.

When I arrived in Jeffrey City, Congress was considering new legislation. The proposed bill reflected a growing consensus among medical researchers that smokers should not be penalized. It extended eligibility to other states as well as to people who had worked in open pit mines and uranium mills, and it offered relief to victims of pulmonary fibrosis and a variety of other potentially fatal lung diseases. The new bill's prospects looked good. The only question seemed to be whether Congress would be willing to finance it adequately. The 1990 trust fund from which compensation payments had been made was empty.

A miner's widow, Mary Lou Music, introduced me to Jeffrey City. I had tracked her down from a newspaper clipping about the plight of local mining families. She invited me to drive with her from her home in Riverton to Jeffrey City, about forty miles away. She wanted me to meet her brother Stanley Wegner, a sixty-seven-year-old uranium miner, who was dying of lung cancer. Stanley had been sick for several years, though he still did odd jobs for one of the mining companies. He had filed a claim for compensation under the 1990 law and after nearly a year had not heard back. Just about all of the men in Mary Lou's family were uranium miners who worked around Jeffrey City in the 1960s and '70s. Her brother Hubert died of lung cancer earlier in the year. Her sister Colette's husband died of heart failure in 1994 after battling lung disease for years. Her brother-in-law, Gerald, was the first to go. He passed away in 1976. Her husband, Carl, was diagnosed with lung cancer the following year. "He'd never been sick a day in his life," Mary Lou said. "First, they said he had a slipped disc. Then they found a lump on his neck. Five weeks later he was gone. He was forty-four." No autopsy was performed. No record of Carl's illness was kept, so when the compensation law was passed thirteen years later, Mary Lou had no way to collect the $100,000 that was due her. After Carl died, she and her three children stayed on in Jeffrey City, living in a trailer. She made ends meet painting houses and cleaning the dormitories where the unmarried miners lived. It was exhausting work but not tiring enough to obliterate the loneliness. "I hated those nights by myself. I'd count each nail hole and knothole. The Bible says you are one flesh when you get married and it's true. I didn't even have anyone to chew out." Now she has her son's health to worry about. Larry followed his father into the mines and worked underground for twenty years. He is forty-five now and permanently disabled. His back was injured by falling rocks. His neck was broken in two places. He'd had a heart attack.

From the highway, Jeffrey City seems uniformly drab. The town site is edged on the north by hard little hills that resemble calcified acne. To the south, toward the Divide, the brown prairie bleeds into a

filmy brown horizon. The curtain of dust is raised by an almost un-
ceasing wind that plays across huge scars in the earth and slag heaps
left by countless mine excavations. The gritty air is also a product of
erosion. Large, unsupervised cattle herds give the range grass a razor
cut every summer. The ranchers around Jeffrey City scoff at environmental critics just as the town did twenty years ago when health experts warned that toxic sludge was leaching into the ground water
from a uranium mill at the rate of 1,000 gallons a minute. Officials
of the Wyoming Health Department said that the state lacked the
authority to force a cleanup, but when the U.S. Environmental
Protection Agency stepped in, the *Jeffrey City News* railed against the
prospect of "crippling regulations." When a miner was buried under
a pile of rock in one of the mines, the newspaper clucked about the
dead miner's poor safety habits. It was almost never the bosses' fault.
But then the bosses owned the town. Until the uranium boom, Jeffrey
City had been little more than a pit stop with a gas station and a post
office dubbed "Home on the Range." In 1957 a prospector on a winning streak named Bob Adams began building the state's first uranium mill and with it a trailer town to house miners and mill workers.
He named his company Western Nuclear and the town after his
biggest investor, C. W. Jeffrey, a physician and oil tycoon from
Rawlins, Wyoming. Jeffrey City was an ideal site for a mill. A dozen or
more uranium mines dotted the mountains east of town and many
more were gouged out of the country to the north. In 1958 Adams's
fledgling company signed a contract with the Atomic Energy
Commission to produce $103 million of milled uranium over the next
seven years. The *Denver Post* dubbed Jeffrey City "an atomic age frontier town."

Mary Lou Music and her husband moved to Jeffrey City in 1960.
They paid $10 a month for a parking place for their trailer. "It was
easy street," Mary Lou said as we crested the hill opposite Snob Nob
where mine executives once lived. From there you can look down on

the curvaceous red roof of the empty $2 million high school gymnasium. The gym was completed just as the town emptied out and was never used. Beyond it, Jeffrey City lay in bits and pieces. A modern ghost town can be deceptive. Looking out at block after block with nothing but curbs, gutters, and water meters, you're not quite sure whether the town is coming or going. The Coast-to-Coast store set there, Mary Lou said, pointing to a vacant lot, the bank there, the supermarket and the beauty salon over there. A few weathered structures remain, including one of the wooden barracks, "Bachelor Apartments Number 2," where unmarried miners lived, the fire hall, a motel, and the Sage Lanes. The bowling alley is closed but its robin's egg blue walls look almost new.

"We had a roller skating rink and Little League. We had a couples' pinochle club, a homemaker club, a Weight Watchers, just about everything a small town in the middle of nowhere could want."

The outdoors was the biggest attraction, though the scenery doesn't advertise itself from the highway. For tourists bound for the Grand Tetons or Yellowstone, the squat mountains around Jeffrey City would barely qualify as a warm-up act. But they were a treasure to local families looking for game to shoot or a quiet canyon to park the RV. "We'd spend a month at a time up there on Green Mountain, living on wild meat," Mary Lou said. "We each of us had an elk permit, and I think a moose permit. We had the dog up there and horses. We had a wood stove. The grub box was our table. We were set up. Unless you've been up there like that, you don't know what living is."

We picked up Mary Lou's brother Stanley Wegner at his mobile home, one of the last occupied trailers in Jeffrey City, and drove to the Green Mountain mining district where Stanley was still on the payroll. The mine where he worked had been on standby status for years, requiring a skeleton crew to keep it operable in case the price of uranium ever went up again. An oil field roustabout, Stanley first went to work in the uranium mines in Shirley Basin south of Casper in 1961. He and his wife moved to Jeffrey City a few years later. Stanley worked underground for seven years when he came down with pneumonia. A lung specialist in Billings, Montana, told him he would likely be dead in a year if he continued working underground. After that, he found a job above ground as a hoistman. He was responsible for moving men and equipment 1,600 feet down the shaft that intersected with the mine's main subterranean corridor or "drift." He learned he had lung cancer in 1998. Slow-moving, short of breath, given to coughing jags, Stanley apologized for sounding sickly and for the time he took getting his big frame in and out of the car. "Only thing the doctors told me was to enjoy the summer. Go visit some of my friends, while I could. I told them I was going out to the graveyard soon enough. I'd see my friends there. One time I tried to figure out how many of the men I knew from the mines around here that had died before me. I came up with a list of one hundred."

At the mine he leaned against the head frame that held the cables that the hoist was attached to and peered down the silent shaft. "I liked it down there, drilling out the rounds, loading 'em with dynamite, going in after you shot it and mucking it out. You could look at the ground and know when it was fixing to go to ore. The high-grade uranium was kind of pretty to look at, several colors at once. Your safety depended on yourself. You had to be checking for cracks. We thought the worst danger was from falling rocks. We didn't give a lot of thought to the radon gas. If you couldn't see it, it couldn't hurt you. Everybody smoked underground. Ignorance was bliss. We were ten feet tall and bulletproof in those days. When a guy got killed, there was always someone to take his place. We didn't whine. If I had known twenty-five years ago what I know today, I probably would have stayed in the oil fields."

We dropped Stanley off at his home and I drove back to Riverton with Mary Lou. "Stanley don't look so good," she said quietly. He died four months later.

The government knew about the health risks of uranium mining as early as the 1940s. Officials also knew that mining companies could virtually eliminate the hazards by installing ventilators in the mineshafts. But they didn't tell the miners, and the government waited years before requiring ventilation. In 1952 the U.S. Public Health Service warned that "certain acute conditions are present in the industry which, if not rectified, may seriously affect the health of the worker." The agency tried unsuccessfully at that time to persuade mining companies to install ventilating systems. According to one estimate, it would have cost the industry one quarter of a cent per ton of ore to ventilate the mines. The health service was able to undertake a long-term survey of conditions in the mines, but only if the researchers agreed not to alarm miners by warning them of the potential hazards of radiation. By 1960, scientists were observing four and a half times more cancers among uranium miners than among miners in general. The health service found radiation exposure in some mines higher than the doses received as a result of the atomic bomb explosions in Japan. Still, the federal government did not step in to regulate for several more years. Finally, in 1967, the Labor Department under President Lyndon Johnson set maximum permissible radon levels. In 1984 a federal court for the first time acknowledged a direct relationship between high levels of radon exposure and lung cancer. The ruling came in a case brought by a group of Navajo uranium miners seeking damages from the U.S. Government. The court wrote that what happened to the miners was "a tragedy of the nuclear age." But beyond words of condolence, the court offered no relief, holding that the federal policy makers who withheld protection from the miners were immune from liability.

In the absence of federal standards, the states where most of the mining was taking place began regulating the mines in the 1950s and early '60s. They didn't do a very good job. David Love, one of the West's most distinguished geologists and a lifelong Wyoming resident, wrote in 1954 that the composition of uranium in mines around Jeffrey City made exposure to it particularly hazardous. "We knew even then of the health hazards," he told a Lander newspaper editor nearly forty years later. "But nobody in responsible positions paid attention." Love called the neglect "criminal." The state's largest newspaper, the *Casper Star-Tribune*, reported in 1990 that state officials had destroyed all mine inspection reports. "However, there is some evidence," the newspaper said, "that Wyoming underground miners were exposed to radon concentrations five to ten times higher than those allowable." In letters to the editor and newspaper interviews over the years, Wyoming miners and mill workers said they breathed air that was fifty times higher than permissible levels, and they accused mine officials of concealing data from state inspectors that would have revealed how bad conditions were. In 1990 a group of miners presented much of this information to Senator Simpson, who was then a member of a subcommittee on nuclear regulation. Simpson had been opposed to the pending legislation to compensate terminally sick miners. He said no one had been able to prove a cause-and-effect relationship between uranium mining and cancer. The Bush Administration also opposed the legislation. But the miners' meeting with Simpson helped turn things around. Wheezing miners showed up with oxygen bottles in tow. Women came with their husbands' death certificates. They had records of forty miners who had died of lung cancer before the age of fifty-five. It was an election year and not the time to be stiffing destitute widows and disabled working men. Simpson softened. "I don't have a reputation as an uncaring S.O.B.," he told the people at the meeting. He added his state to the compensation bill. Wyoming had been omitted from the version passed by the House. President Bush signed the bill into law. In 1992 a fifty-nine-year-old miner named James Adkinson became the first Wyoming resident to be compensated. Adkinson said he would use the money to buy a new set of false teeth, and new linoleum and windows for his house.

By 1982, Jeffrey City was as good as dead. It was lucky to have lasted that long. If the town had been left to the caprices of market economics, it might have been history before Leo Larson and many other miners had arrived. But capitalism in the Western states has traditionally benefited from government intervention. Many of the incentives put in place a century ago to encourage the settlement of the West survived in the form of subsidies and price supports to timber, mining, energy, and agriculture interests. This strange legacy of socialism is one of the abiding ironies of the West. No region of the country is more devoted to the myth of rugged self-sufficiency, none more dependent on federal largesse, and none more contemptuous of the hand that feeds it.

The Atomic Energy Commission kept Jeffrey City alive long after the nation's need for weapons-grade uranium had been satisfied. As the demand declined, the AEC devised a plan to stretch out its contracts by reducing the amount of uranium it bought annually, according to historian Michael A. Amundson. In addition, the commission imposed a total embargo on uranium from foreign countries. The revised contracts depressed prices but kept the mines in business long enough for the civilian nuclear power industry to come on line. As the power plants geared up, the price of uranium took off again, and Jeffrey City experienced the second boom of its short life. It lasted until March of 1979, when the Three Mile Island reactor accident spurred a national reassessment of nuclear power. The price of uranium plummeted from $40 a pound to $7. The Reagan Administration, fearful that a collapsing domestic industry would be unable to meet future demand, lifted the embargo on foreign uranium. People in Jeffrey City had a much simpler explanation for what happened. "It was Jane Fonda and all them Hollywood liberals that caused the panic," Ron Wilmes told me.

"You remember that movie she starred in, *The China Syndrome*? That was a big part of it," he said, referring to the 1979 film about the meltdown of a fictitious nuclear plant.

By 1982, Western Nuclear had laid off over 90 percent of its work force. In just two years the population of Jeffrey City fell from a high of 4,500 to just over 1,000. Western Nuclear hung on for another six years before dismantling the mill, abandoning its mines, and selling the town. The new owner, U.S. Energy Corporation, tried to reinvent Jeffrey City as a second-home destination. When there were no takers, the company promoted the town site as an ideal location for a nuclear waste dump.

"At one time or another, they have tried to turn this place into a private prison, a hunting lodge, and a ski resort," Ron said. He was working behind the bar at the Split Rock when I dropped in the night before the coyote hunt. He was wearing a tam-o'-shanter and plaid suspenders in honor of his Scottish ancestors. The suspenders framed a square torso set off by high, sturdy shoulders. Ron, too, worked in the mines and seemed to be one of the few left unscathed by his years underground. I asked him why he stayed on in Jeffrey City after the mines closed.

"Some of us just stayed. I don't know why. It bothers me sometimes when I think about it. I'm solvent financially. I have mutual funds. I don't need to be here. Jeffrey City is going to die. It's just a matter of time. We're losing a family a month. The gas station just shut down. But where does a fellow like me go? Somewhere else, like in a city, I'd be totally out of my element. I'm not a socializer, and the longer I stay here the more antisocial I get. Maybe I ought to see a shrink.

"I tried to sell this place once, but the new owner went belly up. So here I am, stuck with it. But, you know, it ain't so bad. For one thing, this ain't just a bar. This is an everything hall. People buy and sell cows here. Or washer-dryers, or lawn mowers, or houses. I sell guns.

I even had people pray in here. Of course, they were probably drunk at the time."

Old-timers like Ron date back to the early 1950s when Jeffrey City was still referred to as Home on the Range, before the town boasted seven churches and a Weight Watchers club. All of that is gone now, and the handful of people who are left don't seem to miss it much. "Out here, life is tough," Ron said. "You don't have the government to lean on. It's sixty miles to a grocery store or a doctor. All of us out there have several skills. We take care of each other." Ron's soliloquy drew the attention of the half-dozen people hunkered over the bar, and some of them joined in.

"The big attraction is the solitude," said Joe Stukel, an unemployed miner. "If I want to step out my door and shoot my gun, I can. If I want to stand there mother naked and take a piss, I don't have to worry about nosy neighbors."

"It's the freedom," said another patron. "It don't matter if you drive around with a broke windshield. There ain't no inspections. If you want to hang plastic over your windows in the wintertime, no one is going to complain about how it looks. And if you get loaded at the bar, you know you can make it home without getting arrested."

"We did have a bunch of felons living out here three, four years ago," Ron said. "But the sheriff run most of 'em off. It's pretty quiet now. We don't hardly have bar fights, no more. Not like we used to when the miners and the cowboys would get into it. We did have one guy pull a knife and cut someone. But it wasn't serious, and the guy doesn't live here anymore. I don't think we've had any real excitement since Leo Larson's wife came running after him, firing a .243."

LEO AND I get an early start the second morning of the coyote hunt. He comes out of his house as I arrive at 5:15 and hands me a cup of coffee. When I first met him, he was living in the basement of a ranchette on Snob Nob. But his landlord decided to uproot the house and move it sixty miles west to Lander. Leo had to look for shelter somewhere else. Not an easy task in a town where most of the housing stock is gone. "I know it ain't much, but I was lucky to find this place and not end up freezing to death under a bridge," he says. His new home is a four-room cracker box in a vacant lot flanked by a broken-down corral and an electrical transformer. The house has white pebbly walls that look like cottage cheese and lime green shag carpeting. It is almost empty except for a TV, a handsome log bed, and a set of burled wood table and chairs. Leo made the furniture. Beyond that, his valuables consist of his truck, two rifles, a pistol, a basketful of jade he has picked up while walking in the mountains, and a magnificent coyote hide coat he made from animals he trapped and shot.

We get in Leo's truck and drive toward the Sweetwater.

"We'll try the river," Leo says. "If that's no good, we'll see if we can make it through the snow to Hoffmeister Ponds. Then we can go over toward Muddy Gap or back the other way around Icy Slough. After that, I don't know what the hell we'll do."

The temperature is still hovering around zero, but the wind has stopped, and the fading night sky is clear. Before we start hunting coyotes, Leo wants to check a line of traps he has set along the riverbank. We get out of the truck and go looking for them. He has buried each one in the snow after laying wax paper across the base to cover his scent and pouring antifreeze on the jaws to prevent ice from jamming them open. He placed the traps under the low boughs of juniper trees and hung bait from overhanging branches. An animal that steps in one of the traps as it maneuvers for the bait can die a long and agonizing death. The hanging bait can attract just about anything, including eagles, which are illegal to kill. Leo is hoping to catch a bobcat. He says he can sell the hide for $100. As we approach the river, we see plenty of bobcat tracks in the snow, but all of the traps are empty.

Leo shoulders his rifle and we keep walking down the river as it narrows into a canyon framed by crumbling sandstone palisades. "We'll go on a ways and see if we can't call us a coyote. I've called 'em before down here, so maybe we'll have some luck." By calling, Leo means tooting on a crude pipe that imitates the sound of a wounded rabbit. Making it sound authentic takes a bit of practice. Cold weather can be a handicap because spit tends to freeze inside the pipe, distorting the sound.

"I left my teeth at home, and that should help," Leo says. We take up positions behind two large boulders, and Leo starts to call. The shrill piping reminds me more of a coffeepot than a rabbit, but then I'm not a coyote. Leo gives a two-minute serenade and we sit in silence, watching as the daylight slowly restores bright winter colors to the landscape. White snow pillows up against green juniper and orange sandstone. The canyon wall beside us rises in broad horizontal steps like the pedestal of an ancient temple that has tumbled down around us and created the boulder field where we are sitting.

The previous spring I climbed high in the rocks with an ornithologist, looking for an eagle aerie. We found it in a crevice just below the summit. Like the young royalty they are, two eaglets were feasting off the fat of the land, a dead bullsnake and a baby antelope haunch. We lifted the babies out in a sack in order to band them. At seven or eight weeks, they showed almost no fear, their cloudy blue eyes fixing on us disdainfully. We returned them to their nest just in time to avoid one of their parents who came screaming in behind us like a fighter jet. "You couldn't be born up here and not have a big ego," my companion said. "Look at the world you'd survey from the moment you opened your eyes. It extends for miles, to the Continental Divide and beyond. And then suddenly you are flying over it, and, by golly, you are its lord and master." Searching for another nest, we blundered into a nest of rattlesnakes. They had been hibernating in a small cave and slithered out to enjoy an April sunbath. By the time we were aware of them, their buzzing was all around us. Some were easily visible, stretched out like tapers on the bald rock, but most of them were camouflaged by the low bushes that grew out of the cracks. My friend picked up a stick, stepped in front of me, and flung a writhing viper back into the cave. "Eagle food," he said. "Walk where I walk and you won't get bitten."

I ask Leo if he has seen rattlers here.

"I've killed one pretty near where we're sitting," he says. "But I don't think we'll be seeing any today, not unless it warms up about seventy degrees."

No coyotes respond to Leo's calling. But the sun makes us lazy, and we stay where we are for a while.

Leo grew up one of eight children on a poultry farm in Albert Lea, Minnesota. "My mother raised six hundred to eight hundred chickens every year. My job was to clean the shit off the perches." He fell for a girl from Missouri when he was eighteen, and his youthful passion led him into serious trouble. "I was sitting in the bus station with another fella when I realized I didn't have enough money for a bus ticket to Missouri. He got the bright idea that we ought to go out and steal this car. He kept driving around after we got to Missouri and got caught. The first thing he did was tell 'em about me. He was underage and got off. I did twenty-eight months." Shortly after he was released, he was caught in a post office break-in and sent back to prison. "I was hanging around with the wrong crowd and got to drinking and acting like I was Jesse James." By the time he was paroled the second time in 1965, he had spent the better part of five years in prison. He married the girlfriend from Missouri, had a daughter, and was working as a refrigeration mechanic for a trucking company when he heard about the money uranium miners were making in Wyoming—$130 a day compared to the $4 an hour he was getting as a mechanic. He moved to Jeffrey City and took a room in one of the bachelor barracks. His family joined him a few months later and they found a trailer to rent.

Small, lithe, and fearless, Leo was game for just about any job the mines had to offer. "I could drill, blast, run a mucking machine, whatever they wanted. I was good at it." Toward the end of his mining career, he was pulling pillars, a particularly hazardous job that involves drilling holes and setting off dynamite charges in the support walls or pillars of a shaft that has been mined out. The trick is to extract the last bit of ore and get out before the weakened shaft starts to come down on top of you. A pillar puller is typically the last man out of a tunnel that is being abandoned.

Doing one job or another, Leo spent the better part of fourteen years working underground.

Ventilation requirements were widely in use by the time Leo arrived in Jeffrey City. Fans were installed and stale air pumped out of the mines through ducts that were bored into the mountainsides. But the ventilation systems were only partially effective. The fresh air didn't reach many of the tight corners where miners had to work. When blasting was going on, the gases that were released could be overpowering. Miners were supposed to evacuate places that became thick with smoke from blasting, but many would go back too soon, egged on by bonus incentives that were tied to production. "We'd go to work at seven. The inspector would show up at ten, tell us we had to get out of there for the rest of the day. 'No,' someone would say. 'We just got here.' Then we'd go back. Or we'd be working in some little pocket or up a raise. It would be hotter than a popcorn fart. You'd feel an oily mist go up your nose. You couldn't see, there was so much smoke. Next day, you'd get the shits." Miners working in tight spaces were supposed to carry air bags with them and hang them close by. But the bags got in the way. They had to be moved and rehung every time you moved. For a miner, crawling on his belly, dragging an eighty-five-pound drill, a vent bag was a burdensome accessory. "I worked in places where you wouldn't have a vent bag within a hundred feet. It was a pain in the ass, and it wasn't demanded by the company.

"By the time I got there, everybody knew radon was an occupational hazard. We knew it was a cause of cancer. But you weren't going to change jobs, not when you were making a hundred dollars or a hundred and fifty dollars a day back when that kind of money was like a thousand dollars today. Then there was the contract [bonus] money on top of that. So much a pound or a foot. You cared more about production than about looking after yourself. Besides, there were people dying of cancer all the time that had never been close to a uranium mine."

We walk through the snow back to the truck. Halfway there Leo doubles over in a fit of coughing, then leans against a truck while he catches his breath. "People tell me it's smoking that's going to kill me. Maybe they're right. But I'll say this. It's waited its turn. Just about everything else has tried. I've spent a good part of my life dodging slabs and angry women." We drive through crunchy snow for several miles to the frozen Hoffmeister Ponds, see lots of tracks but no coyotes. Leo grows quiet and slows to a stop. "I ain't feeling so hot. I don't think I can stay awake. Maybe I'm going to kick the bucket." I take the wheel and head east along Lower Sage Hen Creek, familiar territory, while Leo dozes. Something about his words or his fatalism tugs at my memory. My father ran a gold mine for the better part of a decade. It was ancient history by the time I was old enough to be interested in a past that did not include me. My parents had lived at 9,000 feet near the Continental Divide, kept horses, went hunting and skiing out their back door, had the time of their lives. My father, a heavy smoker before and after his years at the mine, developed a chronic cough and, later, a shortness of breath. When he was fifty-one and I was fourteen, he said to me calmly one day while he was teaching me to drive, "If your mother hasn't told you, the doctor says I'm going to kick the bucket." The doctor had given him ten years with no hope of a reprieve. My father showed no inclination to challenge the prognosis. The doctor had a Boston pedigree and an Eastern education, the kind of man my father looked up to. There was a ritual sameness to his checkups. The doctor would measure his flagging lung capacity, refill his oxygen bottle, and reaffirm that things were pretty much on schedule. My mother seethed. She compared them to a pair of train conductors meeting to synchronize their watches. "What do you talk about?" she'd ask. "Certainly not medicine." My father said he had no wish to spend his last good years as a guinea pig, submitting to medical trials or quack cures. "Luckily, I'm not strong enough to travel, or your mother would cart me off to Lourdes," he said to me once. In those days there were no computerized self-help groups. A thousand medical references were not a click away. But there were clinics and specialists whom he might have consulted. My father seemed comfortable, however, in the untested belief that all they offered was false hope. He wanted to live until he was sixty-five, when the pension he would leave us would be substantially larger, and he tried mightily to make it. He died the week before his sixty-third birthday. His stoicism made a great impression on me. I quit smoking the day he died. But as the years passed, I tended to be more appreciative of my mother's Catholic point of view. She believed that the body was a temple of the Lord. You appealed to Him or anyone else who might help preserve it. From someone in the family she had inherited a pope's hat reputed to have healing powers. She made me wear it when I had chicken pox. My father threatened to give it to the dog. She interpreted his sangfroid as resignation. She accused him of having a death wish.

Mining is a destructive business. It wounds the ground and the flesh, and the illness it causes can sap the spirit. The payload rarely lives up to its promise. The miners who came to Jeffrey City were told they would have work for fifty years. Ten to fifteen is what most of them got. Those who escaped an immediate death sentence seemed to be scarred with a fatal dose of pessimism, a mute acknowledgment that damage had been done and a penance was due. The harm is visible around Jeffrey City, especially to the north in an area known as the Gas Hills, where most of the uranium mines were located. It is a ruined landscape, hell with the fire out. *Jeffrey City is going to die*, Ron Wilmes had said. Maybe it should.

Leo wakes up, unrefreshed but alive. He takes over the driving.

Tentatively, I broach the subject of the new legislation that broadens the eligibility of sick former uranium miners for government compensation. Leo would have to have a physical examination to determine if he had one of the qualifying illnesses.

"Where the hell am I going to get the money for that? I got no job, and hardly any money in the bank to get me through the winter. You know what it costs to get a physical? Five, six hundred dollars. No fucking way I could spend that kind of money. Besides, I went to the doctor three years ago when I was getting so sick in the mine. He didn't know what was the matter with me. He gave me some antibiotics that cost me three hundred and sixty-seven dollars and all they did was give me heartburn. Doctors don't know what they're doing. Just a bunch of bullshitters. Live till you die. That's all you can do."

Just west of Icy Slough, Leo sees something moving on the hillside up against a snow fence. It's a fox, not a coyote, but Leo can make some money from the pelt. He makes an abrupt U-turn on the highway and aims the Winchester out the driver's-side window. I lean back to give him room. He fires. It's a good shot, raising a puff of snow right where the animal was sitting. But the fox gets away, scuttling under the snow fence. "Well, if that don't beat all. I can't even hit a fox in a coyote shooting contest. Let's go home and watch the football game."

We pass the Split Rock Bar on the way. Parked in front is a pickup with five coyote carcasses piled up in the back.

Leo doesn't have a cable hookup or a satellite dish, and the images on his black and white TV screen are almost too snowy to make out. He pours us each a cup of coffee, and I bring up another delicate subject. Did his wife really come after him with a hunting rifle? It happened, Leo says. It started with a quarrel over dinner, fueled by too many cocktails. "I didn't like what she fixed, so I threw it on the roof. I was easier to tick off in those days, especially after I'd been drinking. She hit me with a frying pan. I threw her across the room. That's when she decided to come after me with a loaded deer rifle. I about got shot, and she got throwed in jail. She and I got over it, but I had a hell of a time getting my rifle back." The divorce came later, after he accused her of being unfaithful. "I'll give her this much. She stuck with me after I got burned. Family life was OK while it lasted."

Some of the hurt has not healed.

"My daughter stopped calling me Dad. She'd called me that all of her life. Then, all of a sudden, after she turned thirty-four, she didn't anymore. I didn't know what to make of it, so I asked her, and she said she didn't believe I was her real father and she was going to find him, whoever it was. I don't know if her mother put her up to it, and I don't give a rat's ass. I am her father. I raised her and I paid for her child support. But if she ain't going to call me Dad anymore, that's up to her. I enjoyed her when she was young. I wanted to raise a baby girl, and I got to do that.

"I guess things just ain't working out in my favor lately. Nothing you can do. Life goes as it goes."

The next day I drive to Casper to catch a plane home. Just past Independence Rock, where thousands of travelers along the Oregon Trail inscribed their names, a well-fed coyote crosses the road in front of me. A plump target for someone of a mind to shoot, he ambles slowly, looking preoccupied, his breath steaming, his lips drawn back as if in a mirthless parody of Leo's frozen grin.

After I got home, I called the Justice Department office that administers the radiation exposure compensation act to see if Leo could qualify under the expanded provisions of the act, which had just been signed into law. The woman I talked to thought he had a chance and said her office might be able to pay at least part of the cost of a physical examination. But she said there was a hitch. While Congress had broadened the scope of the 1990 act, it had not appropriated enough money to compensate newly eligible miners. She said her office didn't even have enough to pay hundreds of people who qualified under the 1990 act.

Leo would have to settle for an IOU.

THE PONDEROSA

THE CALF'S HEAD appears briefly, like a purple gargoyle, all eye sockets and tongue, before disappearing back inside its mother.

"We're getting there," Jay says, and we start pulling again. He has fastened two chains around the calf's feet, which have also slipped back inside the mother. The two of us are holding on to the other end of the chains, pulling as hard as we can every time the cow goes into contractions. We've been pulling on and off for a half hour. This is the first time we have seen the calf's face. The sun hasn't come up yet, and the only light comes from a bare bulb dangling over the stall. Jay has been out here most of the night. This is his third delivery. The first calf died. The second lies in a corner of the barn, looking plaintively at its mother, who won't come near it.

I have come to a ranch called the Ponderosa about 100 miles west of Laramie to be a part of a vanishing tradition, the Western cattle drive. I'm here at the invitation of the Ponderosa's owner, Mary Hay. She and her family have been running sheep and cattle for nearly a century in the Great Divide Basin, 3,400 square miles of sagebrush and sand dunes in south-central Wyoming as unpeopled and unfenced as any place left in the West.

I'D BEEN ASLEEP in my bunk in a sheep wagon when Jay knocked on the door. "I got one calf its mother won't give it suck. I got another that might be hip locked. I think I might need your help."

He has a pot of coffee brewing in the barn. A radio is playing music from Hot Country Q96, a twenty-four-hour station in Rock Springs, Wyoming. The barn is warm from animal heat, the air thick with cigarette smoke. The floor is slick with offal and afterbirth.

The pregnant cow is a Black Angus cross, but small for the breed. Jay is worried that the calf inside her is too big.

"Her water broke quite a while ago. This shouldn't be taking so long."

The contractions start again, and we go back to the chains. Crouching behind the cow's posterior with our knees bent and our hands outstretched, we look like a grotesque pantomime of water skiers. A cigarette hangs from Jay's mouth. The cow bawls in pain. Her legs buckle. The calf reappears, a forlorn face in a window, and then is gone again.

The radio is playing a love song. Over the cow's bellowing, I catch fragments of the lyrics. "Darling, if you don't want to hear how the waters parted, don't get me started . . . Then we kissed and I saw the light."

A shadow moves across the floor in front of the cow. It's a cat.

"Goddamn. Now we've got a rodeo coming. Hang on."

The cow bucks in her stall, I go down on the slick floor, a pair of flying hooves just missing my forehead. There is more bovine wailing. Then, suddenly, out it comes, *thudding* onto the floor next to me.

"Boy, I'll tell you what," Jay says. "That one's a hundred pounds at least. Just like I figured."

The calf is not moving or breathing.

"Dead?"

"Not durn yet." Jay snubs his cigarette out in the palm of his hand and starts working on the calf. He inserts a straw in one nostril to clear an air passage. He rubs the calf's tongue with a warm wet cloth. He vigorously massages its flanks. After ten minutes, he gives up. "Well, shit."

We rinse the blood and slime off our hands in a pail of water already bright pink from the night's work. Jay picks up the body of the calf by its feet and drags it outside. "We ought to take it over to the boneyard before the dogs get to it. But I can do that later. Right now, I want to get something to eat. You hungry?"

I MET MARY Hay, Jay's boss, the year before at a conference on ranching and the environment at a community college in Rock Springs. She was immediately likable with her warm, sandpapery voice, beseeching blue eyes, and a theatrical compulsion to tell tales on herself. In her mid-fifties, she joked that every part of her was getting old, save one.

"The boys still whistle when they see me from behind. But it's 'Beg your pardon, ma'am,' when they see my face. At the AA meetings, they tell me I talk like a fourteen-year-old. Be better if they told me I look like one."

Her face doesn't look old so much as weathered. It marks her as a ranch woman, that and the Copenhagen she chews and swallows. "It kills your appetite. That's how I keep my girlish figure. Plus, it's not considered ladylike to spit."

I told her I wanted to join her trail crew, glossing over my inexperience.

"You can come," she said. "We love volunteers. In fact, it's just about the only type of help we hire. But you better come this year because I'm getting out of the business. By next spring, I won't own a cow." She said she planned to move to Rock Springs, where she had recently bought a small house.

Livestock economics have been driving ranchers out of business steadily for many years. International competition is largely to blame. It costs about half as much to raise beef cattle in South America and Australia as it does on the Western plains of the United States. For family ranches that operate on tight margins, fluctuating feed lot and slaughterhouse expenses are part of the problem. In addition, laws protecting endangered species and water quality have forced many ranchers to reduce their herds to uneconomical levels. Yet, complaints about middlemen and environmental laws obscure an unfortunate fact of life in the West. It is not an ideal place for cows or their owners to get fat off the land and never has been. The semi-arid rangeland is no pampas. There is too little moisture. The grass is good but sparse. Even when beef prices were hitting their modern peak in the 1970s, returns on capital averaged less than 5 percent. Today, there are about 22,000 public land ranchers left in all of the West, fewer than when Mary was getting started. Still, her leave taking is news. The Hays are one of the more prominent ranching families in the state. Mary is the daughter of Leonard Hay, who in his late eighties can still be described as a cattle baron. He is president of the Rock Springs Grazing Association, which is made up of about forty-five members and has dominion, through a web of deeds and leases, over the better part of two million acres. A group of small Wyoming ranchers, including Leonard Hay's father, formed the association in 1909 as a way of wresting control of much of the countryside from nomadic sheepherders. Over the years, the Hays became prosperous and influential citizens of south-central Wyoming. Their money did not come from ranching, however. It seldom does. Leonard and his brother John branched out into banking and oil and gas. They didn't sell their cattle, and for good reason. The cowboy is still king in Wyoming, albeit a beggar king, and ranching is still thought to be the font of all virtue, not to mention political power. If you are a cattleman in Wyoming, even if it's just for show, you count for something.

Mary has been running Hay cattle, hers and Leonard's, since she was in her twenties, freeing her father to live in town and attend to the family's diverse financial interests.

"I didn't plan to get out of the cattle business," Mary Hay said. "It just happened. We were at the accountant's office one day, Leonard and I, going over the books. I realized it was going to be one of those typical years when I barely made expenses after the calves were sold. Then I remembered I had lost nearly two dozen head. Twenty-three bred cows had flat disappeared. Poof. A bred cow is one that is carrying a calf, which meant I was going to have to absorb all that loss. I wasn't going to make expenses, after all. So I just blurted it out. 'I'm out of here. I'm selling out.' That went over about as well as the day I wrote a newspaper column about alcoholism where I announced that I was a lifelong drunk. There was this very loud silence. Leonard and the accountant looked at me in that patronizing way men will look at a woman who is making perfect sense. I said it again. 'I'm selling out.' Leonard was furious. I reminded him that he himself hadn't had a calf crop in years that did more than make expenses. But that didn't matter. He got all hateful and hurtful, the way he can when you cross him. I went home and cried for a day and a half, and then I was fine. I knew I was making the right decision. I kept wanting to feel badly about it, but badly wouldn't come. It wasn't just the economics of it. Life has a way of making a lot of choices for you. I never set out to be a cowgirl."

Mary gave me directions to the Ponderosa. Drive east on I-80 about fifty miles from Rock Springs toward Wamsutter. Go past Point of Rocks and the turnoff to the Black Butte Mine. Pass the Jim Bridger Power Plant and the C.I.G. gas works at Table Rock. Look for an unpaved, unnamed Bureau of Land Management spur road that will curl back under the freeway and follow it a mile north to the ranch.

The interstate runs east and west across the state, parallel with the Union Pacific's main line. It is Wyoming's busiest industrial corridor. The scenery has been sculpted with dynamite, bulldozers, and backhoes. The landscape bristles with derricks and drill rigs. Wyoming is a poor state tricked out like the boomtown it occasionally becomes. Domesticity is an afterthought, a slip of a curtain for the trailer window, a crocheted sampler from Newberry's that says HOME IS WHERE THE HEART IS. The Ponderosa blends right in. The ranch is a product of the scrap yard, a collection of scavenged metal structures: surplus boxcars from the Union Pacific, shearing sheds converted into tack rooms and machine shops, a Quonset hut for storing winter hay, sheep wagons for the seasonal help, and house trailers for the full-timers and their families. Bordered by a sagging stockade fence, the compound sprawls across a bald hilltop within earshot of the big rigs on the interstate and the incessant rumble of freight trains loaded down with coal, soda ash, and drilling mud.

"So how did it get the name 'Ponderosa'?" I ask Jay over breakfast.

"No idea, but I know what you're driving at. People hear the name and expect to find a big, fancy ranchhouse surrounded by tall trees and beautiful mountain scenery. Then they get out here, and they think it's the most godforsaken place they've ever seen. People will say to me, 'Just what do you see in that desert? How does anything survive out there? What do the animals eat?' To me, it's got a lot more than the pine forests. I like the sands, the sagebrush, and the wind. You may be only a mile from the interstate, but I'll tell you what. You forget the rat race pretty quick."

Jay smokes while he eats, his forearms encircling his food, convict style. He is sixty-one and talks like a man who is glad to be back home after a lifetime in exotic climes. Yet, none of the places he has lived, Pinedale, Denver, or Rock Springs, are more than 200 miles from here. His face could be a bas-relief of the basin, distressed and eroded. A carpenter, he was between jobs when Mary ran into him in Rock Springs and offered him work. In return for room and board, he is playing midwife to a dozen pregnant cows. He checks on them every couple of hours, day and night.

"You go out there at night. You listen to them cows sighing like they do. The stars look like they are only twenty feet above your head. I'll tell you, I wouldn't trade places."

There will be only three of us on the cattle drive. Jay will stay behind with his cows, while Mary Hay, her foreman, Roy Barber, and I gather the rest of the herd and start moving them north toward the Sweetwater River and summer pasture, about sixty miles from the Ponderosa. It will be slow going with such a small crew pushing 300 cows, many of them with calves a week old or less. The route we follow will be determined by where water is to be found. After a wet winter, the basin is dotted with ponds, but this has been an unusually dry year, and we will have to take advantage of man-made water sources, mostly old, balky wells dug years ago by oil and gas crews which have fallen into disuse. Some of them lie well off the traditional route. Getting to them will mean longer days and harder work. We will have to coax the cattle off trails they have been accustomed to following for many years.

The weather is also going to be a factor. A storm is forecast for later in the week. Today, a low fog has settled down around us, obscuring the distant mountains that are the only landmarks in this nearly featureless place.

The Hays are among the last cattle ranchers still making the annual springtime trek across the basin. Most livestock operators transport their cattle in trucks to summer pastures. Trucking them is more expensive but faster and less perilous. In open country cattle can be lost in countless ways. They feast on greasewood and get a fatal case of the bloat. They develop lump jaw from a cactus spine, which causes their jawbones to abscess, and they stop eating. They fall into soap holes, quicksandy death traps topped with paper-thin crusty clay. They hide from storms in abandoned cabins, step through rotting floorboards and break their legs. They freeze to death in spring blizzards. They are struck by lightning. Coyotes eat the newborn. Cows are stolen.

Towing a horse trailer, we drive five miles from the ranch to a gently sloping meadow where we expect to find most of the herd.

Roy Barber squats on the ground by the trailer and draws a map in the sand. Draped over his shoulder are the reins of two horses, which he holds loosely with his other hand. Roy is thirty-eight, short, bandy-legged, and bull-necked with a carapace of dense, bristly black hair that grows down close to his eyes. Bareheaded, he creates the appearance of a man wearing a helmet, like a medieval soldier. The horses pull hard, one way and another, but Roy keeps his balance, moving nimbly on his haunches. He has the fluidity of a break dancer or a snowboarder. I am looking at him when I should be listening.

"We'll gather the cows here at Smiley Draw," Roy says. "That's assuming they haven't drifted back under the interstate. Then we'll cross over Dugout Draw to the well at Two-Dash-One and from there go down to Black Rock Draw, on over Greasewood Flats to the reservoir at the Lower Sands. From there, I am thinking, it ought to be a pretty straight shot to the Sands."

For the first several days, we will come back every night to the Ponderosa. Eventually, we will move trailers and wagons to the Sands and set up camp there. The Sands refers to a grassy indentation in the Killpecker Dune Field, a reef of moving sand that covers 170 square miles. The Sands is only the halfway point, but it's an important destination. The well there provides the first water north of the Rock Springs Grazing Association allotment. The allotment is winter range, and the cattle must be off it by May 18, eight days from now. The native grass in the basin is nutritious but thin, typical of the Western prairie. With cattle numbers declining, it is not overgrazed the way it once was. Still, it needs six months of rest. The May dead-line is a hardship for a minority of association members, including Mary and Roy, who don't truck their stock and who have to drive their calves through tough country in fickle spring weather. Mary Hay may be the daughter of the association's president, but she won't be spared if she breaks the rules. The challenge for her and Roy is to avoid the fine without losing an equivalent amount of money in fatal-ities. They have waited as long as they can to allow the newborns to fatten up before the journey. A week to get off the allotment ought to be time enough, providing the weather doesn't get too nasty.

At the Sands, the herd will be allowed to rest for two weeks. Any calves that have been born along the way will be branded there. From there to the Sweetwater, the trip will be more leisurely. Water will be less scarce. The cattle won't need nearly as much supervision. With his two teenage sons out of school, Roy says he won't need any extra help. Mary Hay will bow out at the Sands. So will I.

Roy wants to take it easy the first day. "I don't figure we'll go past Two-Dash-One today, if that's all right with you," he says to Mary. Two-Dash-One is an oil company cartographer's designation for an abandoned drill site with a water well that is still working. "If there is a storm coming in, we won't be able to avoid it, no matter how hard we go. So there's no point in rushing things."

Mary nods.

"What exactly does Two-Dash-One look like?" I ask.

"It's just a tank on a low hill," Roy says. "When the fog lifts, you'll see a drill rig ahead of you at about eleven o'clock, kind of just off your left shoulder. Work toward it. After you pass it, you'll see a trail bending back to the northeast. You stay on it all the way to Two-Dash-One."

He hands me the reins of my horse, a gray Appaloosa.

"You should like Ap," Mary says. "He's grumpy but steady."

Mary is on a chestnut mare she has not ridden before. She is taking a bit of a gamble. The horse is spooky and known to buck on occasion. The mare is also likely to interest the wild stallions that roam the basin in search of concubines. The harems often include domestic stock, like Mary's horse, that the stallions have stampeded away from their owners.

Fifty feet from where we sit on our saddle horses, Mary points to the skeleton of a calf that had its back broken by a stallion, apparently after wandering too close to the stallion's ladies.

"You watch Ap," Mary says to me. She hands me a can of sardines—lunch. "If you see horses around, you might want to eat this in the saddle. And if you have to go to the bathroom, hold on to the reins. We've had geldings stolen. We had to shoot a stallion last year that ran off with a gelding. Of course, we're not supposed to talk about that."

A roar sounds from inside the horse trailer, startling the horses and me. Ray comes flying out on a green Yamaha dirt bike.

"A cowboy on a motorcycle?"

"Leonard bought it for him. It works better than horses when you're trying to gather a herd that's spread out across the countryside. Roy needs it because he works alone so much of the time."

The motorcycle is symbolic of a deal between Leonard and Roy in which Roy, in effect, has agreed to become the older man's vassal. For looking after Hay land and cattle, Roy is granted use of the ranch and a percentage of Leonard's calf crop each year. If beef prices don't crater again, Roy can look forward to the day he has his own ranch. In the meantime, both men benefit. Roy's stake in the herd will make him a more vigilant caretaker, and vigilance is a cardinal virtue in country where twoscore cows can disappear without a trace. In return, Roy can count on his suzerain's protection when, for example, he needs to get the bureaucrats off his back. Such was the case a year ago when one of them tried to enforce a law against squatting on public land by getting Roy to move his summer cow camp off prime ground on Bush Rim. Roy stayed put.

Mary thinks Leonard is getting the better of the deal. She has seen Roy's budget ("I stole a look at his books one day. He's living in my house, after all."), and she doubts he can borrow enough against his share of the calves to meet operating expenses, let alone sock away a down payment on his own ranch.

"He's taking a chance, and he's putting his family at risk. On the other hand, his arrangement with Leonard allowed him to quit his job at the gas works, which he hated, and his wife hated living there. He grew up on a ranch. So did his wife. He wants the life his dad had. So does she. Be the master of his own life. Be free, even if he has to indenture himself to Leonard. But I'm no one to talk. If Roy weren't taking on the burden of this ranch, it would be harder for me to get out from under it."

Roy IDLES UP out of the fog.

"Days like this, you don't know where you are until you're halfway there."

"You find your markers?" Mary asks him.

"I found Wavy Horn and Matilda pretty close by, so we ought to be in good shape."

Markers are the most independent cows, the ones most likely to stray and take a portion of the herd with them. In unfenced country like this, a herd of cattle will generally stay together if they are bedded down near water. But if they run from a storm or follow a maverick, they may spread out over many miles. Gathering them together again can use up the better part of a day. Wavy Horn, a silly-looking piebald heifer with horns that point in opposite directions, and Wandering Matilda are the two worst offenders. If they are nearby, it's a good sign the herd hasn't scattered.

Roy turns to me.

"The hard part is keeping 'em mothered up. If you let the calves drift to the back, they're going to start missing their mothers. They'll try to run back to the last place they sucked, which is wherever they were last night."

He buzzes off in one direction. Mary rides in another.

I move through groups of softly lowing cows reclining in the sage. Slowly, I'm able to roust them, by moving back and forth among the recumbent shapes, shouting and whistling. They start moving in a ragged line and I tuck in behind them. I look for the drill rig Roy talked about, but the fog is so thick I can't see beyond the rumps of the cows closest to me. I tell myself they know where they are going. When the curtain does part long enough to see the prairie ahead unfold, it all seems the same. The map of the basin is full of colorful place-names that suggest a wonderfully variegated landscape: Cyclone Rim, Honeycomb Buttes, Chicken Springs, Bastard Butte, Bush Rim, Five Fingers Butte, Buffalo Hump Basin, Mowing Machine Draw . . . But where are those rims and buttes? Where are the famous landmarks that kept the emigrants from getting lost, the snowy peaks of the Wind River Range, Steamboat Mountain, or the pointed butte called the Boar's Tusk? How do you distinguish a "draw" from among the endless dips that ripple all the way to the horizon like ocean swells? From my vantage point, atop Ap, there don't seem to be any distinguishing features at all. This is a landscape defined by the absence of scenery, by the absence of the trees and shrubs and the raw material from which scenery is made.

"This is a country that may captivate mad poets," wrote William H. Russell in his account of crossing the basin in 1846. "But I swear I see nothing . . . It is a miserable country." James F. Wilkins, another nineteenth-century diarist, described it as "inhospitable, detestable country."

It is as if Mother Nature herself lost her bearings when she got to the Great Divide Basin. Here the Continental Divide, the grand arbiter of water that flows to the Atlantic and Pacific, splits in two. The line of demarcation forks southwest of Rawlins, one branch making a wide loop to the northeast and the other meandering northwest until they come together again about ninety miles from the point of separation. In between, the little moisture that does fall to the ground stays put, settling into this great windswept oval of sage steppes, alkali desert, greasewood bottoms, and shifting sand dunes. Temperatures ricochet from 40 below zero to 100 above. Eight inches of rainfall a year is the norm. The emigrants who crossed the basin on the way to California and Oregon dubbed it the Great American Desert. But there is water hidden away in seeps and sumps, enough of it to support not only thousands of wild horses but also the largest herd of pronghorn antelope in the world—40,000 to 50,000 of them. On a spring morning, when the darting pronghorn are as thick as locusts, and bands of mule deer are bunched in the draws, when there are fresh bobcat tracks in the mud and coyote kill steaming in the frosty dew under the gaze of a circling golden eagle, it can seem like the ark unloaded most of its North American passengers right here.

The animals are comfortable because civilization isn't. Some 400,000 people made their way across this country between 1840 and 1870. Few tarried, although the basin has always held out the promise of riches. Gold, jade, iron, and uranium have all been mined. At Table Rock, near the I-80 exit to the Ponderosa, a pair of nineteenth-century con artists once planted gemstones like Easter eggs, announced they'd hit the motherlode, and fleeced investors out of $500,000. Eventually, wrote Wyoming historian Mae Urbanek, a camp cook got suspicious. He'd found a diamond in an anthill. Along the Sweetwater River, the graves of pioneers are still being dug open by robbers, looking for antique jewelry. Mary Hay's maternal great-grandfather was a fortune hunter who came to Wyoming from the California gold fields to prospect in South Pass, just north of the basin. According to family lore, he fled south, after being run off by Indians, and eventually settled in Rock Springs, where he operated a profitable coal mine. Today, an oil and gas boom threatens to turn the basin into a giant industrial park. The federal Bureau of Land Management, which administers most of the basin, says as many as 15,000 new wells could be drilled by 2010, doubling the number that has gone in since the early 1900s. Much of the basin could end up studded with compressors, condensate tanks, dehydration plants, pocked with chemical waste pits, crosshatched with pipelines, and roads abuzz with truck traffic. The wildlife wouldn't stand much of a chance. Biologists working for the BLM in Wyoming have said as much. The agency's hands may be tied, however. Over the years, the BLM and the U.S. Forest Service have opened 90 percent of Wyoming's federal land to oil and gas interests. Even though much of that land has not been drilled, it has been leased to energy interests. Officials say it is not always possible to impose new conditions on old lease agreements. Environmentalists argue that federal laws protecting wildlife trump leasing agreements, even when the agreements predate the laws. The courts have yet to rule definitively.

So why do people choose to live here? What prompts a man like Roy Barber to give up a steady job in a growth industry to spend most of the year in a borrowed trailer while his wife toils as a teacher's aide in a town eighty miles away?

For the unwary, it can be a life-threatening experience just getting from one basin to another in a car. When it rains, the clay roads liquefy. Mary Hay once got stuck searching for lost cows during a storm.

She walked five miles, spent the night in an unlocked trailer, and walked another twenty miles to the highway the next day. "I didn't have any water, and I got so thirsty I was racing the dog to the mud puddles. I figured better sick than dead." At AA meetings she tells another story, of going off the road in the midst of an alcoholic blackout, of rolling over and over as her infant children were thrown from the car, of lying unconscious for five hours on a chilly winter afternoon while two little boys, unhurt but dressed in T-shirts, wandered about until a hunter came along.

One hundred and fifty years ago, this was a land that tempted adventurers, men like Mary's great-grandfather, who traveled from one gold field to the next. Roy, though, doesn't strike me as particularly adventurous. He tried competitive bronc riding when he was young. Fractured his neck. That's all part of the rite of passage for a rancher's boy. If you have the build for it and the agility, you are drafted for rodeo, much the way you are drafted for football in rural Texas or Oklahoma.

He says it's the freedom that attracts him, the freedom to do what he wants when he wants. He's not talking about a loafer's freedom, about lounging on the back steps, using up the boss's ammo plinking at prairie dogs. "I can be my own boss. I can do something different every day. I'm a carpenter or a mechanic one day, a veterinarian the next. Then I'm truckin' supplies or cowboying. Of course, I'm not the boss. It's all Leonard's and Mary's. The economics of it can keep you awake at night. It's nip and tuck. Believe me. But it's a kind of a freedom. It lets me do what I'm good at." He is good at improvising, good with bailing wire. He goes about the legerdemain of survival in the middle of nowhere, 100 miles from the nearest Home Depot, with the unhurried poise of the neighborhood handyman, coaxing a calcified water pump back to life or reviving an ancient generator. He doesn't own the land. He doesn't own much of anything. But he owns his life in ways that most of us do not. Such autonomy can make you jealous of a poor man. Roy is not unlike the peregrine falcon that makes its home on the flat rock outcroppings of the basin, scouring out a nest by dragging its belly across the dirt on top of a wind-blown ledge. It's called making a scrape.

By midafternoon, I realize I haven't seen Roy or Mary since leaving Smiley Draw. My cows and I passed the drill rig a couple of hours ago. I check my supplies. I still have a bottle of water and the sardines. The cows move without prompting. They must sense water ahead. Sure enough, a blue nubbin appears on a mound of earth a half-mile ahead of us. It's got to be Two-Dash-One, and it is. I dismount while the cows bury their snouts in a trench full of muddy water. I rest my back against the tank and eat my lunch. I close my eyes, and when I open them fifteen minutes later, I see a spreading sea of cows moving toward the tank with Roy and Mary behind them. Life is good.

The drive goes on like this for the next few days, the cattle moving in unison like plankton on a gentle, steady current. A rank beginner, I am starting to feel like a natural at this business, watching Roy make his diagram in the dirt each morning, nodding knowingly, swinging a leg over Ap's mottled withers, and heading off on my own with a hundred or so dumb animals who represent several thousand dollars of someone else's livelihood. Then the storm hits.

We have moved out to the Sands, trailers in tow. Roy is in his. I am in the sheep wagon. It's not much more than an old-fashioned buckboard with a metal bonnet that looks like a giant mailbox attached to it. Inside, there is a stove, shelves, a foldout table, a built-in bed, and about two square feet of floor space. I wake up shivering and realize that the wind has blown open the tiny window beside me and snow has been piling up on the bed. I fold a towel around the window frame and wedge it shut. The bed is soaked. I light the propane lantern that swings from the ceiling and survey my quarters. The wind has knocked over a box of Hamburger Helper and a carton of Sego evaporated milk. Apparently, that's what woke me. I inherited the commissary from Ramon, an expert cowhand sorely missed but whom Roy can no longer afford. I spread my slicker on the wet bed and lay back down, but the wind is too boisterous. It gets under the wagon and shakes it and rattles its metal sides like timpani.

I step out into the storm to relieve myself, notice a light on in Roy's trailer, and hear the radio playing. I knock on the door. It's a cozy scene inside. Roy is at the kitchen table with a cup of coffee and three dogs at his feet.

"Some kind of weather."

"Uh-huh."

He's leafing through his household account book and listening to a radio theater broadcast of *Gunsmoke*. Trapped in a storm with a frightened widow woman, Marshal Matt Dillon is urging calm as coyotes howl in the background.

"You ever been coyote hunting?" Roy asks. "It's gotta be about right on top of my list of fun. If I could figure out a way to make a living shooting coyotes, I'd do 'er."

It strikes me as odd that I haven't heard a single coyote since I've been out here, and I tell him so.

"Don't you worry. They're here."

I ask him how he'd feel if the coyote were finally exterminated, if it met the same fate that the wolf and the grizzly bear have in so many parts of the West.

"You might as well ask the preacher what he'd do if they did away with sin. The preacher don't have to worry and neither do I. There ain't no way they're ever going to kill 'em all, not out in this desert."

On my way out the door, I ask him about something that I have been admiring for several days. On the wall is an ornate clock framed by an intricate pattern of interlaced leather.

"It's a harness clock," Roy says. "My grandfather made it."

The stiff collar of a harness that was made to fit over the shoulder of a plow horse had been wetted and painstakingly molded around the clock. The collar was overlaid with a decorative latticework of softer leather. It is a marvel of bygone craftsmanship and baroque imagination. I stand puzzling at the thing like an aborigine coming upon a television screen. Here was the perfect symbol of a power I would love to possess—to be able to yoke the pace of time and change the same way you could control the speed of the plow horse. As I stand there dreamily, the face of another long-forgotten clock rises up out of the root cellar of my own boyhood memory. It was a joke clock that ran backward. I hung it in my bedroom, wishing it could turn the calendar backward as summer expired and a new school year loomed.

Roy interrupts my reverie.

"My grandfather was a man who could tell you something about coyotes," he says. "They ate up twenty thousand dollars' worth of his sheep and bankrupted him. If he'd had his way with coyotes, he'd have sewed their butts shut and turned 'em loose."

It is still snowing when we get up in the morning. The storm has chased the cattle east, miles from where we left them the previous day. The calves are lying in wind-buffering clumps amid the greasewood. It will take hours just to get them back on the trail. The work gets off to a bad start. Mary's skittish mare bolts and must be run down. I round up a troop of cattle, only to march them off in the wrong direction, north instead of north by northwest toward the Sands. A half hour later, I hear Mary's voice cutting the wind like a crow's caw. At first, I think she is cursing the cattle. Then I realize it's me.

"Where in the fucking hell are you going?"

I have no answer beyond the truth, which I don't want to acknowledge. I have let the cows herd me. They make the same trek every year, and I assumed they were going in the right direction.

I am only a few degrees off course, but in this ocean of sand and greasewood, minor missteps can lead you badly astray. By the end of the day, I would have been ten miles from water with an exhausted herd. The losses might have been considerable, and I would have borne the cost.

With Mary's help, I turn the line of cows. By noon, we have merged with Roy's band. Now we're headed straight into a thirty-mile-per-hour wind that is slinging frozen rain in our faces. The rolling terrain has straightened into a long, uphill grade. The pace is stop-and-go. The cattle huddle up against the sage whenever the bushes are thick enough to break the wind.

"Keep 'em moving." Roy exhorts us. He buzzes through them like an angry hornet. They bawl in protest, mill around a bit, and quit. It's as if we are driving up a blind alley. I plunge into another bunch, whacking at them with my reins. The bawling acquires a high-pitched, agonized edge to it. My horse stumbles, and I realize I'm on top of them now, about to trample a calf that is too tired or terrified to move. I pull back and the little fellow struggles to its feet, pushing off its knees, wobbling forward before collapsing again in a bush. Three days ago, these spindly-legged babies were gamboling and butting heads with each other. They were like children on the way to a picnic. Now they are exhausted and pitiful. I don't like what this has turned into. Call it a case of Bambi-itis. I come from a long line of animal coddlers. It's been generations, a century at least, since my forebears raised animals to eat. We let the dogs into the bedroom. We put blankets over tables when it storms so they can hide from the thunder and lightning. When they skip a meal or two, we implore them to tell us what is wrong and then trundle them off to the vet. A rancher, on the other hand, might go two or three days without bringing food to a dog that has been left to guard a herd of sheep or cattle. The rancher figures any dog worth its salt will survive off mice and pocket gophers.

Ahead of me, a black calf is on its back kicking its legs and trembling violently. Its eyeballs disappear into its head. It's having a seizure. The mother stands over it, licking its face. A little while later, I start to go after a solitary cow that has strayed a quarter of a mile from the herd. Then I see the ravens circling over her head, and I realize what has happened. She is standing guard over her dead calf.

Mary comes up behind me and suggests we take a break. We dismount and crouch behind a thicket of greasewood, our backs to the wind.

"This is no way to raise livestock, pushing them across the country when some of them are barely able to walk," she says. "They should be down in Kentucky or Louisiana, somewhere in all that lush grass where they'd barely have to move all year. There's no reason to have to drive them like this. We could have waited another two weeks when all these babies would have been strong enough to travel. But no. Leonard says we have to be off the allotment by the middle of the month."

"But Leonard's a cattleman. Some of these are his calves."

"Leonard's not a cattleman. I'm the cattleman," Mary replies. "My father hasn't been on a horse in thirty years. Roy thinks if he were out here and saw the way it is, he'd give us more time. But I doubt that. Leonard's money is not in these few cattle. It's in the land, oil, and gas. Being in the cattle business helps him control all the land he thinks he needs. But you know that. You talked to him."

Leonard Hay grew up on his father's sheep ranch, dropped out of the University of Washington after his first semester, and got a job driving a potato truck. While still a young man, he inherited a 160-acre ranch and 8,000 sheep. In time, he replaced the sheep with cattle and began investing in oil and gas leases and in warehouses along the Union Pacific right-of-way.

Mary had introduced me to Leonard the year before. He was recovering from a long illness that had come close to killing him. He was crossing a street in Rock Springs when we spotted him, a small, neatly tonsured figure, stepping gingerly off the curb, leading a tiny dachshund on a leash.

"This is Fred IV," he said, pointing to the dog, after Mary had introduced me. "All of my dogs have been this breed, all named Fred. I would vote for any one of them, and that includes the dead Freds, before I would vote for that goddamn Gore."

He stared up at me, his head tilted like a baby bird, frail and fierce. "You're not going to vote for him, are you?"

"No," I lied.

The day before the cattle drive, I met Leonard again. He was fully recovered, robust, and merry. He was having dinner at the Log Inn Supper Club on the edge of town, talking to a man from the State Grazing Board about the proliferation of wild horses on the Rock Springs Grazing Association land.

"It's the Democrat," he called out when he saw me walk in with Mary. "I can smell 'em a mile a way."

"You should be able to, Leonard," Mary said. "You were married to one for fifty-five years."

"Who, you say?" Leonard asked.

"My mother."

"Oh yeah."

"Sit down," he said to me. "I'll buy you dinner. What are you drinking?"

He was on his second manhattan and in a professorial mood.

"Let me tell you what this country needs," he said to me. "A depression."

Mary filled the pause that followed.

"Leonard wants to turn the clock back to the time when paper money was no good and all of the wealth came out of the ground."

"If we get a depression," Leonard resumed, "and we will, you can count on it, people are going to start putting a value on natural resources again, and by that I don't mean wilderness or wolves.

"Right here in the ground in southwest Wyoming, we got four hundred to five hundred years of soda ash, four hundred and fifty years of coal, at least one hundred years of oil and gas. A lot of people have forgotten just how valuable that is. But I haven't, and that's why I hold on to as much land as I can."

He let that sink in and then asked me, seeing as I lived in Los Angeles, if I had ever met Doris Day. I said I hadn't.

"She's a peach, isn't she?"

I agreed she was.

The man from the grazing board said he had heard Doris Day was an environmentalist.

"Is that true?" Leonard asked me.

"Well, I don't care if she is," he said. "I'll marry her anyway."

Later, as Mary and I wait out the storm behind the greasewood thicket, she talks about her father. "My whole life, I wanted Leonard's approval, but he doesn't have it to give. It would take away from Leonard. That's OK. I'm used to it. I did ask him once. 'Who are the people you love? Because I know you don't like me.' He said he loved his dog. He said he loved everything that was a part of him, which I guess includes me."

THE CATTLE GET a good rest while we talk, but we can't leave them here for the night. There is no water. We need to get them to the next well before dark. They respond to our commands and begin to shuffle wearily down the trail. Mary talks to them now. "Come on, my dears, not far to go now." She edges up on a Black Angus heifer that has stepped out of line and is nuzzling her calf. "Isn't he a darling?" Mary says. "You have every reason to be proud," she tells the mother cow. "But we've just got to keep going. I know it's hard. I'm an old lady like you. I had my own little boys. I probably wasn't even as good to them as you are."

The plodding cattle remind me of a ragged column of refugees. The heifers wearily lift their hind feet, like the hems of dresses, over the sage, and cast anxious glances over their shoulders, looking for their young.

After another hour, the well appears, and Roy calls a halt to the march. "We're set up pretty good for the Sands," he says. "It's mostly downhill from now on. We should make it there by the weekend, Saturday or Sunday at the latest."

We have to be off the allotment by Sunday.

He says we have lost two or three calves at most. "In weather like this we could have done a lot worse." He estimates we have come about seven miles in just under seven hours.

Saturday is calm, crisp, and bright. For the first time, we have a full complement of trail hands. Roy's wife and teenage boys arrive along with his friend John, an oilfield electrician who, like Roy, grew up on a ranch. Mary's friend Birdie arrives with her two boys and a pair of trained cattle dogs.

Roy is decked out like a bona fide cowboy. He has exchanged his goggles and helmet for a Stetson hat and a pair of boots with fancy red stitching. There will be no need for the motorcycle today, especially not with the dogs. They are fleet, forty-pound Australian shepherds and a marvel to watch. They lay back behind the herd, crouching in wait, their bright eyes peeled for any stragglers. They maintain discipline in the herd better than any of us, quickly closing ranks when the hindmost get to dawdling, hurrying up the laggards, and retrieving every calf that tries to turn tail. Roy's sons practice rope work on the calves, as does John. They snake out the looped ends of their lariats along the ground, catching up the calves' hind legs and jerking them down. *Enough, already*, I think, after every man but me has demonstrated his prowess a half-dozen times and the calves are hiding under their mothers' bellies.

Four hours later, we're at the Sands.

"Ain't it a picture," Roy says. And it is, the whole herd at rest, luxuriating in dune grass completely surrounding Roy's trailer and my sheep wagon, cows leaning up against the hubs, calves poking their heads in the door. We eat fried chicken and potato salad that Roy's wife has brought out. The boys head off on Roy's motorcycle. Roy and John, looking to make mild mischief, invent a pretext for a horse-buying trip to Nevada and begin winking and chortling over the need for rest and relaxation, code for legal prostitution. This is for the benefit of Roy's wife, who smiles and rolls her eyes. Birdie, who had a long drive from Farson, naps against the side of the trailer. I pack up my gear.

When it's time to go, we shake hands all around and Mary does a jig in the sand.

"Oh, happy day, I'm going to be a city girl now."

I get a ride back to the Ponderosa, where my car is parked, and look for Jay to say goodbye.

I follow the strains of Hot Country Q96 and find Jay in the barn, where I last saw him eight days ago. He sees me and brightens.

"Say, you don't think you could give me a hand. I got a calf to brand, and he's such a feisty booger, I know he's going to give me a time of it. You ever use a calf table before?"

A calf table is a heavy, hinged, two-sided iron grill. The calf is locked into it, on its side. Its head is fed through a small round opening at one end. This calf is so small, it can pull its head back and squirm around on the table. Not a good thing to have happen while you are trying to make a legible impression on its hide with a branding iron.

Branding is a catch-all term for a series of torments, beginning with a vaccination and ending with castration. I hold the calf's head steady while Jay gives it a shot and then tags its ears.

"Hold on now," he says as he approaches with the hot iron. With the first touch of heat on its skin, the calf screams and yanks its head free.

"Don't think I made a very artistic impression on that go round. I'll have to try again," Jay says. "But you got to get a better grip on him."

I plant my feet and get the calf in a tight headlock, feeling its fuzzy ears next to my face. The hot iron sizzles against animal fur. I smell singed flesh. The calf bellows again and twists violently against me but doesn't pull free.

"Got him that time," Jay says. "Just one thing left. Keep holt."

Now the calf is looking at me with desperate, imploring brown eyes. I hate to think what he would be saying if he were an E. B. White character, but I suspect the word "SADIST" would appear in a spider's web.

Jay has got his thumb down in the calf's privates, trying to isolate the tiny testicles. He will slip a rubber band around them, and in a month or so they will drop off. "You got to be careful when they're this small. You don't want to tie off his peter."

I look at the calf and want to tell him he could be suffering a worse fate. "Be glad you were born in here and didn't have to make the forced march with the others," I'd tell him. "Be glad Jay is using a rubber band and not a knife the way it used to be done."

Jay is looking over at me. Apparently, I am guilty of a queasy expression.

"You're not a vegetarian, are you, Frank?"

LEAVING THE RANCH, I drive north. I'm going to Lander, about 100 miles across the basin and over the southern tip of the Wind rivers. Lander is an old mining town that has joined the New West. Gaslights and storefront galleries have cropped up on Main Street. The restaurants segregate the smokers and feature gourmet beer with catchy names like Horse Spit and Mule Drool. Workingmen wear shorts downtown on weekends. The sports bar broadcasts women's soccer on the big screen. I have friends there. But I have time to spare and decide to take a detour off the highway to a place out of Mary's past, the Middle Hay Ranch, near the Sweetwater River, where her parents lived when they were first married and where Mary says she was conceived.

I follow one of the old clay roads, more of an overgrown track than a road, nosing my rental car through waist-high sagebrush to the ranch, arriving at twilight.

A dozen sagging wooden structures are clustered along both sides of the road. The windows are broken out. Some of the doors are missing. Most of the roofs, though, are intact. Shards of paint still cling to the walls. Unlike the Ponderosa, this looks like a place built with permanency in mind, back when ranching was still considered a viable way of life and not just a tax shelter or a real estate play. In the background are the Oregon Buttes, the lonely sandstone sentinels that the wagon trains aimed for as they crawled across the top of the basin. A family of pronghorn browse in the front yard of what must have been the ranch house. An eagle has dragged an old tarp into the fork of a cottonwood tree and built a huge nest on top of it. I sit and watch as an adult swoops toward the nest with a small snake dangling from its beak. Two Muppetlike heads appear in the nest at the approach of supper.

Mary said her mother didn't like it here at first. "She was so frightened when Leonard brought her out there she'd pee in the kitchen sink rather than walk to the outhouse after dark. Growing up, I was scared too, scared I'd get lost or lose all of Leonard's cows in a lightning storm. I ran away. I worked as a librarian in Jackson. Then I went to Alaska and got a job as a cook. I even worked for a bank for a while in San Diego. But this country kept calling me back.

"I learned how to get around out here from Leonard. I'd be out hunting for strays, and he would fly over in his airplane, dropping notes tucked into ice cream cartons. I'd see them floating down.

'Twelve head at the bottom of the Little Bar X Canyon,' they would say. I got my bearings that way. But I didn't lose my fear of being out there until I started drinking. I should have known better. My grandfather died an alcoholic suicide. The man I loved most growing up was the same way. He was just a hired hand, but I worshipped him. He was a wonderful, patient teacher. But he got into the holiday wine one Christmas. He was by himself out there. After he drank the wine, he opened a bottle of rubbing alcohol. Leonard found him frozen to death on the storehouse steps.

"I knew when I was fourteen that I was an alcoholic. I took that first drink and felt I had discovered the secret of life. I could do anything when I drank. Herd cows, boss men, raise two little kids. Without liquor, I couldn't have coped. I probably would have committed suicide. I surely would have gone crazy. Drinking mellowed things out. It gave me what I needed to fit in. I would sip a little beer and sip a little more. I didn't stop, even after I rolled the car and nearly killed my children. You would think mother love would be strong enough to stop me, but it wasn't. I drank for another year before I finally reached out for help. That's when I started going to AA.

"It's funny how life can change you. I drank so I could bear the isolation. Later, it was just the opposite. The isolation was what saved me. It was a refuge from temptation. I came to love it. People would say, 'How can you live out there alone?' But I wasn't alone. There must have been at least a hundred different kinds of critters, cows, beaver, skunks, sandhill cranes. People are so full of themselves they don't consider that the animals are on the same plain with them. I have always thought cows are closer to God than I am. But the country is changing. Luckily, for me, I don't need it the way I once did because it isn't ours to do what we please. It belongs to the public, and if they want to claim it, that's their right. I'm not convinced the public knows how to take care of it. I never saw them out there cutting noxious weeds the way I did every summer. I wanted to put up a sign that said: 'These are your public lands. Come and help me rid them of noxious weeds.' But I refuse to moan and groan. My family has been fortunate to have the use of this land for all these years. I feel I belong to it, that I'm part of it, but I look out at the sagebrush or the Sweetwater and I can't feel a sense of ownership the way Leonard does. Maybe it comes from being born on the Continental Divide. My sense of ambivalence."

I poke down the road, looking for the ranch boneyard, the resting place for all of the animals that lived here. It's a good place to find burnished skulls or to shoot scavenging coyotes. Mary said when she dies she wants to be thrown in the Ponderosa's boneyard, next to her dogs.

"Do you believe in heaven?" she asked me one day out on the prairie. "Because I don't see how it could be better than this." She spread her arms as if to take in all 10,000 square miles of the great gray, green desolation around us. "No," she said. "I don't see any need for heaven."

TIERRA O MUERTE

I AM STANDING next to the Rio Arriba County road maintenance yard in Hernandez, New Mexico, peering through a chain-link fence, trying to take a picture of an adobe church, San Jose de Chama. A jumble of cement mixers, backhoes, Caterpillars, generators, and portable privies block the view from most angles. I'm trying to figure out if it is still possible to frame the scene the way Ansel Adams did sixty years ago when he took his famous photograph *Moonrise, Hernandez, New Mexico.* Then there was just the church, a cemetery, a few houses, a sea of sagebrush, and distant snow-capped mountains with a pale moon and silvery clouds overhead.

I am on my way to Vallecitos, an old logging town beyond the mountains in Adams's picture. I am taking my time, unsure of the reception I will receive. The New West of coffee emporia, bed and breakfasts, adventure travel, and all-seasons resorts is not much in evidence in Rio Arriba. The service industry that has been a bonanza for Santa Fe, only twenty miles away, has all the appeal of the plague up here. Recently, the architects of the Continental Divide Trail were told by the county commission that if people want to hike through Rio Arriba, they could walk down the state highway. A sign by the road where I am standing says: NO PHOTOGRAPHS.

The Hispanic residents of rural northern New Mexico have been suspicious of outsiders since the 1700s when the first of them used spears and homemade weapons to fight off Comanche raiders armed with rifles. When I lived in New Mexico in the 1970s, different towns vied for the distinction of being the least hospitable to outsiders—the title going to the town where your car was most likely to be stripped and rolled while you were hiking in the mountains. The villages of Truchas, Cordova, Mora, Chimayo, and Tierra Amarilla were among the perennial contenders. Vallecitos wasn't in the running until recently. For many years, it had a working relationship with the outside world. Protestant missionaries ran the elementary school. A British-owned timber company operated the local sawmill. Residents would proudly tell visitors that the White House Christmas tree one year had come from Vallecitos. Then something happened. The town grew tired of taking orders. It ran the timber company out of the forest, took over its logging contracts, and assumed ownership of the sawmill.

I am going to see the man who led the revolt. He is Antonio "Ike" DeVargas, an unemployed logger and eloquent roughneck who has become the knight errant of this impoverished county, which he likens to a third world colony. "When we were under British rule," DeVargas will say, or "There has always been an outside interest that tries to control the land and resources in the north." DeVargas is the latest champion of a land rights movement that has been going on for 100 years—ever since the U.S. Forest Service took over millions of acres of northern New Mexico that had once been the province of Hispanic settlers. Lately, DeVargas has been doing battle with environmental groups who want to protect what wildlife is left in the forested mountains by putting old-growth trees off-limits to logging. He is also trying to scuttle plans for the Continental Divide Trail. The proposed route bisects the Carson National Forest, passing about eight miles northwest of Vallecitos. DeVargas and his nearly destitute logging company have the rights to the timber. He fears that environmentalists will use the trail to build support for saving the trees. But he faces a greater challenge rebuilding the economy of a town that has been close to death since he intervened on its behalf.

DeVargas was cheerfully noncommittal when I asked to see him. He can be charming or intimidating. An ex-Marine who fought in Vietnam, he is known as an enforcer, a throwback to the days when there was no constabulary in New Mexico's mountain hamlets and authority was often vested in the village strongman. A few days ago, the local newspaper named DeVargas as a suspect in a recent murder. The victim had been shot and his house set on fire. As I prepared to leave Santa Fe and drive north, a friend who had lived in this part of the country much of his life wished me luck. "Have fun with Ike. Try not to piss him off." I have plenty of time to think about DeVargas, and what I'm going to ask him about, on the slow, winding road to his home in the isolated Tusas River Valley. I can't ignore the subject of the newspaper headline. On the other hand, I don't want to get kicked out, or worse. Coming upon the scene of Ansel Adams's photograph, I am glad for the chance to procrastinate.

Adams was not planning to stop in Hernandez or take a picture of San Jose de Chama. He pulled over because the scene was irresistible, the simple village church and the cemetery crosses bathed in beatific light. He had time for one exposure before the light faded. Adams was a wizard with optics, and the black and white photograph owes as much to the genius of an outsider with a camera as it does to the supernal beauty of a nineteenth-century Hispanic village. The moonlight is actually reflected sunlight. The picture was taken in the late afternoon, not at night, as it appears. Adams used a filter to heighten the contrast and create a glorious illusion. *Moonrise* became his most popular picture, more so than his images of Yosemite and the Sierra Nevada. The photograph came to represent New Mexico's idealized past. Today, not much is left of Adams's haunting pastoral. San Jose de Chama has been abandoned for a newer, larger church across the highway. The walls of the old church are cracked and sagging, its waterlogged roof threatening to cave in, its statues and altar screen stolen years ago. Hernandez has become a rural barrio, a tumbledown satellite of Española, the Rio Arriba County seat. The community mirrors much of Rio Arriba—poor but proud, heart-stopping beauty marred by urban sprawl and rural decay. So much ugliness disfiguring the face of a beloved landscape. I confronted the contradiction when I lived here. I couldn't make sense of it. I was susceptible to the expatriate's disease that turns you cynical when the natives don't behave the way you would like them to. Now that I'm back, I am still trying to figure out why people who profess a deep attachment to their surroundings are driven to despoil them. I am hoping DeVargas can shed some light. He rose to prominence as a renegade woodsman who chainsawed a grove of 400-year-old ponderosa trees and carved the name of a local conservationist in one of the stumps. Among the questions that occur to me as I walk around the graffiti-smeared walls of San Jose de Chama is how such a man as DeVargas becomes a local folk hero.

Someone is watching me. I turn around to see a woman, hands on her hips, staring in my direction. I apologize for the intrusion and tell her I am a passerby, curious to see what is left of the scene that Ansel Adams photographed. She points to the sign that says: NO PHOTO-GRAPHS and asks, "Can't you read English?"

. . .

Iᴋᴇ ᴅᴇᴠᴀʀɢᴀs ʟɪᴠᴇs about fifteen miles south of Vallecitos in Servilleta Plaza, a collection of trailer homes and disintegrating adobes strung along a narrow, serpentine road that follows the Tusas River. DeVargas's doublewide perches on cinder block footings about seventy-five yards from the river's edge.

He greets me from his front steps, waving me in the driveway, and wagging a can of beer at me. "Glad you made it, amigo. Come on in and have a cold one."

He is dressed in a snug-fitting turquoise satin shirt. His sleeves are cut off above the shoulders, showing off a lumberjack's fibrous arms. His muscles have slackened only slightly from age—DeVargas is fifty-three. A mane of snow-white hair hangs around his shoulders. He has a matching beard and lively blue eyes. DeVargas has an actor's ability to command attention by looks alone and a kind of manic stage presence. Aloof and patriarchal one minute, loose-limbed and jocular the next. He could play a prophet or a pirate. I wonder how he signals anger, by sudden movement or predatory stillness.

He motions me to follow him down to the river where he is going to get water to boil for coffee. He owns eight acres of lush bottomland, which he bought for a few thousand dollars in 1980. In Santa Fe County, riverfront property like this would be worth close to a million today. Along the Tusas, seventy-five miles north of Santa Fe and a world away, property values have just begun to creep higher. After living here twenty years, DeVargas says he still can't afford running water. We walk through knee-high alfalfa and Sudan grass, past patches of wild asparagus, the wild spinach he calls *quelites*, and *osha*, an herb that is supposed to repel rattlesnakes. Apparently, it has not been doing its job. DeVargas points to an outhouse resting in the high grass between the trailer and the Tusas. "If you have to use it in the night, take a flashlight and watch out for rattlers. I'd loan you my pistol, but it was stolen out of the trailer six months ago."

DeVargas introduces me to his girlfriend, Chon, and we eat a slow supper of take-out fried chicken, ice cream, coffee, and beer. "*Todo en moderación*," he says. "My grandmother told me that. Sex, drugs, eating, logging. Everything you do outside of moderation is too much. I used to drink too much. I'd get sick, wind up in jail. I'm a really headstrong person, and it took a while for my grandmother's words to sink in." But we don't need to worry about anything tonight, he says. We're not going anywhere and if we feel bad in the morning, Chon will fix us *chimaja*, "hangover tea," made from parsley that grows in the mountains. The parsley is just one of many herbs that grow wild and have been used for centuries by people to treat stomach and kidney ailments, to promote sleep and alleviate *susto* (shock) or *envidia* (envy). A tea brewed from lettuce leaves is supposed to quell sexual desire. "When I was young," DeVargas says, "I would kill a deer and drain its blood for my father. *Sangre de venado*. He drank it for his heart. We took what we needed. It wasn't any big deal." He says he still won't buy a permit from the government to go into the national forest and hunt. "I see a deer or a rabbit, I'll kill it, jerk the meat, or can it. I have the same right to supplement my diet that my forefathers had. Most of the people in the villages around here are the same way. They are criminals like me."

After dinner, DeVargas pushes back in a kitchen chair and smokes while Chon sits behind him and weaves his white hair into a long braid.

DeVargas grew up in the nearby village of La Madera, where he was raised mostly by his grandparents. His father was an itinerant musician who hopped freight trains to get from one performance to the next. DeVargas quit school after the tenth grade. "I kind of educated myself. I must have read every Zane Grey story ever written. I moved on to Che Guevara and Mao." He joined the Marines when he was seventeen and became part of an elite unit in Vietnam that operated behind enemy lines. When he returned two years later, he says, he was like a lot of veterans, hurt and bewildered by the reaction to the war. "Lost in our own country." When he returned to the mountains where he had hunted and fished with his grandfather, he found them occupied by strangers. "I never seen so many hippies. I mean, you couldn't go down to the river without coming across some hippie splashing around, usually naked. It was kind of a trip for a while. That's when the drug culture took hold. There had always been people who smoked marijuana. They had their little gardens. Then, all of a sudden, any drug you could think of was available, and it was all out in the open. I bought into it at first because I was totally freaked out by my participation in that stupid war. I did LSD. I did mescaline, a lot of speed, and alcohol like crazy. I did all of it. I just didn't do needles. After a while, though, I realized something was wrong. These people were making a killing, selling their dope and buying up our land with the money they got from us. Most of them came from wealthy families to begin with and didn't have to work. They said they wanted to get back to the land, but they didn't know how. They weren't like us. They started putting up 'No Trespassing' signs and fencing off the countryside. I remember trying to go hunting over across the river in Comanche Canyon where I'd been going all my life. All of a sudden, I had to go twenty-five miles out of my way just to get there because the bastards had closed off the access. But you know, most of them couldn't handle the lifestyle. There is a saying that these mountains take care of their own. Those that fit stay. Those that aren't compatible with the community leave. That was the lesson of the hippies. Some bad shit happened. No doubt about it. Houses were burned out. Some people were killed. Most of them left after that. A lot of them joined the environmental movement and are still trying to mess with us. Most of the hippies that stayed are good hippies. We get along pretty good with them now." He chuckles. "We bring them into our house."

After the war, DeVargas worked at a detention school for boys, fought forest fires, and took a job in a uranium mine. Eventually, he hired on as a tree faller with Duke City Lumber Company, a subsidiary of Hanson PLC, a British conglomerate with worldwide interests in timber, coal, and chemicals. "I fell in love with the woods. I was totally free. I didn't have a boss out there looking over my shoulder. I got paid for what I cut. If I wanted to make a hundred and fifty dollars a day, I could, or fifty dollars. It was my choice." He also became county chairman of *La Raza Unida*, an upstart Chicano rights party that took on a Rio Arriba County political machine and its formidable *patrón*, the county sheriff. *La Raza* leveled accusations of corruption and brutality and eventually unseated the sheriff. It was a bruising campaign. In 1976 DeVargas was charged with drug possession. Sheriff's deputies said they found marijuana and heroin in his home. DeVargas said the drugs were planted. A judge threw out the charges and DeVargas later won a $70,000 civil judgment against the county.

In the '80s he took his activism into the woods. Forming a tactical alliance with Anglo environmentalists, he began accusing the Forest Service and Duke City Lumber of reneging on commitments to provide jobs for residents, to set aside some of the timber for local loggers, and to make sure the forest wasn't completely over cut. The forests around Vallecitos had been so heavily logged the past century that only about 20 percent of the highest grade timber, the oldest ponderosa, and Douglas fir was left. In 1994 DeVargas and a group of loggers sued the Forest Service under the federal Civil Rights Act. The plaintiffs said that by failing to meet its obligations to local people, the Forest Service had discriminated against Hispanics who made up 80 percent of the population. After two years of wrangling, the Forest Service settled the suit, agreeing to pay $40,000 in damages and handing over rights to three fourths of the available timber to DeVargas's fledgling logging operation, *La Compañía Ocho*. The settlement gave DeVargas what many people said he had sought all along, control of the timber business around Vallecitos. Duke City said it could no longer make a profit there. The company abandoned its sawmill and left town.

With Duke City Lumber out of the picture, the Hispanic loggers and Anglo environmentalists were soon at each other's throats. The environmentalists accused DeVargas of breaking an agreement to stay out of the most pristine areas of the forest. DeVargas countered that the conservationists were trying to shut down logging altogether by using the Endangered Species Act to protect a bird, the Mexican Spotted Owl, that did not nest in the woods around Vallecitos. DeVargas said the environmentalists' strategy was a racist attempt to separate Hispanics from their ancestral land and force them into urban barrios. He organized a march on the Santa Fe headquarters of the Forest Guardians, his principal adversaries, and hung the group's leaders in effigy. DeVargas became an overnight celebrity, with his gift of gab, his raffish stage presence, alternately modest and menacing. People said he reminded them of the late actor Lee Marvin. DeVargas's words carried all the way to San Francisco, to the national headquarters of the Sierra Club, where his message caused dismay at the highest levels. It is one thing to go after corporate polluters, quite another to bully a bunch of poor Chicano loggers trying to feed their families.

DeVargas exposed a weakness at the core of the environmental movement, its own version of expatriate's syndrome. What do you do when the natives—poor, indigenous people, don't behave the way you want them to, when they insist on cutting down old growth forests or killing whales or drilling for oil in a wildlife refuge? How do you reconcile love of nature with reverence for tradition or sympathy for the downtrodden? The Forest Guardians stood their ground. They argued that barely 5 percent of the forest was still capable of providing good wildlife habitat, withstanding catastrophic fire, and retaining ground water. They said DeVargas was out for himself, and not for the betterment of the Hispanic villages. The Forest Guardians were branded as cultists, nature worshippers who sought to purge the wilderness of human beings. Someone put a bomb in the group's mailbox and left a lit cigarette beside the fuse. The cigarette burned out before the fuse could ignite.

DeVargas didn't just win in the court of public opinion. A federal judge ruled against the Forest Guardians when they sued to try to stop logging on a ridge known as *La Manga*. Because it was so inaccessible, *La Manga* had remained a virgin stand, a symbol of forest majesty, the trees dating back 400 years to the time when DeVargas's ancestors arrived in northern New Mexico. DeVargas celebrated the ruling by cutting down several of the biggest, oldest trees on the ridge. He said he wanted to get started before the environmentalists could appeal the ruling. The loggers sectioned the fallen trees and stacked them in piles. They call the big ponderosa "punkins" for their rusty orange bark. In a final flourish, they carved the name of the Forest Guardians' director in one of the stumps. It didn't matter that there was no way to get the timber out, that DeVargas didn't have the money to build a road into *La Manga* or a way to process the wood. No one in the crew knew how to run the sawmill. The mill itself lacked vital equipment, including debarkers, planers, and a drying kiln.

Three years have gone by since DeVargas cut the trees down, and the logs are still there, spoils of a hollow victory. A fungus is turning the punkins blue and slowly robbing them of their market value. In the interim, DeVargas hasn't been able to hold his small logging company together. One faction took possession of the sawmill, the other, which he heads, claimed the rights to most of the timber. Neither side can afford to go it alone. When I arrive, the woods are silent, and there is little prospect of full-scale logging resuming soon. The only work in Vallecitos is a nonprofit craft cooperative run by Sandra Zamora, a logger's wife. It is a shoestring operation, employing three people, and funded by a $35,000 grant that makes use of small, low-grade timber that can be harvested close to town.

DeVargas meanwhile is struggling to reunite the members of *La Compañía Ocho*. He needs to raise $500,000 to pay the company's debts and build the road into *La Manga*, but he can't refinance the debt without the sawmill as collateral. Once *La Compañía Ocho* is back in business, he says, there will be work for fifty people. But mending fences won't be easy. There is a lot of bad blood between the factions. In a letter to the Secretary of Energy, DeVargas has accused two of his former colleagues of misusing $200,000 in federal economic assistance funds. There are plenty of people hoping to see him fail, who tend to agree with the Forest Guardians that DeVargas is less interested in spreading the wealth than in taking over Duke City's timber contracts with the Forest Service.

"Sometimes it seems like it is in our nature to be envious," DeVargas says. "There is an old saying that the only thing better than having a good crop is when your neighbor has a bad one. It all goes back to exploitation and to our feelings of cultural inadequacy. We don't have any heroes in our community.

"We're going to have to learn to get along better, if we're to have any kind of economic hope for these communities. They're basically broke right now, except for what Sandra and them are doing. Sandra is an old-time hippie who married Joe Zamora. Joe is a member of *La Compañía Ocho*. The trouble with Sandra is she still believes in grants and government handouts. I can't convince her there's no future in that small diameter shit. But she's good people. You should go up and meet her."

I GO TO bed listening to the bubbling Tusas and thinking about hippies. I moved to Santa Fe in 1975 as the last of the rural communes were breaking up. The young people who fled the suburbs for Rio

Arriba's adobe villages were coming out angry and disillusioned. One couple, still trying to hold on, came into the newspaper where I was working with a bizarre tale of woe. The home they had built amid apple and apricot trees near the village of Chimayo in the foothills of the Sangre de Cristo Mountains was being systematically dismantled. The thief had taken most everything of value from their drawers and closets and was now concentrating on the furniture and fixtures. He had recently made off with their front door. The couple had appealed in vain to the county sheriff. They then had sought the protection of a local politician, the patriarch of one of the oldest families in the area. The politician said he was powerless to help. He said the thief was a young man who was a *brujo*, a witch, who could turn himself into a dog or a coyote and elude anyone trying to capture him. The newspaper published the story of the couple's ordeal. It didn't help them recoup their losses, and they moved away.

The story had a postscript.

In time the young thief was caught and sent to the New Mexico State Penitentiary, where he was known as the Dog Boy of Chimayo. He was still there in 1980 when an inmate takeover led to one of the bloodiest prison riots in history. Thirty-three people were killed and much of the prison was burned down. The Dog Boy was the first to die, beaten by a convict murder squad. The assassins had commandeered two-way radios from the guards, and reporters covering the riot could hear the pleas and screams as convicts armed with cudgels and acetylene bore down on their prey. "Let's see you try to escape. Let's see you turn yourself into a dog." The Dog Boy was suspected of being a snitch, someone who had turned on his own kind. According to Roger Morris, who wrote a book about the riot, as the ambulance that carried his body away passed waiting police dogs, the animals, usually disciplined and quiet, began to howl. Their handlers had difficulty calming them.

· · ·

IN THE MORNING Chon tells me there has been a change of plans. She and Ike are going camping with friends in the San Pedro Mountains, sixty miles away. DeVargas is outside, watering a patch of squash and chili and talking to some neighborhood children. I figure it's now or never if I'm going to ask him about the murder he is being investigated for. I pick up the newspaper with the account of the crime and go out to confront him. The paper said the murder victim had assaulted a friend of DeVargas and suggested that DeVargas may have sought revenge. According to the story, neighbors of the victim recalled seeing some- one vaguely resembling DeVargas near the murdered man's house the night of the shooting. Sheriff's deputies were quoted saying that tire tracks at the scene matched the treads of a spare they found in DeVargas's truck. According to the newspaper, DeVargas had replaced the other tires and refused to say what he had done with them.

"I wasn't there. I didn't kill the guy," DeVargas says to me. "It's politics. I ran against the sheriff a couple of years ago. I accused him of mishandling evidence. Now he's trying to get me back."

I ask him about the truck tires, and he gives me a long hard look.

"What do people usually do with old tires when they get rid of them? You want to get into that, talk to my lawyer. I'm tired of this bullshit. They put my name in the paper to embarrass me. Pure and simple. You don't know how things are done around here. I do. I've been framed before, my friend."

One of the neighborhood children appears from behind the trailer and interrupts. He says DeVargas's dog, a playful cocker spaniel, tried to bite him.

"He did?" DeVargas kicks at the dog, delivering a glancing blow, then picks up a branch and says to the boy, "You take a stick to that dog's head and make it crack like when you hit a baseball." He hands the branch to the boy.

"Come here," he says to me. "Help me get some water on my radishes."

We part amicably. DeVargas invites me to stay in his trailer while he and Chon are away. I decline, spooked by thoughts of the dead man's friends descending on the place in the middle of the night. Instead, I head up the road to Vallecitos, where I hope to find Sandra Zamora, the good hippie.

The road to Vallecitos is a time tunnel, taking me past old men walking behind plodding cows and little boys fishing with bamboo poles from narrow bridges. June foliage camouflages the dusty hills, spreading a light green wrap over the incised stream banks that have been broken down by cattle, gravel excavations, and spring floods. Then the road lifts out of the Tusas valley to an elevation of about 7,500 feet, and the country becomes dry and Western again. Long stretches of New Mexico rabbit brush, called *cham'isa*, have replaced grass in overgrazed meadows. Pine forests stripped of the grandfather trees now bristle with "dog hair" thickets, dense, spindly growth that is tinder for forest fires. This is the small diameter "shit" that DeVargas disdains because it has little commercial value.

Vallecitos sparkles prosperously in the dewy morning light. But the glow is purely illusory, like the moonlight over Hernandez. You don't get a true picture until you have turn off the highway, cross the Vallecitos River, and start up the empty dirt streets toward Gallegos Hill and the cemetery beyond. The departure of Duke City, the closure of the sawmill, and the collapse of *La Compañía Ocho* have driven out all but a handful of families. The houses are hybrid derelicts. The original wattle and daub construction sprouts junkyard annexes made of plywood and sheet metal. The only store in town, the Vallecitos Mercantile, is closed, the walls swabbed with black graffiti, the roof caving in. The last tenant kept her horse in the building with her. The town plaza is graced by spreading cottonwoods, but the sturdy adobes that formed the perimeter have been gutted. The community center is boarded up. It was the headquarters of the *Sociedad de Hermanos Unidos en Protección Vallecitos*, a relief society and labor organization during the logging heyday. Even the *morada*, the traditional house of worship for village men and the place where bodies were prepared for burial, has been plundered. Still, there are signs of life. A cluster of hollyhocks grows out of a spare tire someone is using for a planter. I can hear chickens. A small monkey-faced dog follows me at a safe distance. A mother and child watch silently from the steps of their house as I make my way through town.

Vallecitos was established in 1824 when a group of twenty-six farmers were given title by the Mexican government to the Town of Vallecitos de Lovato land grant. The grant conveyed small plots to each of the twenty-six farmers and thousands of acres of common land for the town to own collectively. There is no written history of Vallecitos, only a melancholy folklore full of stories about misfortune and loss, ghosts and witchery. In one tale the town's decline is blamed on the disappearance of the church bell, made of gold and other precious metals by a mysterious stranger, a gringo, who gave it to the town before disappearing himself. In another the village is thrown into a *susto*, a scare, by the lamentations of a ghost. It is the spirit of a girl who broke her parents' hearts by losing the rosary and scapular given to her by the parish priest at her first communion. The stories belong to the period when Vallecitos and many other mountain settlements were being dispossessed of their vast commons, where they planted their crops and pastured their livestock.

Yankee speculators were the villains, along with the United States Government, which broke its promise to honor the land grants. In the 1848 treaty of Guadalupe Hidalgo that ended the Mexican War, the United States pledged to respect the property rights of all former Mexican citizens living in the newly won territories of the Southwest. However, Congress and the courts balked at validating many of the grants. They said the boundaries were not clearly drawn, that claims overlapped or that ownership was not properly documented. The U.S. Supreme Court nullified the Town of Vallecitos grant in 1899. The court said it could find no written evidence that a land grant had ever been made. In Rio Arriba County settlers lost over 60 percent of the nearly three million acres conferred to them by Spanish and Mexican officials. The wholesale divestiture made tenant farmers out of Hispanic land owners and opened up millions of acres to Anglo entrepreneurs, mostly itinerant cattlemen and loggers, who poured into the mountains in the late nineteenth century. The land was overgrazed and overcut and much of it eventually abandoned when its resources were exhausted. Several million acres wound up under the control of the U.S. Forest Service.

By the 1930s, forage in the mountains was so scarce that cattle were beginning to starve to death. The per capita income in Vallecitos was just over $200. Unable to support their families, village men left to take jobs as cowboys, sheepherders, and miners in Colorado, Utah, and Arizona. Many residents came to see themselves as victims of an Hispanic diaspora that began with the invalidation of the land grants. Some people fought back. Rebel bands calling themselves *Las Gorras Blancas* (White Hats) and *La Mano Negra* (The Black Hand) reacted to the loss of ancestral lands by cutting fences, burning haystacks, barns, and houses belonging to the Anglo usurpers. The insurgency simmered for decades, never amounting to much until the 1960s, when people were inspired by the national civil rights movement and emboldened by a charismatic leader, Reies Tijerina, popularly known as *"El Tigre."*

Tijerina was an Assembly of God preacher, originally from Texas. He and his followers called themselves the *Alianza Federal de Mercedes*—the alliance of land grant heirs—and began a campaign of civil disobedience. They held a series of marches and sit-ins on Forest Service property, demanding that the land be returned to them. Meanwhile, a new outbreak of arson fires once again targeted barns, houses, and hayricks belonging to Anglo ranchers in Rio Arriba. Fearing an insurrection, the county district attorney tried to derail the movement by rounding up a number of its leaders. He had the opposite effect. In June of 1967 about twenty armed *Alianza* members, led by Tijerina, descended on the Arriba County Courthouse in the little town of Tierra Amarilla about forty miles north of Vallecitos. Tijerina's plan was to place the district attorney under citizen's arrest. The *Alianza* accused the official of illegally detaining members of their organization. A gun battle erupted in which a jailer and a state policeman were wounded. The attackers fled, some on foot into the mountains. The National Guard was summoned. Soldiers in armored personnel carriers patrolled the countryside in what became the largest manhunt in New Mexico history. Eventually, most of the *Alianza* leaders were taken into custody. Some of them served time in jail, although no one was convicted of wounding the two officers. The injured jailer accused Tijerina of shooting him, but the man was beaten to death before he had a chance to testify at a trial. His murder was never solved. Tijerina was found innocent of all charges related to the courthouse raid. The episode did prompt a reassessment of Forest Service policies. Grazing restrictions were eased. No land was given back, however, and the pressure for restitution continues today. The battle cry of the *Alianza* is still etched on road signs. TIERRA O MUERTE. Land or Death. "The land belongs to he who works it," DeVargas had said to me, quoting a line from the Mexican revolutionary Emiliano Zapata. It doesn't matter that only a tiny minority of people in Rio Arriba County still make a living off the land or that the residents of mountain villages like Vallecitos usually work elsewhere if they work at all. "It's the cultural connection that matters," DeVargas said. "It's the dream of what we had. I'll die before I'll lose that dream."

I find Sandra Zamora in her office in the vestry of the abandoned Methodist Church. She is a heavyset, middle-aged woman in a green pantsuit. It is hard to imagine her as a hippie. Easier to mistake her for an Hispanic matron, except for her avian wariness. It's the look of the *afuero*, the outsider, of someone who is never going to be entirely at ease in her surroundings, like a spy. She gives me a prolonged once-over before deciding I am safe to talk to. It's not been a good day. She is president of the local water association and has been getting nowhere trying to raise the money for a new filtration system. Public health inspectors have detected high levels of fecal coliform in the tap water. "We need three hundred thousand dollars to fix it. The EPA's threatening to fine us twenty-five thousand dollars a day if we don't, and I can't even get people to pay their water bills. When I tell them to pay, they threaten me. One of them came over, drunk, yelling obscenities. Joe, my husband, hit him. The man fell down with a bloody nose. Then Joe got served with a restraining order." On top of that, she says, people on the east side of the river are feuding with people on the west side over irrigation rights. The respective *mayordomos*, or ditch masters, refuse to talk to each other, even though they are next-door neighbors. One has taken to firing his rifle in the air as a warning. "This town always had a tradition of sharing," Sandra says. "But for some reason it's broken down. We've got such bad blood, such *envidia*. Everybody's got to be number one, and no one winds up with anything."

Outside, Joe and a neighbor, Manuel Gurule, are building a greenhouse out of poles and planks they have made from "dog hair" timber. They plan to grow vegetables that do well in the short mountain growing season—lettuce, tomatoes, beans, chili, pumpkins. Sandra wants to hire village women to run it. Her hope is to get enough people interested in growing vegetables to sell to restaurants in Santa Fe. At the moment, she is worried that work on the greenhouse is going too slowly to start any plants before the season is over, especially chili, which needs to be in the ground early at this elevation. "I'd love to hire another guy to help Joe and Manuel, but the men around here turn up their noses at the money. They just lay around waiting for the fire season when they figure they can make the big bucks fighting forest fires. It doesn't help to have Ikey running us down, either. This is women's work, as far as he's concerned. No one is going to go up against Ike. He's a rough, tough guy who always wants an argument. That's about all *La Compañía* did, sit around and argue with each other until they split up. Ikey couldn't hold them together, and he is about the only authority figure we have left up here."

Sandra has no opinion about DeVargas's possible role in the recent murder. She hopes he was not involved and doubts anything will come of the suspicions. She is right about that. No charges have been brought against DeVargas or anyone else. The case remains unsolved.

Sandra and Joe moved from Tierra Amarilla to Vallecitos seventeen years ago after seeing an ad in the *Thrifty Nickel* newspaper for a small house. It cost $10,000, as much as they could afford. Joe had been kicked in the groin by a steer and disabled while working as ranch hand in southern Colorado. The injury never healed properly. One complication followed another: liver damage, renal failure, and, most recently, a stroke. His voice is high and hoarse. He moves slowly, leaning on a cane, though if you bump into him, he feels as hard and resistant as a fence post. "Joe has terrible nightmares, about killing and burning," Sandra says. "He won't talk about them. I think it may go back to when Tijerina was around. Or before, when he was a little boy. There was a horrible accident. Two of his brothers were killed. Joe blames himself for it."

Now Joe and Sandra get by on his disability payments, on the $200 monthly stipend he is paid for reading electric meters, and the $10 hourly wage each receives from the $35,000 coop grant. While Joe builds the greenhouse, Sandra does the meter reading. She invites me along on her rounds. The route leads from Vallecitos south to Ancona and La Madera and then up through Petaca and several other villages where people have looked to the forest for their livelihoods.

"When Joe goes by himself, he takes his pistol," Sandra says. "I just don't stop at some houses."

We drive out over Jarita Mesa, past old mica mines and the vestiges of a wild horse herd. The villages are ragged clusters of cinder block and stucco, haphazardly arranged atop bare brown hillocks. Doors open at our arrival. Dogs slink out, while barefoot men in undershirts peer out from the shadows. No one comes outside or says anything. Sandra nods at three crosses below one of the houses. "They're for three guys who got shot. Don't stop. The killers still live around here." We pass the home of two brothers Sandra says were charged with beating their mother and raping their sister. She says one of the brothers is in prison. "That house was bought by a big shot lawyer from Santa Fe, but he was burned out," she says, pointing at a charred hulk. Her commentary continues, through Petaca and Las Tablas. "The guy that lives in the house with the red roof had his face shot off . . . The big house over in the trees belongs to a drug dealer." East of La Madera, we pass a walled compound of three large houses, conspicuous for their grandeur. Sandra says the compound belongs to an Anglo family who built the wall rather than move away after a bomb was detonated outside one of the houses. "You have to be tough to live up here. I learned that lesson when I moved to northern New Mexico. I got to be pretty rough just to protect myself. I learned to carry a gun and use it. I caught a guy trying to steal gas from my car and I shot at him. People respect you if they think you are crazy enough to shoot at them."

Back at her house in Vallecitos, we are joined by Joe and Sandra's sister, Cindy, who lives nearby. The house is adobe, cool and shadowy on a bright summer afternoon. It is a hodgepodge of collectibles that Sandra buys and sells at flea markets—massive sideboards perched on claw feet, voluptuous sofas, rococo birdcages, indigo glassware, soft drink bottles, and alabaster figurines. Cindy introduces herself. She is younger than Sandra and cheerier. She says she was marooned in Vallecitos by the second of two abusive ex-husbands. Both of them went to prison, she says, one for selling heroin, the other for trading in contraband weapons. "I've had a knife held to my throat, and I've been shot at."

"Cindy's been to hell and back," Sandra says.

Sandra and Cindy are the daughters of a nuclear scientist who moved from Ohio to New Mexico during the Cold War. The family settled in Socorro, south of Albuquerque, where the two sisters rebelled by hanging out with poor Hispanic kids. "I was told I was a bad kid from the time I could think," Sandra says. "So, I thought, why not prove it. But it wasn't just that. I was drawn to the Spanish culture. It seemed so welcoming, and mine seemed cold, critical and dry. I didn't like the idea of war, and my father's work had a lot to do with it." Divorced from her first husband when she was still in her twenties, she moved with her two children to Tierra Amarilla in 1976. She was not welcome there. "We were hippielike, me and my longhaired kids. They told us we better learn Spanish or leave. I didn't feel safe until I met Joe. He came from a well-respected local family. His dad was a good friend of Tijerina."

Sandra fixes a pot of tea and we sit in a darkening room full of the sounds of clocks ticking, caged birds twittering, and Joe softly snoring. Cindy has the look of someone who has entered a private garden.

"If I were a wealthy woman," she says, "I would build my own greenhouse. I'd grow orchids. Then I'd build a guesthouse. It would be stocked with fresh linens and groceries. I would have a horse-and-buggy and ride into the mountains or I'd travel. I've never been to the East Coast. I've never smelled the ocean. I'd like to see the different colors in the fall, the reds. I'd just like to drive down a winding road and hear the sound of the wind."

Sandra returns with the tea. "Sometimes I feel I could have a better life somewhere else. But I don't know where it is. Sometimes we think someone rich should come in and buy out this town," Sandra says. "It's kind of a treasonous thing to say, I suppose. But it could be so beautiful here if only someone cared."

Before I leave, she says she wants to show me something. She picks up a key and leads me across the street to the Methodist Church. "We're kind of proud of this. It's the one place that's stood the test of time." She is right. The church is in mint condition, the wooden pulpit and pews polished and dust-free. Hymnals in place. There is a working pump organ, a hand-carved baby's bier, and burial records that date back fifty years. A grave cost $5 in 1950. The Methodist Church was a force in Vallecitos. It ran a mission school until the 1970s. A visiting minister held Sunday services until 1990. Students who did well went on to a church-run high school in Española and from there to a Methodist college in the Midwest. There is a secret, unwritten history of Vallecitos that has nothing to do with the poverty, the crime or the labor strife, Sandra says. It is about the doctors and lawyers and businessmen who grew up in the town and then went away. "The smart ones got out. Isn't that the way it always works."

I PICK UP the Continental Divide Trail about ten miles southwest of Vallecitos near Magote Peak in the Carson National Forest. The route through the forest is less a trail than a series of landmarks—a fence line, a streambed, a jeep road, a ridge. It is easy to get lost, easy to wind up somewhere, at the Canjilon Lakes, for example, where a stranger with a pack on his back may not be welcome. The forest is public land in name only in this country. It is part of the ancient commons where local people continue to pasture livestock, collect firewood, and hide out when they have to. I take my time getting oriented, reminding myself that I've rarely been able to rely on my own internal compass in northern New Mexico. For all the years I have come back, for all the attachment I have, it remains *terra incognita*.

A friend of DeVargas, Moises Morales, who lives in Canjilon and serves on the county commission, says he guided Reies Tijerina and a small group of fugitives from the courthouse raid through this country. I had interviewed Morales the year before when I first heard of the commssion's opposition to the Continental Divide Trail. He spoke of the high country between Vallecitos and Canjilon as a place that should be left to local people, as a kind of refuge. Morales said that he and Tijerina and his men had followed an old stock trail, then hid out on Old Women Mesa, huddling under a grove of trees during a rainstorm. From there, they watched National Guard troops make their way up State Highway 84 to Canjilon, where a makeshift prison camp had been set up to hold *Alianza* members.

The mesa offers a commanding view. Someone standing there 400 years ago might have caught a glimpse of the first European settlers in northern New Mexico. They would have been among the 130 families recruited by Juan de Oñate, a Spanish explorer and fortune hunter. This part of New Mexico is crisscrossed with trails, its destiny bound up with them. Onate followed the *Camino Real* north from Mexico. In the 1820s the Santa Fe Trail brought Missouri fur trappers, who wiped out the beaver, opened up trade with the United States, and awakened the young nation to the rewards of westerly expansion. In 1846, one month after the United States declared war on Mexico, General Stephen Watts Kearney and his Army of the West marched down the Santa Fe Trail to stake America's claim to all of New Mexico.

"The Continental Divide Trail is just an advertising gimmick for the businesses that sell hiking shoes and camping equipment," DeVargas said to me. "Our people don't need trails. Besides, the Continental Divide doesn't even go through here." He is right. The Divide runs thirty miles to the west, through the Jicarilla Apache Reservation. But when the trail builders couldn't get permission from the Jicarilla for the project, they sought to reroute it through the Carson and Santa Fe national forests, cutting a seventy-five-mile swath down the center of Rio Arriba County. Now county officials are demanding that the Forest Service tear down trail signs that have been erected and move the trail out of the forest and away from mountain villages. "The recreationists have their own agendas. They come with a preconceived notion of wilderness," DeVargas said. "They don't think people should be living in the wilderness, but our people have been living in it for four hundred years and we're going to stay."

I follow the trail down Magote Ridge, over a brushy plateau to a cleft in the sandstone palisades of the Canjilon Mountains. Wind moaning in the narrow canyon is supposed to be the ghosts of the Archuleta brothers, outlaws who were murdered in a family feud in the 1870s. Off to my left, below a sandstone pulpit known as Orphan Mesa, is the site of an extraordinary archeological discovery. In 1934 paleontologists found a twenty-foot-long coiled skeleton of a phytosaur, a dinosaur that roamed the Earth 220 million years ago. Sheepherders had come upon the bones of the ancient reptile and given the thing a nickname, *Vivarón*, the child-eating snake.

Below the palisades, the country opens up and the trail leads south across the Chama River to the Piedra Lumbre, a sleepy river valley of silvery cottonwood and yellow-tipped rabbit brush. Just beyond the river crossing is the husk of an early twentieth-century homestead. The split cedar uprights of the house are still standing. Scattered about in the undergrowth are the seats of a buckboard, the wheels of a Model T, and the toothsome cylinder of an old corn grinder. The machine is stamped with the name of a Scotch-Irish merchant who foreclosed on several Hispanic families in the valley, uprooting them from their land grant.

The trail swings west and meanders ten miles through broken country past the tiny ranching community of Youngsville. Tijerina and the men with him came this way after descending from Old Women Mesa. They found refuge at the home of Ubaldo Velasquez, an

Alianza member. Velasquez is still living there when I come by. He is in his early eighties and walks slowly and stiffly. But his memory is sharp. He opens a drawer in an old brown chiffonier and pulls out a sheaf of documents that he says prove that his family was among the original recipients of the land grant for the Piedra Lumbre when it was issued by the Spanish territorial governor in 1766. Although the courts have rebuffed him countless times, Velasquez continues to petition, hoping he will live long enough to find a sympathetic judge.

"A lot of people say these old *hijuelas* [deeds] are worthless, but if you believe in them like some of us do, then they have a great deal of power. I think they are what keep me going."

During the past year, he tells me, a developer has acquired several hundred acres of the Piedra Lumbre. The land has been subdivided and fenced, blocking a stock trail that Velasquez and his neighbors used to lead their herds to summer pastures in the hills north of the valley. "We had to get rid of the cattle," Velasquez says. "It was going to be too expensive to trailer them over there, which is what we would have to do now."

No homes have been built yet in the subdivision, and Velasquez still enjoys looking out over the unblemished landscape. To get a better view, he maneuvers his pickup truck up a dirt track to a knoll above his house. Back-lit by a flaming sunset, the terraced uplands of the Piedra Lumbre glow green and orange like the gaudy layers of a child's birthday cake. This is the country that Georgia O'Keeffe painted, describing it as a "wonderful emptiness." Velasquez points to a spot in the foreground where the Rio Chama and another stream, the Rio Puerco, converge. "Over there is where they are going to build, right smack on our land. People from California, Texas, New York, all over. People like you, amigo," he says, patting my shoulder.

THE BOOTHEEL

Just past a faded mile marker, where the unsigned road to his ranch veers off New Mexico 81, Andy Peterson gets out of the truck and squats in the dirt. Someone has formed an arrow out of small stones in the center of the road. It points toward the Petersons' place and the Mexican border beyond. Peterson gets back in the truck beside his wife and says nothing. He drives the eight miles to their ranch house, walks into the kitchen, pours himself a glass of milk, sits down at the dining room table, places his hands on the tabletop, and spreads his fingers wide.

"Is it smugglers, Andy?" his wife, Louise, asks. He looks at her blankly, shrugs, and gets up.

"Ace," he calls as he walks back outside toward the truck. A younger man follows him. A screen door bangs. A dog barks, and father and son drive off into the night.

Andy is short and compact, his lightly lined face makes him seem younger than his sixty-three years. In profile, he looks a bit like a frowning Andy Griffith. Ace, in his mid-twenties, is taller and rangier. He is an accomplished calf roper who recently turned down a rodeo scholarship to Western New Mexico University so he could help his parents run the ranch. Louise, rounding into late middle age, speaks with the deliberate calm of someone soothing a case of nerves.

"I imagine they're going down to the Mexico border to check on the cattle or pull one of the corrals so it doesn't get stolen," she says. "Someone may be coming through tonight with a load of drugs or wets. That's what the arrow in the road was about."

I came upon the Petersons' place, by accident, early in my travels. I had been on the Continental Divide Trail for two days, hiking north from the Mexican border through thickets of mesquite and spiny cholla. The ranch house materialized out of the noonday haze, its cool veranda a miracle of shade—the house itself a monument to some vainglorious past, an adobe mausoleum. I learned that the Hatchet Ranch is all that remains of a cattle empire that spread over much of southern New Mexico during the early 1900s, and that it was once controlled by the family of Albert Fall, Secretary of the Interior under President Warren Harding, whose career was brought down by the Teapot Dome scandal in the 1920s. Sheltered by a thin screen of scraggly salt cedars, the ranch today seems exposed and vulnerable, a place still subject to frontier forces, more like a kibbutz or a white farmstead in Zimbabwe than an American household. Few Americans outside the Alaskan bush have a frame of reference for this sort of life. Call it extreme existence. I have returned after a year to experience a few days of it, to better understand the nameless longing that drew me back. The Petersons know something about the feeling. They don't have to be here. They have been ranching for many years, but they bought the Hatchet several years ago when they were in their late fifties, assuming a mountain of debt at a time in life when most people are contemplating retirement. To help make ends meet,

Louise operates a school bus franchise, which requires her to drive the longest school bus route in the state—sixty-seven miles one way. "I don't know if it was the challenge of making something out of a wilderness or just the feeling you get out here of fullness or peace, of being part of something that is so much bigger than you are, of being close to God."

The hatchet is no longer an empire, but it is still quite large, spreading across 250 square miles of whiskered desert in Hidalgo County at the spur tip of New Mexico's "Bootheel," the ledge in the state's southwestern corner and the only place in the United States where you face east to see Mexico. The ranch is 70 miles from the nearest law enforcement, 100 miles from the nearest hospital, two mountain ranges away from the closest neighbor. It is surely one of the more forgotten regions of the country and, consequently, one of the more attractive to illegal commerce. As the U.S. Border Patrol tightened security in the major towns along the border, the amount of illicit traffic diverted to rural areas in New Mexico has grown by 100 percent a year. At that rate, the value of drugs seized in Hidalgo County will soon exceed the assessed valuation of all personal property in the county. Tractor trailer trucks, eluding customs with their loads of tires, toys, livestock, or frozen food, rumble down the dirt road toward the four-strand wire fence and the unguarded gate that leads from the Petersons' property into northern Chihuahua. The "wets"—short for wetbacks—come the other way, on foot or stacked like fence posts under sheets of plywood in the back of pickup trucks. Bands of drug couriers, ten or twenty at a time, dressed in black and carrying backpacks stuffed with marijuana, cocaine, and occasionally guns troop by the Petersons' ranch. One form of trespass leads to another. Fences are cut and water lines severed by thirsty migrants. Cows are butchered or stolen. Equipment disappears. At neighboring ranches, windmills have been dismantled and hauled away. Just over the Peloncillo Mountains in Arizona, a family that led the Border Patrol to a cache of drugs on their ranch was awakened by night visitors warning them to leave well enough alone. The scorched shell of a drug runner's car pokes out of the sand on the side of a dirt road to the Petersons' house. Andy found a dead body recently.

The border country has always been a haven for fugitives. It was the Apache Indians' last stronghold. Members of the Clanton gang who fought Wyatt Earp and his brothers at the O.K. Corral kept a hideout here. In 1916 Pancho Villa staged his famous raid on Columbus, New Mexico, about thirty miles east of the Hatchet Ranch. Andy Peterson is a descendant of Mormon outcasts, polygamists who established a string of colonies in northern Mexico, only to be driven out during the revolution of 1910. The Petersons have lived on the border all their lives. They speak of the danger as though it were a feature of God's plan for them, accepting it as they would a prolonged drought or a disabling injury. "We have a deep awareness," Louise says, "that God is our provider, that no matter what happens, if the cattle all die, or that if something were to happen to one of us, that it is all part of His will."

The Bootheel was part of the last chunk of Mexico to be annexed to the United States. Along with a slice of southern Arizona, it was included in the Gadsden Purchase of 1854. Mexico was nearly bankrupt after its war with the United States and was willing to part with 45,000 square miles of seemingly worthless desert for less than $3 an acre. The United States wanted the land for a transcontinental rail route across the southern tier of the country. The railroad wasn't built until 1880 and aside from connecting local ranches to West Coast livestock markets, it was not much of a civilizing influence. The Bootheel has remained one of those places that people pass through wondering why anyone would choose to stay. From a train window, it is a vacuous landscape, a series of bleached basins rimmed by a flat line of distant mountains. Outside Lordsburg, the county seat and a town of about 3,000, the population density is still less than one person per square mile. During the time I am there, crisscrossing hundreds of miles, I pass no more than a dozen cars. Half of them belong to the U.S. Border Patrol. The isolation suits the Petersons, especially the men in the family who are famously reclusive in a county where it is hard *not* to be by yourself. Andy Peterson speaks so seldom and so softly that divining his moods and intentions can be like reading signs or dowsing for water. "He's like most everything else that lives in this desert," his wife says. "He communicates without talking. The first time he took me out on a date, he and his dad picked me up and drove forty miles to the show house in Lordsburg without saying a word. When we were first married, I'd think, 'Why can't he just tell me what it is he wants me to do?' After a while, I realized he would rather deal with a cow than people. But I got used to it."

Andy and Ace return at suppertime, a portable corral resting in the back of the pickup. Louise rings a wrought-iron bell in the front yard under a spreading mulberry tree and groups of dusty men in twos and threes come in out of the coral twilight. They include the Petersons' other son, Jay; Andy's two brothers, Hugh and Pete; brother-in-law Ronnie Ward; nephews Nate, Veao, and Joe, and two Mexican hands, Beto and Ramon, who have come over from the Rodriguez Brothers' *ranchería* a mile south of the border fence. The men have been here all week, camped out in the Petersons' living room, gathering calves for market from a cattle herd strung out across 160,000 acres. Tomorrow is the last day of the roundup. Relief shows in tired faces. Ace limps slightly where his horse fell on him, doing no harm, he assures his mother. Jay holds his ribs where a cow kicked him while he was probing to check if she was pregnant. Louise suspects his ribs are broken and urges him to take it easy. "Only one day to go," Jay replies. Grace is said. We stand for it in a circle, men holding hands. "Dear Lord, we thank Thee . . ."

Supper is pot roast and pineapple upside-down cake. The men bend to it, and the room resonates with the sounds of earnest consumption, not unlike noshing cows. Conversations are sidebar occurrences, rarely enveloping the whole table. The accents are out of West Texas, where many of New Mexico's early cowboys came from. A calf is a *cy-ef*. A yearling is a *yerlin*. Moisture is *boisture*. A pig is *pay-ig*, a litter of which has gone missing.

"Sow et 'em?"

"Don't know. Maybe."

"Anybody looked for 'em?"

"Nope."

Searching for three piglets or their remains is a daunting prospect. The ranch house is at the center of a maze of unoccupied bunkhouses, cabins, barns, and sheds, dating to the ranch's early days when it supported a dozen full-time hands and served as a bivouac for cavalry troops guarding the border during the Mexican revolution. Established in 1880s, the Hatchet Ranch eventually became part of a land and cattle business that encompassed one million acres scattered across the Southwest, from Mexico to Colorado. Albert Fall held a controlling interest in the operation. He was in his prime then, about to become one of New Mexico's first U.S. senators and, shortly thereafter, Secretary of the Interior. In 1923 Fall was convicted of taking a $100,000 bribe in return for secretly leasing government oil reserves at Teapot Dome, Wyoming, to friends in the oil business. He was the first Cabinet officer ever sent to prison. To his dying day, Fall insisted the money was a loan, not a bribe, though he admitted lying about who gave it to him. He intended to use the $100,000 to expand his ranching operations in New Mexico. Much of Fall's life was the stuff of Western movies. Educated as a lawyer in Kentucky, he had gone west for health reasons and there reinvented himself, punching cows, prospecting for gold, and becoming handy with a gun. He told friends that his greatest ambition was to be a crack shot, and, in time, he did become known for his audacity with a firearm. When he was thirty-four, Fall was arrested for wounding a deputy sheriff during a gunfight on a street in Las Cruces, New Mexico. Fall's cronies argued that the deputy fired first, egged on by politicians who wanted Fall out of the way. But Fall insisted that politics had nothing to do with it. He said that he never liked the deputy and that when he saw him coming down the street he just decided to shoot him. The deputy was indicted. Fall was released.

After his bribery conviction, Fall's cattle empire was split up among creditors and family members. The Hatchet stayed in his son-in-law's family until it was sold to the Petersons. With just the Petersons living here now, struggling to run a place that used to require seven or eight full-time hands, neglect has been inevitable. The lawn has gone to seed. Jackrabbits have colonized the vegetable garden. The desert is lapping at the outbuildings. The crumbling adobes are filling with sand and sagebrush, their metal roofs held on by stacks of old tires.

After dinner, the Peterson men adjourn to the living room, a dim cavern hung with enough antlered heads to furnish a museum of taxidermy. The room also boasts a television set, a luxury missing from most of the family households, I am told, and the men gather around it. It's an election year, and one of the presidential debates is on, but the entertainment of choice is a faded videotape of deer hunting in Mexico. After a bit, a deck of cards is produced and a poker game begins. Someone closes the double doors to the dining room where Louise and I are sitting. "They won't shut you out after they get to know you," Louise says to me. "Or maybe they will," she chuckles. "You want to see your room?" she asks brightly.

The rooms of the house are hitched together in the order in which they were built, all facing out on a covered walkway, its rumpled tin roof barely held up by tilting columns. I head down the long portal with a flashlight, mindful of a warning from Louise to watch out for rattlers. The house ages inward like a tree. The deeper you go, the older it gets. The walls become thicker, the mosaics of inlaid Mexican tile more elaborate, the fireplaces more numerous. The portal is a flea market of cast-iron stoves, iceboxes, and broken furniture. Louise apologizes for the clutter. "This house has been more than we can handle. I love it, but Andy doesn't really care. He's just looking for a home for a cow." At the door to my room, she hands me a thick album. "I thought you might like to look through this," she says. "It's the story of Andy's family." The album overflows with letters, diaries, photographs, and genealogies. It is a selective recounting, told through tributes and testimonials. People are remembered the way they would like to be. Still, it is a lifting of the veil. Tragedies are revealed. Failures and disappointments alluded to, confidences shared. Much of it is about the Mormon exile in Mexico, one of those small upheavals barely noted by historians but enshrined in the memories of the people who experienced it. Bequeathed from one generation to the next, the survivors' stories of sacrifice and perseverance become part of the private history that defines and energizes a culture. "This will tell you a lot more about the Peterson family than I could," Louise says.

Andy Peterson's great-grandfather fled Utah and settled in the polygamist community of Colonia Díaz in northern Chihuahua in 1887. Colonia Díaz was one of eight "cities of refuge" established for families of plural marriage who faced prosecution in the United States. Joseph Smith, the founder of the Mormon Church, said polygamy was a form of worship. An abundant posterity, Smith said, gives glory to the Lord. Outside the church, the practice stirred outrage and mob violence that led to Smith's murder in 1844. Congress passed laws imposing fines and jail sentences as well as depriving polygamists of the right to vote, hold office, or serve on juries. Posing as peddlers and census takers, federal marshals began searching for lawbreakers. In 1879 church officials instructed Mormon missionaries in Mexico to look for land where practitioners of plural marriage could live in peace. With a gift for turning an ordeal into an opportunity, the Mormon expatriates set out to build a new Zion much as they had in the arid wilderness of nineteenth-century Utah. From the beginning, Joseph Smith had told his followers that the frontier was the antechamber to paradise. The final gathering place, Smith said, "shall be in on the borders . . . The glory of the Lord shall be there." Colonia Díaz was set along the flood-prone banks of the Casas Grandes River on land no one else wanted. Believing as they did that a righteous community would be taken up to heaven in the Last Days, the colonists set about building a city worthy of eternal renewal. Colonia Díaz consisted of about 1,000 people, their houses, stores, and businesses clustered in a compact grid of 140 blocks surrounded by orchards and pastures. The colonists prospered, but in the process they sowed the seeds of their own destruction. Perhaps, they had too much success in a land of want or talked too much about being God's chosen people. They were there barely twenty-five years before the Mexicans ran them off.

Soon after the revolution broke out in 1910, guerillas under Pancho Villa and other rebel leaders began making demands on the Mormon colonies for provisions. The rebels were landless peasants, already deeply suspicious of gringos. Farms were burned and stores plundered. When the residents of Colonia Díaz tried to organize their own defenses, they were told to turn over all of their guns or face a full-scale assault on their communities. In July 1912 Colonia Díaz and the other Mormon communities in Mexico were evacuated and the colonists became exiles again. "The work of twenty-five years had never seemed so precious, but we turned our backs on everything," Rachel Mortenson Jensen wrote of her last morning in Colonia Díaz. "We turned the cows and calves out together, broke down the pig-pens, opened the chicken-run, and watched the creatures gingerly find their way about. Our bins were bursting with freshly harvested grain, our cupboards full of bottled fruit, and our loved ones buried out there in the cemetery."

With less than twenty-four hours' notice, a line of eighty-five wagons and buggies formed up and began the journey from Colonia Díaz north across the border. The caravan came to a halt a week later in Hachita, a dusty railroad town eighteen miles north of the Hatchet Ranch. A tent camp was erected in a vacant lot that came to be known as Poverty Flat.

In her account of the Mormon flight from Mexico, author Annie R. Johnson wrote that the refugees were not universally welcomed. "Those wagons belched children like jackrabbits," someone said. There was much speculation about how many wives each man had. One little girl remarked to a new arrival, "Are you a Mor-min? My mama says her don't like Mor-mins."

From Hachita, Andy Peterson's great-aunt Elsie wrote to relatives in Utah. "Everything is gone or destroyed in the way of horses, saddles, clothing, bedding, provisions, and household goods. They have taken the mill, money, flour, wheat, and everything. Ever since I wrote you before, we have been living in a tent. Rain one day. Wind the next. Cold, then hot. Our worldly goods consist of a tent, a few goods boxes, and two suitcases. It's not so bad now, but I don't know what we are going to do."

In 1913 Colonia Díaz was burned to the ground by revolutionaries and never rebuilt.

Letters and newspaper stories preserved in Louise's album describe what happened to the Petersons after their escape from Mexico.

Elsie Peterson eventually moved to Mesa, Arizona, but her brother, Andrew, Andy Peterson's grandfather, decided to stay. He found work at a nearby ranch, married, and fathered three children. Five years later, with the U.S. Army under General John Pershing chasing after Pancho Villa, Andrew Peterson disappeared. A search party found his body and pieced together what happened. Peterson, his brother-in-law, and a friend had gone looking for cattle that had strayed across the border. They had not gone far when they apparently were accosted by a band of rebels. The three cowboys were then stripped, mutilated, and executed. One man was found with his penis stuffed in his mouth.

The murders provoked a spasm of saber rattling in Washington, but it didn't come to anything. The killers got away. The suspected ringleader was someone many of the Mormon colonists had known as a boy. He had attended their schools and once courted a Mormon girl. Hundreds of people attended a funeral service for the three cowboys. An El Paso newspaper reported that Andrew Peterson's dog refused to leave his grave when the service was over. In 1947, the graves all but obliterated, Bernard Whiting, an old man who had grown up in Colonia Díaz, set about laying headstones for the three Mormon cowboys. Forty years later, the Peterson family, some thirty strong, began holding reunions at the spot where Andrew Peterson was buried. Apparently, it is an unquiet grave. Louise says the men in the family never forgave their grandmother for remarrying. She says Andy didn't want to invite her to his own wedding (she came anyway), and, to this day, he resists going to Mexico, even though it is just across the back fence. "It's because of what happened to his grandfather."

I AM AWAKENED before dawn by the stutter of diesel motors and the sound of men loading horses into trailers. We drive for an hour and a half down a dirt road to a spot about a quarter mile from the border, where we set up the corrals. The horses are unloaded and I am handed the reins of a tall gelding named High Stepper. The men gather in a mounted caucus and, without uttering a complete sentence, seem to agree on a strategy for rounding up the cattle. The herd is scattered across a 20,000-acre expanse of greasewood, mesquite, and cholla that, up close, make the desert suddenly appear like a pygmy forest. I don't see a single cow. Andy eases up beside me and makes a looping, fishhook motion with his arm, says something about "that draw" and "those hills" and rides off. I think he means for me to stay along the east side of a long arroyo, as the cattle are being pushed along the west side, and turn back any that make a break for the hills. I quickly realize that High Stepper knows what he's doing, if I don't, and I give him his head, enjoying the tom-tom percussion of hoofbeats on the dry, desert floor.

Although it has not rained in four months, the Bootheel is not officially in a drought. Droughts in this part of the country are epochal, not seasonal. They are reminiscent of the natural disasters that the God of the Israelites visited on the Egyptians. The decade of the 1930s was a drought. Likewise, much of the '50s. Local people pronounce the word "drouth" as if mouthing an ancient curse. The county looks desolate even for the Southwest. Much of southern Arizona and New Mexico are creased by green canopied rivers, the Gila, the Blue, the San Francisco, and the San Pedro. But in the Bootheel, there are no rivers. Mountain runoff spreads out in broad shallow lakes, inches deep, and quick to evaporate. The water is laden with salts and alkali from the decomposing mountains and where it collects, little vegetation can take hold. The effect is preternatural, all blowing sand, shimmering horizons and bone white playas. Conjuring images of Armageddon, the novelist Cormac McCarthy described it as a faultless void. He wrote: "The sun in the west lay in a holocaust where there rose a steady column of small desert bats and to the north along the trembling perimeter of the world dust was blowing down the void like the smoke of distant armies." The passage is from *Blood Meridian*, McCarthy's biblically cadenced novel about the wanderings of a band of scalp hunters and the inexorable brutality of life along the border.

During the drought of the 1930s, government agents bought up the Petersons' cattle for a few dollars a head and shot them so the starving animals wouldn't strip the ground of what little forage was left. After the slaughter, according to Louise, people tried to make a little money by scavenging the bones of the dead cattle and selling them to fertilizer factories in California. The drought of the '50s is blamed for the collapse of the bighorn sheep population in the Hatchet Mountains. Herd numbers fell from around 1,000 animals to fewer than 50 today. But a century of poor livestock management also contributed to the loss of good sheep habitat. Overgrazing brings to mind Dust Bowl imagery of bald, wind-raked pastures and manure-splattered stream banks. The long-term effect is less dramatic but equally injurious. Over time, the grass is replaced by a different kind of vegetation. It is bushier, hardier, and less nutritious. And, in deserts, it often provides ideal cover for mountain lions. The lions prey on bighorn sheep. The Petersons, who have lived in the wilds all their lives, say the experts are a little too eager to blame ranchers for the ravages of nature. Moreover, if mountain lions are killing off the bighorns, ranchers argue, why not declare open season on the lions, instead of protecting them as game animals that can't be poisoned or trapped? "Scripture says that God created man to work the earth and the animals to be subjugated to man's needs, and we believe that," Louise tells me.

I am shooing cows back across the draw when Andy crosses my path at a gallop, then just as suddenly gallops back in my direction and pulls to a stop. "I apologize for cutting in front of you," he says. "I wasn't looking." Although it hardly matters to me, it does to him. It is a breach of conduct that he would not tolerate in someone else. A cowboy doesn't cross in front of another, even if the other is only a cowboy for a day. It is part of the etiquette by which men who work alone acknowledge one another. Words matter little in a place where men are judged almost entirely by their deeds. It helps explain why you are not absolved, apologies notwithstanding, if you leave a gate open or a well pump running. Except in small children, such carelessness is a sign of disrespect. It's like telling another rider you didn't see him, which, to a cowboy, is like telling him he was too in-consequential to notice.

I drive back to the ranch at dusk with Ronnie Ward and two Petersons, Nate and Pete. There is a twitchy silence, and I sense they are working up to asking me a serious question. Earlier in the day, another member of the crew asked me if I could explain to him what the television show *Survivor* was all about. This time the question is about money. Coming from a big city, might I have some financial tips on how a working man could get a slightly higher return on his money? Higher, in other words, than it is currently earning in a sav-ings account at the Western Bank of Lordsburg?

I figure I can satisfy them by mentioning a few of the standard choices: stocks, bonds, etc. I get as far as the phrase "money market mutual fund."

"I don't know what that is," Ronnie Ward says quietly.

We are distracted by a small cyclone of dust, such as a car might stir up, spiraling toward the ranch house, about a mile away. We stop and watch the dust plume, looking for a telltale glint from a familiar vehi-cle. We can hear the dogs barking at the house.

"Drug runner?"

"You never know."

"Louise is home alone."

It turns out to be a false alarm. The vehicle belongs to the local hay merchant, a family friend.

The cowboys are eager to draw their pay and head for home. They may be relatives but they still get a daily wage.

Sixty-five dollars a day. Poverty level.

"They get their meals, too," Louise says.

I SPEND THE evening alone with Louise and Andy. They have some things they want to show me.

Louise points to a water tank that was spray-painted by an environmental group. The graffiti reads: COWS OFF PUBLIC LAND. The Petersons are public land ranchers, meaning that most of their grazing occurs on land leased from the state and federal governments.

"How do they expect to promote respect for the environment when they make an ugly mess like that?" Louise says. Ahead of us along the road is another development distressing to the Petersons, a blue and white sign marking the route of the Continental Divide Trail. Beginning at the border, the trailheads west across the desert and through the Big Hatchet Mountains. For twenty miles or more, the trail crosses some of the public land that the Petersons lease for grazing. At one point, it comes within a mile of their home.

"They never thought to inform us they were putting the trail through here," Louise says. "First thing they did was drive one of their signs through a water pipe and drain one of our stock tanks. Then they intentionally put one up facing the wrong way, so that we had all kinds of people trooping down our road, through our corrals, and past our house. They drank out of the hose, without asking. They came into the house when we weren't there and used the phone. One fellow sat out there in his car, blowing his horn and yelling at Andy to move the cows out of his way. These people feel superior to us. They act like we're the trespassers, and they have all the rights."

"But why would anyone face a trail sign the wrong way on purpose?" I ask.

"You tell us," Andy says, giving me a hard look.

I had hiked the trail through the Big Hatchets. At the time there was no sign pointing toward the Petersons' house, but I had walked on in anyway, intrigued by the drooping old adobe and hoping to fill my water bottle. I had knocked on the door, met Louise, and proceeded to ask a lot of questions. She responded graciously, showing me the house and pouring me a glass of ice tea. Later, when I asked if I could come back, she hesitated. I was a stranger from the city, a journalist no doubt addled by environmental superstitions, someone who would get in the way. "Be prepared for the fact that no one is going to trust you," she said.

I told her it was an occupational hazard. We talked some more. Would I be willing to pay room and board? Of course. And when I wrote up my stay would I try to convey what she meant when she said that she and her husband felt besieged? I assured her I would, mistakenly assuming she was talking about the waves of migrants and smugglers making their way north across the Bootheel.

"I don't blame most of them," Andy says when the subject arises. "They're poor, desperate people. If they have to cut a pipeline to get a drink, I can understand. It gets pretty thirsty out there. If they're hungry and need a cow, I'll give them one. I can cope with them. You factor in the losses. That's the way it's always been."

Andy knows firsthand what it's like to be alone and hurt in the desert. The year he turned fifty his horse fell on him while he was riding out of a steep arroyo. He broke his pelvis. Bleeding internally, unable to walk, he wasn't discovered until the next morning. By then he had managed to crawl to a pipeline and bore a hole in it with his pocketknife. A trickle of water had kept him alive.

"Those poor Mexicans aren't what get me," he says. "I'm not worried about them. I'm talking about people like . . ." He hesitates and looks away. "Hikers, bird-watchers, butterfly hunters, sheep counters. You name it, they're here. They're the ones who will try to run all over me because they think they can, because I'm some sort of hermit or a hick. And folks wonder why I get ringy out here."

Andy's grumpiness speaks for thousands of ranchers across the West who are losing control of the land they depend on. The Petersons have title to a small fraction of the ranch they call their own. They lease the rest of it. Yet, the value of the ranch is based on the productivity of all 250 square miles that they graze. Reduce the number of cattle on the land, as some environmentalists would like to do, and the Petersons will be stuck with the same debt but fewer cattle with which to pay it down. Similar circumstances have forced some ranchers in the Southwest to go out of business. It has also allowed thousands of acres of desert range to begin recovering from a century of overgrazing.

For a long time, ranchers had the Bootheel to themselves. The Continental Divide Trail hadn't been built. The environmentalists were busy elsewhere. The arguments that wildlife have the same rights as cattle or that grazing land ought to be set aside as wilderness weren't made in this area until recently. The Hatchet country still hasn't attracted a lot of people or been subject to a great many demands. But the people who do come tend to be opinionated and outspoken. They are the bird-watchers, the "butterfly hunters," the archeologists, and the bighorn sheep biologists that Andy and Louise fret about.

The Petersons do have cause for worry. A consultant for the New Mexico Department of Game and Fish, who has made frequent trips to the ranch, is recommending that they move their cattle out of the Little Hatchet Mountains. The cattle share the mountains with one of New Mexico's last native bighorn sheep herds, and the long-term effect of livestock grazing is to make the mountains uninhabitable for the sheep. But if the Petersons can't use the Little Hatchets or find substitute pasture, they will have to cut the size of their herd.

Many ranchers tend to get furious over such interference. They claim a frontier variant of *droit du seigneur*, a right to control the destiny of land that they and their ancestors have used for 100 years or more, even if they haven't actually owned it. They have gone all the way to the Supreme Court with this argument and lost. The Petersons are taking a more conciliatory approach. They are installing a water system that will allow them to shift the location of their cattle by shutting off water at one spot, where grazing should be discouraged, and turning it on somewhere else. The system will also provide water for wildlife. But it is a costly solution, requiring about seventy miles of water lines and a network of pumps and tanks. "We need forty thousand dollars, at least, to get it done," Louise says. "It's really not more than a dream."

Meanwhile, some people are catering to the tourists. Signs have gone up in Hachita welcoming hikers coming off the Continental Divide Trail. For the first time since the early 1940s, when the Southern Pacific Railroad operated a bunkhouse for engine crews, the town can boast of overnight accommodations. The Hachita Bed and Breakfast is a simple place, a couple of slab-sided modular units with a common bathroom set in a scruffy field that might well have been the original Poverty Flat. But by the bedside when I visited, there was a basket of magazines, among them *The New Yorker* and *Vanity Fair*. *Whose spoor was this?* I wondered. *Who had slept here last? A movie location scout? Wan models from Ralph Lauren or Neiman-Marcus posing for a shoot amid the tumbleweed? What would this place be like in ten years?* Perhaps it could be the backdrop for a New Age spa, a comfortable haven for the retro ascetic, the buildings arranged unobtrusively around the water tower, the windmill, and the two or three privies that are still standing. It is not likely, though by no means impossible, given what guidebooks are beginning to say about the Bootheel country. "True mountains of mystery . . . blank spots on the map that have always attracted adventurers . . . distant desert ranges with an almost mystical glow . . ."

"When you write your story," Louise says to me, "please just don't tell people how to get to our place."

"He'll write what he wants to write," Andy says.

We eat dinner in silence. I'm about to make my way out to the back bedroom when Andy appears at my side, his hand outstretched. "You were a help with the cattle." He turns and goes out the kitchen door. I don't see him again.

The next morning, Sunday, Louise asks me if I would like to accompany her to church in Hachita before I leave. With no Mormon church nearby, she attends Methodist services. They are held in a small house fitted out with a half-dozen pews and a pulpit. The minister makes the rounds of four Bootheel communities every week.

On the way, I coax Louise into talking about her own past.

"Oh, my history doesn't amount to much," she says.

She came to New Mexico from El Paso with her parents in 1948 when she was a little girl. Her father wanted to be a cotton farmer and had enough money from the sale of a dairy to buy a field but not a house. At first, they lived in a dugout, a hollowed-out space in the ground with a roof constructed of railroad ties, tar paper, and dirt. They cooked their meals outdoors. "You don't know what poor is until you have to get your water out of a dirt ditch without even a siphon tube." Their first house was a section of Army barracks that had been used to shelter German prisoners during World War II. "We still didn't have any heat. Daddy tried to stack bales of hay against the walls for insulation, but Momma thought they were a fire hazard and made him move them. I could tell it was cold in the morning when I'd look over and see Daddy's bushy eyebrows frosted over.

"I just feel God's hand in so much of life because there's been so many times when anything could have happened. There are too many things you are not in control of out here, you have to have faith. The first year on the ranch Andy and I didn't think we were going to make it. We had a really bad drought, and I didn't think we were going to come up with the payments. We did, and I just know God had a hand in that."

Including Louise and me, six people attend the church service, about 20 percent of Hachita's population.

We sing three hymns, our voices badly mismatched, and the minister reads from the Gospels. The lesson is the verse from Luke, Chapter 9, in which a man who wishes to follow Jesus asks if he first might go home and bury his recently departed father, and Jesus replies: "Let the dead bury the dead," and a another man asks if it would be all right if he finished plowing his field, and Jesus replies: "No man putting his hand to the plow, and looking back, is fit for the kingdom of God."

After the lesson, the minister leads a prayer for rain and then begins his sermon.

"I am convinced we are in the latter days. Maybe they will come in one hundred years, maybe sooner. But they are coming."

On the way home, I ask Louise if Jesus appeared today would she drop everything to follow Him, would she walk away from the ranch and from her husband.

"Of course I would. I wouldn't hesitate for a moment. That's if He would have me. Wouldn't you?"

HEADING WEST, ALONE, I cross the Continental Divide, a barely noticeable swell under the desert blacktop, and pass Playa, another Bootheel hamlet on the verge of ghostdom. I could cut north to the interstate, but the urge to linger pulls me south toward the Animas Valley and the Geronimo Trail, which winds over the Peloncillos through Apache and outlaw country. Where the pavement turns to gravel, some poet of the road has attached corny postscripts to the road signs. A sign says DIP. The addendum reads BUT NO CHIPS. Another sign says RUNNING WATER with PRAY FOR inscribed above it. This goes on for a while, the messages on limp cardboard and barely legible, leftover whimsy from before the end times, I suppose. Endings are a subject of interminable debate among students of the West. The 1890 national census proclaimed the end of the frontier, although large pockets of unsettled territory survived well into the next century. Others point to the end of the Indian wars, the fencing of the open range, the damming of the wild rivers, the virtual destruction of the big carnivores, the wolf, the jaguar, and the grizzly bear.

In the Animas Valley the landscape changes dramatically. Now I see what the guidebooks are rhapsodizing about. The Old Testament barrens give way to grassland, savannah, and oak-studded hills. To the east, ponderosa pine and Douglas fir darken the yellow crest of the Animas Range, a wrinkled band of mountains that Cormac McCarthy said look like crumpled butcher paper. Off to the west, a sea of waist-high buffalo grass grows out of an ancient lakebed three times the size of Manhattan Island. A bear cub scuttling across it is like a black billiard ball disappearing into a football field.

Crossing into Arizona, I pause at the crest of the Peloncillos and look north past green-tinted rhyolite cliffs toward Skeleton Canyon, where Geronimo surrendered to General Nelson Miles in September of 1886, formally ending a half century of warfare with the Apaches.

I stop for a late lunch at the stately Gadsden Hotel in Douglas, an Arizona border town founded in 1900. The Gadsden is what an old hotel should be, an oasis of cool marble, deep shadows, and grand staircases. Missing only are the people to fill the ghostly spaces, men like Albert Fall, Black Jack Pershing, and Nelson Miles, whom Teddy Roosevelt called the "brave peacock." Instead, the hotel has been commandeered by a senior citizen bus tour on its way to Chihuahua. I am shown to a long table already occupied by members of the tour group, including a pair of gents trying to decide if they will need to buy toilet paper before venturing into Mexico.

There are more signs along the road leaving Douglas, signs of the times.

WE'RE BEING INVADED, the first one says. SOMETHING MUST BE DONE NOW.

TONS OF DRUGS, THOUSANDS OF ILLEGALS PASS BY THIS SIGN, says another.

The sequence goes on like this for several miles, plaintive and petulant. Hereabouts, more than one million people are crossing the border illegally every year. The Ku Klux Klan was here in the spring, offering aid and comfort to any rancher who took up arms against the invaders. Television crews from Mexico arrived, pointed their cameras indiscriminately at ranch houses, and announced, "Come through this door and you will be killed. The people who live here are waiting to kill you." The cowboy, it seems, is getting hoisted on his own petard, accused of living up to the old rough-and-ready stereotype—the one we used to romanticize, the one embodied by Albert Fall, coolly shooting down a man simply because he didn't like him. The Mexican media exaggerated, but it did not fabricate. Along the border, recently, several ranchers have pulled guns on foreign trespassers and held them hostage until the law could be summoned. One migrant was injured by gunfire. A neighbor of the Petersons rode into Mexico with a group of men to retrieve cattle they believed had been stolen. But the Petersons and most of the people I have met along the way have stayed out of the fray. They go about their business, unassuming and unarmed. They ride cautiously into the new century, keeping their heads down, trying not to cut in front of anyone. They heed the lesson of their own history and its frequent reminders of their own vulnerability. As Louise put it, "There are so many things you are not in control of."

I slow down for a deer standing in the highway ahead of me and see another sign, this one hand-lettered on a piece of cardboard lying on the shoulder, probably discarded by some needy traveler. It says: HELP US.

OH, CANADA

"So he's going with crazy Mike, eh?"

The words drift across the wooden counters in the Beaver Mines general store where I am picking up supplies for a pack trip into the Canadian Rockies. I am going with Mike Judd, a former cowboy and hunting guide, best known lately for his acts of defiance against the oil and gas industry. A year ago, he was confined to the county mental hospital after he made off with a Caterpillar and threatened to tear up a road that Shell/Canada had built in one of the last unspoiled canyons in southern Alberta's Castle-Crown Wilderness.

I look over at the four men joking in the front of the store, one of them jerking a thumb in my direction. "You think he knows what he's in for?"

When I was growing up in Minnesota, Canada beckoned like Atlantis. It was a boy's world, right out of the fictional wilderness I had immersed myself in—Kenneth Roberts's *Northwest Passage* and novelist Joseph Altsheler's tales of a band of daring frontier lads paddling silently across indigo lakes and sleeping on the forest floor. In my eyes Canada was all forest and indigo lakes. I went with my father almost every August. It took us all day to reach the border, a slow, hot drive past farm fields and lakeside tourist courts with their riot of homemade billboards hawking night crawlers and all-you-can-eat crappie suppers. The clutter disappeared when we crossed into Canada at Lake of the Woods. My father referred to the country north of the border as the Canadian Shield. It is the name geologists gave to the nucleus of the continent, the first part of North America to rise permanently above sea level. For me, it was the great granite battlement beyond which all familiar trappings and responsibilities dropped away and the realm of summer began. The forest massed in front of us. A breeze rose off the water. The air smelled like gin, my father said.

"I don't want to disappoint you," Mike Judd says to me as we climb into his truck and head for his horse camp on the South Castle River. "I'm afraid you're going to find that this isn't the Canada of your youth. The oil companies, the timber companies, the cattle ranchers . . . they've all had their way with this country, and it shows it."

But this trip isn't just about Canada. It is my last stop, a time of reckoning. I had gone from border to border and a bit beyond, spent the better part of two years exploring an endangered landscape. I had listened to the arguments about why it was so and who was to blame. The world of the Divide was animated by feuds—between cowboys and conservationists, sheepherders and coyotes, wolves and elk—and it would be a lesser place for the loss of any of the antagonists. Its appeal comes not only from mountain meadows and sculpted canyons, but from the relics of history—the bones of homesteads, the names of immigrant herders carved in aspen bark—and from the sinuous architecture of broken country, whether shaped by wind and drought, by a miner's dynamite or a rancher's cows. If there is a common element to it all, it is threadbare grace. You see it in the desert bighorn that goes without water for six months or the shepherd who supports a family on $5,000 a year. The West that captures the imagination is often an impoverished landscape, poor in moisture and nourishment, exposed and distressed, worn to burnished bedrock. Yet, it is possible to get carried away with graveyard aesthetics, like Shelley's desert traveler contemplating the majestic wreckage of Ozymandias and its inscription: LOOK ON MY WORKS, YE MIGHTY, AND DESPAIR.

Mike Judd does not encourage such thinking. He is not ready to accept the role that society has scripted for him, as a refugee from the nineteenth century or an expatriate from the wilderness. "I'm going to show you the good, the bad, and the ugly," he says. "And when you've seen it, I hope you'll want to do something about it."

I had heard about Mike from environmentalists in the United States. They called him a cowboy Cassandra, a prophet of ecological ruin, ignored in his own country. A scold to neighbors and a worry to his family, he had eventually taken his message south of the border, where he found a more responsive audience. Five years ago, his warnings about the industrialization of wilderness along the Continental Divide helped persuade U.S. Forest Service officials in Montana to put a chunk of the northern Rocky Mountains off-limits to logging, mining, and oil drilling.

Canada hadn't weakened its environmental policies since I was a boy. It just hadn't seen the need to pass strict laws. There was so much country, bigger than the United States, even counting Alaska, and so much of it unspoiled. The first paved cross-country highway wasn't finished until the 1960s. Even after Canada became a force in international timber and energy markets, and the Western provinces began to exhibit scars that did not heal, there was no push for wilderness preservation comparable to U.S. efforts. Indeed, the absence of such laws has given Canadian companies a competitive advantage. For example, by the year 2000, they were meeting about 35 percent of the U.S. timber demand. They are not about to trade market share for stronger environmental protection. Meanwhile, the Ministry of Environment dutifully looks for ways to protect Canada's endangered species, which now number around 300, but can't come up with a law that provincial politicians will agree to. All of Canada's provinces have gained power over the past thirty years as the central government in Ottawa sought to placate separatists in Quebec. As a result, it has become increasingly difficult for the federal government to exert authority on any number of issues. Eventually, Canada's inaction on the environment is bound to have repercussions.

"It'll affect you guys in the lower forty-eight," Mike says to me. "Our wildlife is your wildlife. They don't stop at the border. A lot of them—the bears and the wolves, mainly—come from up here. If we stop growing them, you'll stop seeing them."

Mike steers his truck up a rough gravel road toward his camp. The old Ford rides low and slow, piled high with saddles, panniers, and boxes of frozen food and portable kitchen equipment. His three-year-old husky, Keeper, sits between us in the cab alongside his 12-gauge, his copy of *The Gulag Archipelago*, and a bullwhip he uses to chase the neighbors' cows out of riverside vegetation. "If they have their way, they'll eat all the grass along the river. If I have mine, they'll go out a little thinner than when they come in."

Just past fifty, Mike is slight and wiry, with a grizzled face and eyes that twinkle and fade. He grew up on his father's small ranch, rode a horse to school in Pincher Creek, finished the twelfth grade, and lit out across the mountains for a job with the biggest cattle operation in British Columbia. He returned after five years to help his brother run the family's ranch and start a wilderness-outfitting business. But southern Alberta was changing. The wilderness was being fragmented and the game scattered. You could drive a pickup into places that not that long ago were accessible only by horse or a mule. The changes weighed heavily on Mike. He withdrew from the company of the cowboys, roughnecks, and loggers whose colorful society he had craved as a boy. "Every time an issue of conservation came along, they were on the other side. That was not helpful to me because as a guide my living depended on these mountains. I tried to point out the value of leaving them alone, but the more I did that, the more I became an alien."

The first gas wells were drilled in 1902 inside the boundaries of what is now Waterton Lakes National Park, just north of the Montana border. Today, there isn't a major valley for fifty miles north of Waterton without an access road servicing a well, a pipeline, or a processing plant. Nearly 300 miles of roads have been built into the narrow canyons that run perpendicular to the spine of the Rockies. Most of them dead-end against the flanks of the Divide, where Mike and I are headed. Half of the elk habitat has been destroyed in the mountains around Pincher Creek and Waterton. Less than a quarter of the grizzly bear's home range is still intact. Its numbers have declined by more than 90 percent over the past century. Biologists predict southern Alberta will be the next place where they go extinct.

The human population of southern Alberta is deceptively sparse. It is an unhurried, uncluttered place of tidy, clapboard towns, English gardens, and a sea of green hills lapping against the mountains that float in the distance like gray-barnacled leviathans. Words like "nice" and "just so" come to mind when describing the bright red window boxes plump with geraniums or the wooden door knockers in the form of a hand-painted Canada goose. To a lot of people, the term "wild" is a pejorative, something to be washed out of the dog's fur like skunk odor. It brings to mind the "black wind" that rakes these hills in the winter or the thin, stony soil that broke the spirits of the North Dakota farmers who thought they were coming to an agricultural paradise—which is how the Canadian Pacific Railroad advertised it in the 1890s. For most people, there's wilderness enough five miles up the dirt road the oil industry built along Scarpe Creek, where you can fish for trout with your cooler of Molsons within arm's reach on the seat of your all-terrain vehicle. Rural Canada has fallen head over heels for the ATV or "quad" as it's known in these parts. The machines can tackle the most primitive oil and logging tracks. They make their own trails, dispersing wildlife, despoiling habitat, fouling streams. They aren't supposed to be in the Castle-Crown Wilderness, but people ignore the regulations. From the traffic and the noise, you'd think most of Calgary was motoring around the forest roads on a summer weekend. We find a pair of quads parked outside the one-room cabin Mike built for hunting clients. The two teenage drivers are fast asleep inside. Mike rousts them with a sharp knock and a stern warning about the penalty for trespassing. He won't press charges. He can't take the risk. His isolated camp is too vulnerable to reprisal. He asks the boys if they are familiar with the signs prohibiting ATVs in the backcountry.

"Them yellow ones?" one of the boys answers distractedly. "Yeah, my dad is on the committee that drew up the rules."

They board their machines and sputter off. Mike goes looking for his horses.

We ride two and pack six. I bring up the rear on a stout Appaloosa named Traveler, and it's my job to make sure no one turns tail and heads for home. Mike doesn't believe in keeping his horses roped, one behind the other. A conventional pack train would become hopelessly snarled in the forest, especially on the bushwhacker's route Mike prefers to better-traveled trails. We thread our way through dense stands of lodgepole and larch, the packhorses maneuvering expertly, their cargo of wooden grub boxes barely brushing a tree trunk. I'm not so agile. Before I know it, both sleeves of my shirt are shredded. My hat is gone and my forehead bleeding. "What's keeping you?" Mike asks, only half in jest, when I catch up with him. "I thought you said you could ride a horse." He points to the ground, where a pile of bear shit glistens in the afternoon sun. "The old man of the mountain has been here and not that long ago. Good sign."

The pine trees give way to a jungle of shoulder-high huckleberry and lacey white bear parsnip. At one point we are surrounded by water, like a bayou—Louisiana in the Canadian Rockies. The packhorses spread out in all directions, snacking on green clumps that float like hyacinth. Mike is out of sight, and I am no longer sure which way he is headed. I push on, down a watery aisle of giant, swaybacked cottonwoods, taking my cue from Traveler, who seems in no particular hurry, clip-clopping through the shallows. I am not worried about getting lost. That would take work in a place where every canyon defaults to a road. Besides, the point of wilderness is not so much to get lost as it is to lose yourself, to be immersed in the ecology of Genesis, the world before the Fall. Or so it seems to me as I stare down at the red and green pebbles of argillite—compressed sandstone, baubles from the Pleistocene—that form a shimmering, tiled avenue through the cottonwood.

"There's no good argument for wilderness," Mike says that evening after supper. "There simply isn't one. If there were, we'd be winning. I've spent the better part of my life arguing for it and having no success. We can't even keep a little band of wolves alive in these mountains. The ranchers shoot them on sight. You'd think people would want to keep a bit of this wild country preserved. It's part of their heritage. But they're afraid of it. They think progress will cease, and they will be back living in dugouts on the prairie like their great-grandparents."

It's an enduring preoccupation, part fear, part fascination. How else explain the perennial popularity of movies from *King Kong* to

Jurassic Park that conjure worlds where the apes and dinosaurs are back in charge? Thomas Cole, the first American artist to glorify American wilderness, warned against trying to destroy it. In the *Course of Empire*, painted in 1836, Cole presented a sequence of four tableaux in which civilization transforms wilderness in one scene, only to succumb to it in the last. Cole's point was that as society turned its back on its wild origins, it lost the strength and vigor needed to sustain itself. Yet, Cole himself was uneasy in the wilderness. "The sublime features of nature are too severe for a lone man to look upon and be happy," he wrote in his journal. Cole captured America's ambivalence toward wilderness in his painting *The Oxbow*. On one side is a scene of rugged, storm-lashed mountainside. On the other side, across a meandering river, is a serene, sunny rendering of farms and fields. I had stood at such a divide often enough in the past two years, avoiding judgment, acknowledging the allure of both places, granting the cowboy his due while ruing the damage he has done to the wilds. But you can get a little too comfortable occupying a neutral vantage point. Sitting by a campfire in Canada, I recall the Texas political adage about what you find in the middle of the road: yellow stripes and dead armadillos.

It takes an ex-cowboy like Mike Judd, himself a weekend painter, to distinguish between art and life. In actuality, the two sides of Cole's famous canvas do not abide peacefully and never have. The Continental Divide north of the U.S. border to Banff National Park is no different. On the map, it is a 200-mile-long ribbon of green, denoting protection, that bulges expansively as it passes through areas like the Castle-Crown Wilderness, Crowsnest Provincial Park, Kananaskis Country, and the Elbow Sheep Wildland. In actuality, much of that land is open to real estate development, roads, ski resorts, dams, mines, logging, off-road vehicles, and, of course, oil and gas.

Mike made his position clear sixteen years ago when he blocked a line of Shell Canada bulldozers in the process of gouging a road to the 7,000-foot summit of Corner Mountain. There the company planned to sink gas wells in the middle of some of the best remaining bighorn sheep habitat in southern Alberta. The area had been designated a "Prime Protection Zone" for wildlife, making it illegal to tear up the ground without a permit from the chief forester for the region. Mike believed that if he could hold off the bulldozers, his friends in the Alberta Wilderness Association could secure an injunction barring Shell's intrusion. He was wrong. After a brief standoff, someone from the oil company produced a permit from the chief forester's office, clearing the way for the bulldozers. A constable who had been summoned to the confrontation was a neighbor. He put his arm around Mike and tried to comfort him. "I know how you feel . . ." But Mike would have nothing of it, according to author Sid Marty, who was also there and who described the scene in his book, *Leaning on the Wind*. "It's greed," he yelled. "After all the bullshit, it gets down to one thing: just greed."

Mike quit the Alberta Wilderness Association. Of its 2,500 members, four had shown up to lend support on Corner Mountain. Later, he resigned from another environmental group, the Castle-Crown Wilderness Coalition, accusing the leaders of terminal timidity. He grew testy and aloof. Friends feared he was spoiling for a fight he couldn't win. Mike's homestead in the Screwdriver Valley is surrounded by gas wells, pipelines, and relay stations. There are six sour gas wells within two miles of his house. Sour gas is so named because it contains hydrogen sulfide. The gas that comes out of Screwdriver Valley is rank with H_2S. You can taste the sulfur in the tap water. Up close, a whiff of sour gas can kill you. A fatal dose is undetectable because it deadens the sense of smell. A concentration of .06 of 1 percent or 600 parts per million is lethal. One part per million can cause spontaneous abortions. People who had known Mike for a long time worried about the neurotoxic effects of living around sour gas. They wondered aloud if chronic exposure was the cause of his bursts of anger and his curt dismissals of old friends.

Mike has a different explanation for his conduct. "Nobody wants to be perceived as not being nice. I guess I got over caring about that when I watched the bulldozers tear up Corner Mountain. It was the most beautiful place in the world. When I saw them go up there, I knew they'd go anywhere for a cup of gas."

In 1997 one of Mike's neighbors found a dead cow and calf near a gas line. Shell investigated and found a perforated pipe and a leak. During the next two years, they found forty more leaks. Mike and his neighbors argued that the network of lines that crossed their land was rotten with corrosion and should be shut down. The Alberta Energy and Utilities Board eventually ordered Shell to move part of the system, a junction where five pipelines came together, and faulted the company for being unresponsive to the fears of local residents. The board gave Shell two years to relocate. In the summer of 2000, with the pipeline junction still in place, the company began work on another well near Mike's property. "It was a pretty tense summer. At the end of it, my girlfriend moved out. I couldn't blame her. She had two kids and this was no place to raise them. It was around that time, I took things into my own hands, you might say."

He "borrowed" his cousin's Caterpillar and started driving toward the South Castle River, where a road was being punched into the wilderness to provide access to the newest well site. "Being a little bit drunk, I wasn't exactly sure what I was going to do, just something to stop the bastards." His cousin and the police found him parked at the head of the road and coaxed him down. "They said I was depressed and needed to be hospitalized. That's when they put me in the county unit in Lethbridge. They kept me there for three weeks. The nurses could see I wasn't crazy. They asked me what I was doing there. I said I was a political prisoner."

We stop the first night in Calamity Basin and set up camp across a teardrop lake from an amphitheater of sandstone that soars 1,000 feet, straight up to the Continental Divide. We sit outside our tents, swatting mosquitoes, waiting for the long July twilight to drain the heat from a hot, tired day.

"So what are the colors you see in that rock?" Mike asks, nodding at the cliff wall. "Do you see purple?"

"It's gray."

"I would paint it purple."

The wall is so close and so vast, you can only take in a piece of it at a time. Binoculars add dimension but not color. There are niches and apses; side altars and catwalks; soundless waterfalls and tiny landslides that tinkle like wind chimes. Halfway up the cliff, three white specks, mountain goats, forage on a fringe of green.

We see what we see. John Muir compared the Sierra Nevada to a cathedral. James Watt, President Reagan's Interior Secretary, pronounced the Grand Canyon a bore.

The rock is purple. The air smells like gin.

Up here, the Continental Divide becomes the great wall of the imagination, crowned by crumbling domes and turrets as it zigzags its way north and disappears into the clouds. This is the mythic Divide, the one that made conquering heroes of the first explorers to breach it: Escalante, Lewis and Clark, Pike, Carson, Frémont, and the Canadians: Thompson, Palliser, and Blakiston. To the southwest is Kootenay Pass, where the Kootenay Indians tried to sneak by the Blackfeet, fierce guardians of the Divide country, to hunt in the game-rich valleys of the east-facing Rockies. Barely visible on the southern horizon is Chief Mountain, the sacred summit of the Blackfeet. Like a long, jagged reef, the Divide remains the last bastion of the ancient world. But we have laid siege to its flanks, like an army of carpenter ants. Roads reach high up the sides from all directions. Loggers' clear cuts have shredded the forest canopy. From up here, the vast sweep of bare ground looks like a fairway for giants.

Industry blights the American side of the Divide, as well. Thousands of oil and gas wells dot the Great Divide Basin. More are contemplated in the heart of grizzly country in the Bridger–Teton National Forest and and just outside the Bob Marshall Wilderness in Montana. Acid rain falling over Wyoming's Wind River Range is poisoning the largest herd of bighorn sheep in the Rockies. Cattle still scavenge for sprigs of grass along the butchered tablelands of the Rio Puerco valley in northern New Mexico, an area so overgrazed it has been described as the worst example of desertification in the United States.

Public opinion polls in Alberta say 80 percent to 90 percent of the people want the remaining wilderness preserved. Polls in the United States tend to reflect similar views. So why don't the politicians heed them? Because the politicians don't believe the polls? Because when they watch the television news and see Mike Judd standing virtually alone against the bulldozers on Corner Mountain, they realize his cause lacks a certain force *majeure?* In the United States public support for wilderness often weakens if people believe that protecting it will cost jobs. That argument is often made, but the truth is there aren't that many jobs left in the wilderness. The national forests have been shorn of much of the oldest and most valuable timber. Technology and automation have steadily reduced employment in the mining and oil and gas industries. Often, the people who lose their livelihoods are the ones who depend on wilderness, outfitters and guides, people like Mike Judd.

"At some point, you come to the conclusion that most of your fellow citizens don't really mind this shit," Mike says, gesturing at the ravaged Kishinena Valley below us.

We reach the top of the Divide the next morning and travel along it for the next several days, moving along a game trail around Kishinena Peak to Kootenay Pass, then doubling back through Waterton Park and over Sage Pass. In a dense fog we follow a route that is more ledge than trail, a misstep from oblivion, along the roof of the Divide. The fog is so thick, I have trouble seeing the horse in front of me. Chalky buttes and hoodoos appear and disappear in the mist. Suddenly, we plunge knee-deep in a terrace of snow. My horse snorts and shudders violently. Ahead, Mike dismounts and examines a set of tracks in the snow. "Grizzly," he says. "And not too far ahead of us."

We skirt a series of low peaks and passes named after obscure British civil servants, Font, Matkin, Jutland, and Scarpe, ending the week in a fragrant meadow called Onion Basin. We pitch camp, eat what there is left to eat, and lay back in the coarse grass against our saddles. A wilderness doesn't always wear an Old Testament scowl. Onion Basin makes me think of A. A. Milne's 100 "Aker" Wood. It is one of those strangely egalitarian places, like a demilitarized zone, where nature feels safe enough to let down its guard. Baby animals wander out of their dens. Elk wallow in the dirt. Here the horses shed their soldierly demeanor as they roll on their backs, bicycle their feet in the air, and nicker quietly.

I go to bed chewing on a comment Mike made several days ago. "There's no good argument for wilderness," he said. But why should we have to justify wilderness? We get pleasure from it. Isn't that enough? Is there a better argument for building more golf courses or buying bigger cars or having more children?

I didn't grow up in the wilds. I'm a product of suburbs who gravitated to cities, the bigger, the better. I discovered wilderness on weekends and vacations, but I never thought of those trips as retreats or escapes. I found wilderness, in its own way, to be as as vibrant and stimulating as a big city. Urbanites are addicted to stimuli, their antennas restlessly probing for some intriguing discovery—be it food, fashion, architecture, knowledge, or experience. We go through life the way a child explores a new house, in search of wonder. It may take us to different places because we don't have the same tastes. Yet, I cannot imagine that if the design of the world were ours to do over that we would leave out wilderness any more than we could conceive of Athens without the Parthenon, Paris without Notre Dame, or New York without the Statue of Liberty.

At one point on this trip, riding across the top of the Rockies, looking down at the roads and the clear cuts and all of the places where civilization was carving its initials, I remembered General Electric's famous slogan. "Progress Is Our Most Important Product." I first heard it in the 1950s on my parents' G.E. television set, which itself was the most visible sign of progress in our house at the time. The words of the commercial were usually accompanied by scenes of a sleekly modern kitchen, its seamless ensemble of built-in cabinets and appliances a stark contrast to our homely assortment of wooden cupboards, freestanding icebox, chipped Formica, and faded linoleum. Today, G.E.'s slogan might well be the mantra of global capitalism, certainly of the industries that are marching up these mountainsides, relentlessly mining the resources and transforming the environment, making it more accessible, more familiar, and safer. But is that what we want, to purge the world of all traces of its ancient unruliness, to wean society off its primal longings and tribal leanings, to alienate the animist and the tree hugger, to tidy up the planet? The roots of our own culture are in wilderness. The stories of our history and the legends of our heroes are entwined with it.

Wilderness is the swamp we drained to build a mall before we understood that swamps absorb our waste water and filter out the toxins. It is the urban forest we cleared away before we learned that its root system held the city's watershed in place. Wilderness is the unquantifiable, unfungible asset, the one the accountants scratch their heads over when they are trying to value the estate. It is a tree lying across the path to the future, a place to pause long enough to remember Thomas Cole's vivid warning about the perils of progress. The headlong rush to the future, Cole suggested, can cut us off not just from nature, but from our better nature. We took this land from people who believed that the mountains were the realm of gods, who came here for divine inspiration. Today, as we watch the grandest buildings disintegrate in fiery clouds, is there not some reawakened impulse for simple sanctuary, for the places that remind us of what God first wrought, of "purple mountain majesty"?

THE GRIZZLY COMES in the night. I hear his footfalls, but I don't fully awaken. I remember wondering semiconsciously what large animal would walk so softly. I have been visited by grizzlies before. It is an experience that can leave you babbling to yourself, as if a meteorite has landed in camp. But this bear in this place does not rouse me and I fall back to sleep, as if the whole thing had been an animated dream inspired by Dr. Seuss of pachyderms on tiptoes.

"Did you see the bear?" Mike asks the next morning. "He must have walked right between our tents." Keeper, his dog, had noticed first, bristling and staring at the wall of Mike's tent, but not moving or making a sound. Mike stepped outside. At first, he saw nothing, but as his eyes adjusted to the dark, his gaze was drawn to a large form about fifty feet from the camp. Mike and the bear looked at each other for a long moment. Then the grizzly turned and disappeared into the forest.

We search the ground for tracks, but the grass is thick and we don't find any. Still, the bear has its hooks in us, and we can't quite ignore the temptation to follow unseen footsteps. How long would it take, I ask Mike, to get to the high north, to the country beyond the settlements and the parks and the roads—up there where the bears still number in the thousands? He gets out a map, flattens it out on a stump, and moves his finger slowly up the Divide. We have enough horses and probably enough time. It's early July. We could resupply at Crowsnest Pass and Bow Valley, make it through Banff and Jasper to the Willmore Wilderness by September. It's not the Yukon, Canada's northwestern frontier. But it's the antechamber.

Thunder mumbles in the west, a gentle warning. It is the first sign of the summer storm season and Mike wants to be down in the low country before it arrives. He takes a last wistful look at the map and puts it away. "We'll do it next time," he says. We saddle the horses, load the boxes, and head down a steep, rocky trail, our backs to the Divide.

BIBLIOGRAPHY

Abbey, Edward. *Desert Solitaire*. New York: Touchstone Books, 1968.

Alberta Energy and Utilities Board. *Public Inquiry Operational Review of the Shell Carbondale Pipeline System License 23800 Waterton Field Shell Canada Limited*, Decision 99–24, Proceeding No. 980058, October 12, 1999.

Alberta Environmental Centre and WDA Consultant Inc./K.U. Weyer. *Impact of the Petroleum Industry on Cattle Production: Critical Review of the Scientific and Other Literature*, April 21, 1995.

Alinder, Mary Street. *Ansel Adams*. New York: Henry Holt and Company, 1996.

Ambrose, Stephen E. *Undaunted Courage*. New York: Simon & Schuster, 1996.

Amundson, Michael A. "Home on the Range No More: The Boom and Bust of a Uranium Mining Town, 1957–1988." *Western Historical Quarterly* (Logan, Utah) 26, Winter 1995.

Anderson, Larry. *Benton MacKaye: Conservationist, Planner and Creator of the Appalachian Trail.* Baltimore: Johns Hopkins University Press, 2002.

Anderson, Terry L. "Conservation Native American Style." PERC Policy Series, PS-6, July 1996.

Arrington, Leonard J. *Brigham Young.* New York: Alfred A. Knopf, 1985.

Ashby, Christopher S. "The Blackfeet Agreement of 1895 and Glacier National Park: A Case History." Masters thesis, University of Montana, 1985.

Bartlett, John R. *Personal Narrative of Explorations and Incidents in Texas, New Mexico, California, Sonora, and Chihuahua, During the Years 1850, '51, '52, and '53.* 2 Vols. New York: D. Appleton & Co., 1854.

Beal, Merrill D. *The Story of Man in Yellowstone.* Caldwell, Idaho: The Caxton Printers, LTD, 1949.

Best, Allan. "Vail and the Road to a Recreational Empire." *High Country News* (Paonia, Colo.), December 7, 1998.

Blum, John M., ed. *The National Experience.* New York: Harcourt, Brace & World, Inc., 1963.

Bogue, Allan G. *Frederick Jackson Turner.* Norman, Okla: University of Oklahoma Press, 1998.

Bragonier, Dave. *Wild Journey.* Cody, Wyo.: WordsWorth, 1999.

Bullchild, Percy. *The Sun Came Down.* San Francisco: Harper & Row, 1985.

Calvin, Ross. *Sky Determines.* Albuquerque and Silver City, N. Mex.: University of New Mexico Press and High-Lonesome Books, 1993.

Carlson, Alvar W. *The Spanish-American Homeland.* Baltimore: Johns Hopkins Press, 1990.

Chadwick, Douglas H. "Grizzly Cornered." *National Geographic*, Vol. 200, No. 1, July 2001.

Cleaveland, Agnes Morley. *No Life for a Lady.* Lincoln, Nebr.: Bison Books, University of Nebraska Press, 1977 (reprinted by special arrangement with Houghton Mifflin Company, copyright 1941).

Clifford, Frank. "Maverick Babbitt Mending Fences on Range Reform." *Los Angeles Times*, December 25, 1993.

———. "Opening Parks to All of America." *Los Angeles Times*, November 25, 1994.

———. "Firewood Issue Fuels Battle in New Mexico Mountains." *Los Angeles Times*, December 1, 1995.

———. "Blazing a Trail Down America's Spine." *Los Angeles Times*, December 6, 1997.

———. "Exploiters or Stewards of Nature." *Los Angeles Times*, January 10, 1998.

———. "Old Animosities, New Battles." *Los Angeles Times*, August 15, 1998.

———. "West's Recreation Areas Face Dilemma." *Los Angeles Times*, November 13, 1998.

———. "Oil Field on Reservation Fuels Dispute." *Los Angeles Times*, June 28, 1999.

———. "Fighting Battles for Grizzlies." *Los Angeles Times*, November 5, 1999.

Coil, Jill L., et al. *"Tierra o Muerte*—Land, Water, and Community in the Rio Chama Valley." *Collected Research Papers of the Advanced Natural Resources Seminar*. Boulder, Colo.: University of Colorado School of Law, 1997.

Deaver, Sherri. "Blackfeet Use of the Badger-Two Medicine." Report prepared for the Lewis and Clark National Forest, Great Falls, Mont., 1988.

deBuys, William. *Enchantment and Exploitation*. Albuquerque, N. Mex.: University of New Mexico Press, 1985.

Diem, Kenneth L. and Lenore L. *A Community of Scalawags, Discharged Soldiers and Predestined Stinkers? A History of Northern Jackson Hole and Yellowstone's Influence 1872–1920*. Moose, Wyo.: Grand Teton Natural History Association, 1998.

Donahue, Debra L. *The Western Range Revisited*. Norman, Okla.: The University of Oklahoma Press, 1999.

Dowie, Mark. "With Liberty and Firepower for All." *Outside Magazine*, Vol. XX, Number 11, November 1995.

Duncan, Dayton, *Miles from Nowhere*. New York: Penguin Books, 1994.

Ebright, Malcolm. *Land Grants and Lawsuits in Northern New Mexico*. Albuquerque, N. Mex.: University of New Mexico Press, 1994.

Egan, John W. "Home on the Range No More: Boom and Bust in Jeffrey City." In Roberts, Phil (ed.), *Readings in Wyoming History*, Laramie, Wyo.: Skyline West Press, 2000.

Everhart, Stacy. "The Survival of a Ranch 1902–1989." Unpublished paper. Deming, N. Mex.: William Everhart papers, 1989.

Everhart, William C. *The National Park Service*. Boulder, Colo.: Westview Press, 1983.

Faden, Ruth, et al. *Final Report of the Advisory Committee on Human Radiation Experiments*. New York: Oxford University Press, 1996.

Fitzgerald, F. Scott. *The Crack-up*. New York: New Directions, 1945.

Gunther, Kerry A. "Grizzly Bear-Human Conflicts, Confrontations, and Management Actions in the Yellowstone Ecosystem." Yellowstone National Park, Wyo.: *Interagency Grizzly Bear Committee Yellowstone Ecosystem Subcommittee Report*, 1980–1997.

Guthrie, A. B. *The Big Sky*. Boston: Houghton Mifflin, 1965.

Hafen, Leroy R., and Ann W. *Handcarts to Zion*. Lincoln, Nebr.: Bison Books, University of Nebraska Press, 1992, in association with the Arthur H. Clark Company, Glendale, Calif., 1960.

Haines, Aubrey L. *The Yellowstone Story*. Vol. 2. Yellowstone National Park, Wyo., and Boulder, Colo.: The Yellowstone Association for Natural Science, History & Education, Inc., in cooperation with the University of Colorado Press, 1996.

Hardy, B. Carmon. "Cultural 'Encystment' as a Cause of the Mormon Exodus from Mexico in 1912." *Pacific Historical Review* (Portland, Ore.), November 1965.

Hayes, Alden. *A Portal to Paradise*. Tucson, Ariz.: University of Arizona Press, 1999.

Hess, Karl, Jr. "Homage to Catron County." *Northern Lights* (Missoula, Mont.), Vol. 9, No. 4, Winter 1994.

Hillard, George. *A Hundred Years of Horse Tracks*. Silver City, N. Mex.: High-Lonesome Books, 1996.

———. *Adiós Hachita*. Silver City, N.M.: High-Lonesome Books, 1998.

Horejsi, Brian L. *Ecosystem Wide Habitat Fragmentation by the Oil and Gas Industry in Southwest Alberta* (testimony presented to the Energy Resources Conservation Board Hearing, Pincher Creek, Alberta, regarding the Shell Canada Limited Carbondale Pipeline application), December 8, 1994.

———. "Uncontrolled Land-Use Threatens an International Grizzly Bear Population." *Conservation Biology*, Vol. 3, No. 3, September 1989.

Hummels, Mark. "Longtime Activist Running for Sheriff." *Albuquerque Journal*, April 11, 1998.

Johnson, Annie R. *Heartbeats of Colonia Díaz*. Salt Lake City, Utah: Publishers Press, 1972.

Julyan, Bob. *New Mexico's Wilderness Areas*. Englewood, Colo.: Westcliffe Publishers, Inc., 1998.

Keleher, William A. *The Fabulous Frontier*. Albuquerque, N. Mex.: University of New Mexico Press, 1962.

Krech, Shepard, III. *The Ecological Indian*. New York: W. W. Norton & Company, Inc., 1999.

Knight, Richard L., and Landres, Peter B., eds. *Stewardship Across Boundaries*. Washington, D.C., and Covelo, Calif.: Island Press, 1998.

Lamar, Howard R., ed. *The New Encyclopedia of the American West*. New Haven, Conn.: Yale University Press, 1998.

Larson, T. E. *Wyoming*. New York: W. W. Norton & Company, Inc., 1984.

Leopold, Aldo. *A Sand County Almanac and Sketches Here and There*. New York: Oxford University Press, 1987.

Lyon, Tolbert James "Shorty." *Lyon Hunts and Humor*. Santa Fe, N. Mex.: Sunstone Press, 1990.

Marty, Sid. *Leaning on the Wind*. Toronto, Canada: McClelland & Stewart, Inc., 1995.

Macalady, Ali, and Mockler, Karen. "Recreation Drives a Forest." *High Country News* (Paonia, Colo.), October 11, 1999.

Mayhood, David W. *Some Effects of Natural Gas Operations on Fishes & Their Habitats on Canada's Rocky Mountain East Slopes*. Report prepared for the Rocky Mountain Ecosystem Coalition, Technical Report 95/1, March 1998.

McCarthy, Cormac. *Blood Meridian*. New York: Vintage International Books, 1992.

McClintock, Walter. *The Old North Trail*. Lincoln, Nebr.: Bison Books, University of Nebraska Press, 1968.

McConkie, Bruce K. *Mormon Doctrine*. Salt Lake City, Utah: Bookcraft, Inc., 1978.

Miller, Char, and Rothman, Hal., eds. *Out of the Woods*. Pittsburgh, Pa.: University of Pittsburgh Press, 1997

Moffatt, Karl F. "DeVargas Questioned in Murder." *Rio Grande Sun* (Española, N. Mex.), June 15, 2000.

Morris, Roger. *The Devil's Butcher Shop*. New York: Franklin Watts, 1983.

Nabokov, Peter. *Tijerina and the Courthouse Raid*. Albuquerque, N. Mex.: University of New Mexico Press, 1969.

Nash, Roderick. *Wilderness and the American Mind*. New Haven, Conn.: Yale University Press, 1982.

Nikiforuk, Andrew. *Sabateurs: Wiebo Ludwig's War Against Big Oil* (manuscript). Toronto, Canada: Macfarlane Walter & Ross, 2001.

O'Connor, Richard. *Pat Garrett*. New York: Doubleday & Company, Inc., 1960.

Owen, Gordon R. *The Two Alberts: Fountain and Fall*. Las Cruces, N. Mex.: Yucca Tree Press, 1996.

Page, Jake. "The Bountiful Beauty of New Mexico's Gray Ranch." *Smithsonian*, Vol. 22, No. 11, February 1992.

Phillips, Gregory E., and Alldredge, A. William. "Reproductive Success of Elk Following Disturbance by Humans During Calving Season." *Journal of Wildlife Management*, Vol. 64, Issue No. 2, 2000.

Polling-Kempes, Lesley. *Valley of Shining Stone*. Tucson, Ariz.: University of Arizona Press, 1997.

Power, Thomas Michael. *Lost Landscapes and Failed Economies*. Washington, D.C., and Covelo, Calif.: Island Press, 1996.

Raban, Jonathan. *Bad Land*. New York: Vintage Books, 1997.

Riebsame, William. *The Great Western Range: A Cultural Landscape* (unpublished manuscript). Boulder, Colo.: Department of Geography, University of Colorado, 1999.

Riley, Carroll L., and Manson, Joni L. "The Cibola-Tiguex Route: Continuity and Change in the Southwest." *New Mexico Historical Review*, Vol. 58, No. 4, 1983.

Roberts, Pamela (producer). *Backbone of the World: The Blackfeet*. Bozeman, Mont.: Rattlesnake Productions, 1997.

Robbins, Michael. *Along the Continental Divide*. Washington, D.C.: National Geographic Society, 1981.

Rothman, Hal K. *Devil's Bargains: Tourism in the Twentieth-Century American West*. Lawrence, Kans.: University of Kansas Press, 1998.

Schneider, Keith. "Fund Set Up to Pay Civilians Injured by Atomic Arms Program," *New York Times*, October 16, 1990.

Schullery, Paul. *Searching for Yellowstone*. New York: Houghton Mifflin, 1997.

Schultheis, Rob. *The Hidden West*. New York: Lyons & Burford, in arrangement with Random House, Inc., 1996.

Shoumatoff, Alex. *Legends of the American Desert*. New York: Alfred A. Knopf, 1997.

Simmons, Marc. *The Last Conquistador*. Norman, Okla.: University of Oklahoma Press, 1991.

Sniffin, Bill. "Warnings of Uranium Mining Dangers First Issued in 1954," *Lander Wyoming State Journal*, May 14, 1990.

——. "Simpson Gives a Glimmer of Hope," *Lander Wyoming State Journal*, May 30, 1990.

Sprague, Marshall. *The Great Gates*. Boston: Little, Brown and Company, 1964.

Stegner, Wallace. *Mormon Country*. Lincoln, Nebr.: Bison Books, University of Nebraska Press, 1981.

Thoreau, Henry D. *The Maine Woods*. Princeton, N.J.: Princeton University Press, 1972.

Torrez, Robert J. *La Mano Negra*. Guadalupita, N. Mex.: Center for Land Grant Studies, 1994.

Tullis, F. La Mond. *Mormons in Mexico*. Logan, Utah: Utah State University Press, 1987.

United States Forest Service, Rocky Mountain Region. *Continental Divide National Scenic Trail Comprehensive Plan*. Washington, D.C.: United States Department of Agriculture, 1985.

United States House of Representatives, Committee on Natural Resources. *The Changing Needs of the West*. Hearing held in Salt Lake City, Utah, April 7, 1994. U.S. Government Printing Office, Serial No. 103–80, 1994.

Udall, Stewart L. *The Myths of August*. New Brunswick, N.J.: Rutgers University Press, 1998.

Urbanek, Mae. *Wyoming Place Names*. Missoula, Mont.: Mountain Press Publishing Company, 1988.

Walker, Bryce S. *The Great Divide*. Alexandria, Va.: Time Life Books, Inc., 1973.

Whipple, Dan. "Radiation: Difficulties of Measuring Exposure." *Casper Star-Tribune*, July 2, 1990.

White, Richard, and Limerick, Patricia Nelson. *The Frontier in American Culture*. Berkeley, Calif.: University of California Press, 1994.

Wilkinson, Charles F. *Crossing the Next Meridian*. Washington, D.C., and Covelo, Calif.: Island Press, 1992.

Wilmsen, Carl. "Fighting for the Forest: Sustainability and Social Justice in Vallecitos, New Mexico." Ph.D. Diss., Clark University, Worcester, Mass., 1997.

Wissler, Clark, and Duvall, D. C. *Mythology of the Blackfeet Indians*. Lincoln, Nebr.: Bison Books, University of Nebraska Press, 1995.

Worster, Donald. *Under Western Skies*. New York: Oxford University Press, 1992.

Yetter, Bob. *The Last Stronghold*. Missoula, Mont.: Rocky Mountain Front Advisory Council and Garden City Printing, 1993.

Young, Karl E. *Ordeal in Mexico*. Salt Lake City, Utah: Deseret Book Company, 1968.

SOURCES AND ACKNOWLEDGMENTS

Forty years ago, Jules Loh, a wire-service reporter with a poet's touch, wrote about the glittering promise of the barren West. Loh was writing about Texas, but what he had to say could have applied to Wyoming's Great Divide Basin or New Mexico's Bootheel. From the days of Coronado, the siren song of the badlands has been irresistible. To someone caught in the spell, Loh wrote, "there is no barrenness here, there is beauty. At night the alkalai dust clings to the scrubby greasewood and the moon turns the prairie into an endless sea of silver." The people whose work helped launch me on this project shared similar views, whether they were describing pioneers, pilgrims, treasure seekers, artists, or preservationists. To all of them, the West held out the prospect of completion. "The glory of the Lord shall be there," declared Joseph Smith. "More sky than earth," said Georgia O'Keeffe.

My initial inspiration came from several sources: Roderick Nash's *Wilderness and the American Mind*, Charles F. Wilkinson's *Crossing the Next*

Meridian, Marshall Sprague's *The Great Gates*, William deBuys' *Enchantment and Exploitation*, and Donald Worster's *Under Western Skies*.

Dayton Duncan's *Miles from Nowhere* helped me establish the boundaries of my journey. Authors Thomas Michael Power and Debra L. Donahue contributed to my understanding of the changing economics of the West and of the damage that has been inflicted on the landscape.

In Montana, Pamela Roberts helped me get started with her moving documentary, *Backbone of the World: The Blackfeet*. Bob Yetter's monograph on the Badger-Two Medicine provided an excellent summary of the cultural and environmental attributes of the region. I also learned about Blackfeet language and culture from tribal educator Darrell Kipp and from writers Percy Bullchild, Christopher S. Ashby, and Sherri Deaver. Shepard Krech III's book *The Ecological Indian* offered a fascinating deconstruction of the myths surrounding the American Indian's relationship with nature. In a similar vein, Terry Anderson's unmasking of the myth of Chief Seattle was highly instructive.

For background on Yellowstone National Park, I found Merrill D. Beal's *The Story of Man in Yellowstone* especially helpful as well as Aubrey L. Haines' two-volume history of the park, *The Yellowstone Story*. Historian Michael Amundson and former *Wyoming State Journal* editor Bill Sniffin went out of their way to provide me with material they had published about the history of Jeffrey City. John W. Egan's history of the short-lived boomtown was also helpful. Much of the information about the health effects of uranium mining came from a study commissioned by former President Bill Clinton and directed by Ruth Faden. I wouldn't have met Leo Larson without the intercession of Lance and Jill Morrow, who put me up and made it their business to educate me about the ecology and geography of the Great Divide Basin.

Mary and Leonard Hay were generous, painstaking hosts, willing to share a family story that is intertwined with at least one hundred years of Wyoming history. At Vail, I relied on Hal K. Rothman's rich history of recreation in the West, *Devil's Bargains*, along with Allan Best's articles about Colorado ski resorts in the *High Country News*. My thanks to Nick Theos in Meeker for a short course in sheepherding. In New Mexico, I was lucky to find Carl Wilmsen's dissertation on Vallecitos. I relied on William deBuys' unsurpassed history of northern New Mexico, on Malcolm Ebright's extensive research on New Mexico land grants, on Mary Street Alinder's biography of Ansel Adams, Lesley Polling-Kempes's history of the Abiquiu region and Peter Nabokov's account of the courthouse raid in Tierra Amarilla. Roger Morris's *The Devil's Butcher Shop* brought back memories of New Mexico's savage 1980 prison riot and helped me place it in the context of the region's cultural tensions.

I am grateful to William Everhart of Deming for sharing his knowledge of the early history of the Hatchet Ranch. Annie R. Johnson's book *Heartbeats of Colonia Diaz* provided a wealth of material on the history of that Mormon settlement in Mexico. Writers Karl Hess, Jr., and Mark Dowie were astute and sympathetic authorities on the prickly culture of Catron County. I couldn't have completed the chapter on Mike Judd in southern Alberta without Brian Horejsi's research on grizzly bears, Andrew Nikiforuk's analysis of the dangers of sour gas, or Sid Marty's wonderful memoir of his life around Pincher Creek.

This book is a product of many years of reading, countless interviews, and personal experiences. In the process of recollecting, assembling, and documenting material, it is possible for oversights to occur. For any omissions or errors of fact or interpretation, I would like to apologize in advance. The work that went into this book would not have been possible without the assistance of the Alicia Patterson Foundation. I am indebted to Tony Day, Keith Love, Dick McCord, and Kit Rachlis for their letters of recommendation. I am grateful to the *Los Angeles Times* and especially Susan Denley, Roxane Arnold, and John Carroll for their indulgence and support.

A long weekend with Bruce and Paula Ward at the Continental Divide Trail Alliance helped me understand how the social, political, and environmental forces that are shaping the modern West have come to intersect along a simple foot trail through the mountains. Jim Wolf, who conceived of the trail nearly 25 years ago, reminded me how much of our history was acted out along the Continental Divide.

There are people whose names don't appear in this book whose knowledge and generosity of spirit contributed to the writing of it. I would single out Ed and Betsy Marston, David Love, Tom Bell, Barrie Gilbert, and Bill Riebsame Travis.

For all of the frigid nights spent in sleeping bags, for all of the meals of stale bread and boiled mutton, there was no shortage of civilized comfort, of evenings around kitchen tables in front of crackling fireplaces. For warm hospitality, good company, and wise counsel, my thanks to Joseph Gendron, Jim and Joy Williams, Courtney White, Jim Winder, Dutch Salmon, Mike Gardner and Ruey Darrow, Hugh McKeen, Ben Brown, Warner and Wendy Glenn, Bob Trapp, Lauren Reichelt, Maria Varela, Larry Torres, Sam Hitt, Kirk Winchester, Virgil Trujillo, Freddie Velasquez, Martha Yates, Tom and Laurie Barrow, Fred and Joan Clifford, Mac Blewer, Ray Hanson, Todd Guenther, John Mionczynski, Lars and Susie Michnevich, Linda Baker, Rob Shaul, Albert Sommers, Bob Schuster, Rone Tempest and Laura Richardson, Louisa Wilcox, Lou Bruno, and Carol Murray.

In Alberta, where I knew no one, Dave Mayhood and James Tweedie and his family treated me like an old friend.

The first 40,000 words were a leap of faith. They grew into a book, thanks to the encouragement and coaching of Betsy Amster of Amster Literary Enterprises and to the guidance of Charles Conrad, executive editor of Broadway Books. If an editor can be a personal trainer, Kit Rachlis was mine. "Put more of yourself into this book," he told me in the early going. "Don't worry," he said, "I won't let you embarrass yourself." Kit has stood under the high wire for a lot of writers. Without his gentle cajolery, many of us might not have found our balance or our nerve.

If this book has a source, it is on the Yukon River, not far from where the Continental Divide swings west into Alaska. There, one summer several years ago, John Balzar, friend and goad, told me to quit talking and start writing.

Readers interested in learning more about the Continental Divide Trail can do so by writing the Continental Divide Trail Alliance at P.O. Box 628, Pine, CO 80470, or by viewing the Alliance website at www.cdtrail.org.

© BARBARA ANDERSON

About the Author

Currently the environment editor of the *Los Angeles Times*, Frank Clifford has been a journalist for more than thirty years. Before coming to California, he wrote about the American West for newspapers in Santa Fe, Tucson, and Dallas. A native of Minnesota, he lives in Los Angeles with his wife.